AF754568

Amalie Frese | Julius Schumann (eds.)

Precedents as Rules and Practice

New Approaches and Methodologies in Studies of Legal Precedents

HART

Nomos

Onlineversion
Nomos eLibrary

The Deutsche Nationalbibliothek lists this publication in the Deutsche Nationalbibliografie; detailed bibliographic data are available on the Internet at http://dnb.d-nb.de

ISBN 978-3-8487-6757-1 (Print)
978-3-7489-0829-6 (ePDF)

British Library Cataloguing-in-Publication Data
A catalogue record for this book is available from the British Library.

ISBN: HB (Hart) 978-1-50993-850-6

Library of Congress Cataloging-in-Publication Data
Frese, Amalie | Schumann, Julius
Precedents as Rules and Practice
New Approaches and Methodologies in Studies of Legal Precedents
Amalie Frese | Julius Schumann (eds.)
242 pp.
Includes bibliographic references.

ISBN 978-1-50993-850-6 (hardcover Hart)

1st Edition 2021
© Nomos Verlagsgesellschaft, Baden-Baden, Germany 2021. Overall responsibility for manufacturing (printing and production) lies with Nomos Verlagsgesellschaft mbH & Co. KG.

This work is subject to copyright. All rights reserved. No part of this publication may be reproduced or transmitted in any form or by any means, electronic or mechanical, including photocopying, recording, or any information storage or retrieval system, without prior permission in writing from the publishers. Under § 54 of the German Copyright Law where copies are made for other than private use a fee is payable to "Verwertungsgesellschaft Wort", Munich.

No responsibility for loss caused to any individual or organization acting on or refraining from action as a result of the material in this publication can be accepted by Nomos or the editors.

Inhalt

Introduction: Precedents as Rules and Practice

1. *Introduction: A New Methodological Framework for Studies of Precedent*

"[T]here is no better way for a lawyer to get at the heart of a legal system than to ask how it handles precedent", MacCormick and Summers wrote in their renowned volume *Interpreting Precedents*.[1] Understanding precedents as "prior decisions that function as models for later decisions"[2], the authors convincingly demonstrate that the significance of precedents in the legal system does not mark the border between the civil and the common law world[3] as precedents play a vital part in legal practice in both worlds.[4] Thus, while there is no formal doctrine of binding precedent at an international level, nor in most Continental European legal traditions, studies of legal practice show that some kind of precedent is in operation and is an integrated part of practice also in these legal contexts.[5] As Raz stated, adjudicative institutions' "practices are usually the product of informal traditions and slow evolution".[6] Nonetheless, there is still a certain preponderance of studies discussing the question of a formal binding effect of precedent. In other words, the majority of studies take the *rules* of precedent as a starting point. Despite the obvious research interest in the formal binding effect from a normative perspective, this approach entails a theoretically and methodologically limited examination of judicial *practice*.[7] Where practice does not match a rule of precedent, legal scholarship

---

1 MacCormick and Summers, 'Introduction' in MacCormick and Summers (eds), *Interpreting Precedents: A Comparative Study* (1997) 1.

2 Ibid 1.

3 There may be reservations about this differentiation per se: ibid 2–3.

4 Ibid 12.

5 Frese and Olsen, 'Spelling It Out–Convergence and Divergence in the Judicial Dialogue between CJEU and ECtHR' (2019) 88 *Nordic Journal of International Law*, 429; Derlén and Lindholm, 'Peek-A-Boo, It's a Case Law System!: Comparing the European Court of Justice and the United States Supreme Court from a Network Perspective' (2017) 18 *German Law Journal*, 647; Jacob, *Precedents and Case-based Reasoning in the European Court of Justice*, Cambridge University Press, 2014.

6 Raz, *The authority of law: Essays on law and morality* (1979) 180.

7 Rottleuthner, 'Rechtswissenschaft als Sozialwissenschaft' in Hilgendorf and Joerden (eds), *Handbuch Rechtsphilosophie* (2021) 266.

tends to simply arrive at the conclusion that there is a "de facto"[8] binding effect.[9] Yet, the consequence of this assumption is that the concrete practical importance and operation of precedents remains a blind spot[10] and may even obscure the broader view on rules governing precedents.[11] Therefore, the aim of this book is to widen the lens of scrutiny from the normative pull of precedents to socio-legal perspectives on the practice of precedents, thereby offering a combined view of rules and practice.

This book is the result of a collaboration between researchers with a common interest in the topic of precedent. As part of this collaboration, a workshop was held at the University of Vienna in January 2019. The idea of the workshop, which is also reflected in the book, was to bring together researchers contributing a range of new perspectives to the study of precedent.

As demonstrated by the chapters in this edited volume, novel approaches to the study of precedent allow not only for criticism of long-standing assumptions about the role of precedent in common law and in civil law traditions but offer new research questions that go beyond the focus on the dichotomy between binding versus non-binding precedent. Thus, in using these new approaches, our volume brings new insights to questions such as the legal authority of cases, the role of legal agents like judges and other court staff as well as legal cultures and languages in choosing precedents, the influence of the institutional design on decision-making practices, and the role of precedent in international adjudication and whole legal systems.

The contributions inter alia supplement doctrinal approaches to precedent with socio-legal approaches that make use of methods and technology not typically applied in legal studies, such as linguistics, sociology, and computer science, to show how the combination of both sets of methodologies can provide vital insights into the mechanisms of legal

8 Also referred to as "faktische Präjudizwirkung" or "faktische Geltung" in German literature, e.g. Larenz, 'Über die Bindungswirkung von Präjudizien' in Fasching (ed), *Festschrift für Hans Schima zum 75. Geburtstag* (1969) 249; see also on this: Payandeh, *Judikative Rechtserzeugung: Theorie, Dogmatik und Methodik der Wirkungen von Präjudizien* (2017) 124–132.

9 Jacob (n 5) 30.

10 Peczenik, 'The Binding Force of Precedent' in MacCormick and Summers (eds), *Interpreting Precedents: A Comparative Study* (1997) 465–467; Payandeh (n 8) 128–132 deplores a resulting lack of methodology.

11 Ridi, 'Rule of Precedent and Rules on Precedent', forthcoming in Brabandere et al (eds), Comparative Procedure in State-to-State Disputes (2020), Available at SSRN: <https://ssrn.com/abstract=3697226> accessed 12 July 2021.

decision-making and precedent and cross-fertilize legal inquiry. Hence, the structure of the book is based on the idea of introducing different research approaches such as sociological, linguistic, legal-technical, and also doctrinal research. By combining studies that apply different legal empirical and theoretical approaches from different national and international systems, this edited volume exposes structures that affect the different roles and functions of precedent in practice.

While the book is not intended to be exhaustive in its theorized view on approaches to the study of precedent, its original contribution does lie in bringing together research approaches which are based on new methods and perspectives. The strength of the book lies in the diversity of approaches to an object of study that is at the core of legal practice while simultaneously remaining insufficiently examined. The contributions provide substantive insights into the particularities of legal practices, national and international, and into how different legal actors and the designs of different legal systems interact with practices of precedent.

2. Content

The book is divided into three parts. Each represents and illustrates different methodological vantage points and approaches to the study of precedent and seeks to capture different streams of research design. Part I presents, in three studies, new approaches in the methodology of precedent research. Part II focuses on the agents of precedents and the communities in which they are embedded. Part III offers two analyses of precedent in different legal systems, one focusing on the ICC and the other on Germany, France, and Austria.

Part I: Precedent as authority: Broadening the Range of Research Methods

Part 1 takes the construction of authority as an entry point to the exploration of precedent. The four authors suggest the use of methods outside the "usual canon" to investigate precedent. In chapter 1, *The Weight of Precedent: From Abstract Theorizing to Concrete Application*, Henrik Palmer Olsen and Martin Lolle Christensen propose taking the step from theorizing the authority of precedent to measuring this authority with novel technologies. Palmer Olsen and Christensen regard precedents as a recognized source of law in almost every legal system and see their wide acceptance as closely linked to the almost universally accepted ethical principle that like cases should be treated alike. Although precedents are often taught to students in legal theory and juridical methods classes, the focus frequently lies on discussing the theoretical definition of precedent. Only rarely are students provided with efficient methods for identifying and assessing the weight and relevance of precedent in relation to individual cases. In their contribution, Palmer Olsen and Christensen show that recent advances in network analysis and natural language processing have made it possible to introduce new metrics for identifying precedents based on the citation practice of courts. These metrics provide ways of navigating very large corpora of case law and can be used to both guide qualitative inquiry and to operationalize new ways of analyzing court practice, thereby adding new information that is important to both legal academics and legal practitioners. The chapter provides the reader with an overview of how network analysis can be used in law, both in basic research and as applied legal analytics, on the basis of an illustrative example from a Danish Supreme Court case and outlines a number of research projects that have utilized these new methods to identify and characterize precedents.

Chapter 2 is an empirically based exemplification of the method advanced in Chapter 1. Amalie Frese's study demonstrates the use of case law citation network analysis to address *The Practical Construction of Precedent in the Jurisprudence of the European Court of Human Rights*. By mapping all references and citations between cases in the jurisprudence of the European Court of Human Rights (ECtHR), Frese shows how the ECtHR itself creates 'authorities' in its jurisprudence as it cites some cases very frequently and others less so. These authorities are, however, 'mathematical authorities'; by constructing a paragraph-to-paragraph network, which allows the researcher to gain insight into the cited content in the judgments, the chapter furthermore tests the extent to which the network approach can identify 'judicial authorities' that can reasonably be considered precedents for a given legal domain. The chapter shows that the network approach to the study of precedent is a highly useful method that has the specific advantage of providing a shift in the viewpoint on which cases are authoritative from the scholarly perspective to the perspective of the Court itself by tracing the references and citations to past cases which the Court itself makes in its judgments.

In chapter 3, William Hamilton Byrne in *Reconstructing Scholarly Authority in International Law* explores the nature of the authority of legal scholarship in international law and argues for turning to hermeneutical philosophy to understand that authority is more than a legal construct. The chapter considers prominent theories of the authority of the sources of international law in order to understand the authority of legal scholarship as it comes before international courts. Firstly, Byrne asserts that legal formalism as the dominant theory of sources has trouble in accounting for the paths of changes in international law, which often occur outside formal channels. Secondly, the author argues that naturalist theories equate the authority of scholarship with other types of authority, at the expense of looking past empirical phenomena. Thirdly, he states that sociological theories face difficulties arising from the heterogeneity of legal scholarship and its function in providing knowledge. Finally, Byrne argues that only a hermeneutic understanding can capture authority as a situated and relational concept between legal traditions and the horizons of the interpretative subject. The chapter concludes with reflections on what the reader can take from a turn to hermeneutics in terms of making sense of legal precedents as vessels of the past in service of the present amongst competing claims to authority in international law.

Part II: Actors and Languages of Precedent: Courts and their Communities

In Part II, three authors investigate the actors of precedents and their environment. In chapter 4, *Culture Clash: The Sociology of WTO Precedent*, Harlan Cohen explores the communities of practitioners that give precedent its force. As precedents exert their force within arguments, understanding that force requires, according to him, an understanding of the groups of actors who interact and argue over specific rules. Cohen shows empirically how different international law regimes involve different mixes of actors – diplomats, military personnel, scientists, economists, international lawyers, and domestic lawyers. This chapter accounts for how each of these actors bring their own professional norms and biases to the debate, and how different mixes of actors will agree on different norms or operating assumptions. Cohen's theoretical and empirical reconstruction of these communities of practice helps explain why certain prior interpretations act as precedents, framing or shaping debates, while others do not.

In chapter 5, Elina Paunio investigates the linguistic and institutional factors that constrain the reasoning and the construction of precedent in the case law of the Court of Justice of the European Union (the Court). In her chapter, *Reasoning with past cases at the CJEU: linguistic, institutional and systemic* constraints, she therefore explores the impact of multilingualism, the Court's set-up and its role in the EU legal system on judicial decision-making and the understanding of precedent as a matter of EU law. The Court, the institution charged with ensuring the uniform interpretation of multilingual EU law, is itself both a multilingual and a monolingual institution. Its judgments are published in all official languages while the internal working language is French. Because of its linguistic setup, translation is omnipresent in proceedings before the Court. Paunio explores the linguistic diversity within the judges' chambers, the use of French as the working language, and the important role of translation in proceedings before the Court opposite institutional factors which include the Court's structure, the collegiality of decision-making, as well as the Court's caseload. Paunio shows that all of these factors help explain certain features of the Court's style of legal reasoning, a style often described as formalistic and authoritative, and heavily reliant on statements from past cases. In a Weberian sense, the case law method employed by the Court is based on formulae, on building blocks from past cases, which hide the irrationality of the law and judicial decision-making. Exploring these factors sheds light on the judicial practices that inform the elaboration of precedent at the highest court of the European Union.

The third contribution to Part II is *Precedents – A Question of Memory* by Julius Schumann, who explores how a court can make its own past usable. By regarding precedents as past events, he examines the formation of an institutional memory by supreme courts. Taking into account the organization of different supreme courts in Central Europe, *Schumann* identifies archives, along with individual judges, as central repositories of such an institutional memory. However, the author argues that archives have undergone considerable change in recent decades, which also suggests an impact on the daily work of decision-making. The chapter points out in general terms the importance of memory for the construction of precedent and, at the same time, offers some reflections on the transformation of courts' institutional memory in the digital age and its need for curation.

Part III: Identifying Concepts of Precedents in Legal Systems

The third part offers two views on international and national courts as agents of precedents in their legal framework. Chapter 7 by Georg Kodek on *Precedents in Private Law – A Civil Law Perspective* focuses on the legal systems of France, Germany, and Austria. Starting from the common assertion that only legislation is binding for all, the author searches for traces of 'binding' precedent. For this purpose, the author analyzes different factors such as the institutional framework, the organization of the court system, the motivation of court decisions, the publication of decisions, as well as procedural mechanisms that ensure consistency of court decisions. On this basis, *Kodek* sees court decisions as bridging the gap between abstract laws and concrete cases, contributing to the content and understanding of statutory provisions, and reducing the uncertainty that comes with abstract-general legal provisions. For him, the development of 'case law' is a multi-faceted process that can in the end only result from the contribution of many actors. According to the author, the effect of precedents depends on the extent to which courts, the legislature, administrative authorities, and other "users" of the law accept these decisions and base their own decisions on them.

Chapter 8 by *Raphaëlle Nollez-Goldbach*, entitled *The Precedent in the ICC Jurisprudence*, discusses the specific role that precedent has for the International Criminal Court (ICC), as the Court "may apply principles and rules of law as interpreted in its previous decisions" (Art 21.2 of the Rome Statute). Nollez-Goldbach examines the complications related to identifying what 'a precedent' is in ICC case law, as almost every judgment brings a new interpretation of the statute, since it is usually the first one in which a given article is applied. The chapter thus focuses on the conceptual practices of the ICC and the legal tools and techniques specific to the 'young' Court and pays special attention to two landmark decisions, namely the Bemba acquittal and the Rohingya decision.

Final Remarks

The chapters in this book contain a highly diverse set of introductions and accounts of research designs, approaches, and methodological reflections on precedents. Our aim is to inspire and guide new research agendas and methodological strategies not only limited to the legal systems that serve as the objects of inquiry in the studies of this book. Moreover, practitioners in judicial bodies and international organisations may attain useful perspectives on the mechanisms of judicial decision-making and precedential authority from this volume.

During the workshop in Vienna, we observed an extremely fruitful exchange between different methodologies and approaches all concerned with the object of precedent. The necessity for a pluralism of methods becomes particularly evident with regard to this topic. Precedents, as this volume shows, are shaped not only by formal, binding rules but by an entire institutional framework that keeps the object of research dynamic. Based on the versatile research on precedent from a variety of perspectives and in a range of contexts that are represented in this book, it is our conviction that a combination of quantitative methods together with qualitative as well as doctrinal legal analysis indeed opens up new and innovative avenues of research.[12]

We would like to express our sincere thanks to the authors who have enriched this book with their contributions. Likewise, we would like to express our gratitude for a financial support from the Faculty of Law of the University of Vienna, which made this book possible. And finally, we would like to thank the publishers Hart and Nomos, who provided excellent support in the printing of the book.

Amalie Frese
Julius Schumann

12 See also Šadl and Olsen, 'Can Quantitative Methods Complement Doctrinal Legal Studies? Using Citation Network and Corpus Linguistic Analysis to Understand International Courts' (2017) 30(2) *Leiden Journal of International Law*, 327.

Bibliography

Mattias Derlén and Johan Lindholm, 'Peek-A-Boo, It's a Case Law System!: Comparing the European Court of Justice and the United States Supreme Court from a Network Perspective' (2017) 18 *German Law Journal*, 647

Amalie Frese and Henrik Palmer Olsen, 'Spelling It Out–Convergence and Divergence in the Judicial Dialogue between CJEU and ECtHR' (2019) 88 *Nordic Journal of International Law*, 429

Marc A Jacob, *Precedents and case-based reasoning in the European Court of Justice: Unfinished business* (Cambridge University Press, Cambridge 2014)

Karl Larenz, 'Über die Bindungswirkung von Präjudizien' in Hans W Fasching (ed), *Festschrift für Hans Schima zum 75. Geburtstag* (Manz, Wien 1969) 247

D. Neil MacCormick and Robert S Summers, 'Introduction' in D. Neil MacCormick and Robert S Summers (eds), *Interpreting Precedents: A Comparative Study* (Ashgate 1997) 1

Mehrdad Payandeh, *Judikative Rechtserzeugung: Theorie, Dogmatik und Methodik der Wirkungen von Präjudizien* (Mohr Siebeck 2017)

Aleksander Peczenik, 'The Binding Force of Precedent' in D. Neil MacCormick, Robert S Summers and Arthur L Goodhart (eds), *Interpreting Precedents: A Comparative Study* (Taylor and Francis 1997) 461

Joseph Raz, *The authority of law: Essays on law and morality* (Clarendon Press, Oxford 1979).

Nicollo Ridi, 'Rule of Precedent and Rules on Precedent', forthcoming in Eric de Brabandere et al (eds), Comparative Procedure in State-to-State Disputes (Cambridge University Press, Cambridge 2020), Available at SSRN: <https://ssrn.com/abstract=3697226> accessed 12 July 2021

Hubert Rottleuthner, 'Rechtswissenschaft als Sozialwissenschaft' in Eric Hilgendorf and Jan C Joerden (eds), *Handbuch Rechtsphilosophie* (2nd edn, J.B. Metzler Verlag, Stuttgart 2021) 264

Urška Šadl and Henrik P Olsen, 'Can Quantitative Methods Complement Doctrinal Legal Studies? Using Citation Network and Corpus Linguistic Analysis to Understand International Courts' (2017) 30(2) *Leiden Journal of International Law*, 327

The Weight of Precedent: From Abstract Theorizing to Concrete Application: The case of the ECtHR

Henrik Palmer Olsen and Martin Lolle Christensen

A. *Precedent and the law*

The aim of legal doctrinal scholarship is to answer the question "what is the law?" within some defined area of the law, at a defined point in time and in a defined jurisdiction. Identifying and interpreting relevant sources of law is what determines the content of valid law in doctrinal scholarship. Case law is generally one such recognized source of law, which must be taken into account where it is relevant. The role and use of case law varies across both jurisdictions and fields of law, but generally case law represents the use of law in practice, and therefore cannot be ignored by either academics or practitioners. Judicial practice is in many ways central to the understanding of what law is.[1]

Judicial practice is however sometimes plentiful. Some courts issue several hundreds of decisions every year, over the span of a few years several thousand decisions and over a few decades tens of thousands. In an account of the law, not every decision can be included. A selection must take place. This gives rise to a difficult question: Which methodological considerations justify the inclusion of one judgment (or set of judgments) over others (which will be excluded) in a doctrinal account of law?

Using the European Court of Human Rights (ECtHR) as example, this chapter will show how traditional understanding of precedents are lacking in answering these questions, and how citation network analysis and natural language processing (NLP) can provide complementary answers. In order to understand why these auxiliary methods are necessary we must first present the problems with conventional understandings of precedent.

---

1 By this we do not seek to embrace legal realism, which is often characterised by its focus on "law in action", but is simply an observation that across jurisdictions, judicial practice plays an important role in defining what law as a practice of judging social behaviour in accordance with pre-defined legislative texts and principles is.

The concept of precedent is complex and relates to long jurisprudential traditions that extends beyond different sub-traditions linked to legal cultures of the world. In common law countries, the doctrine of *stare decisis* has been firmly established in legal theory. The doctrine has been developed over many centuries and is based on a distinction between *ratio decidendi* and *obiter dicta*, where *ratio decidendi* is defined as the reasoning that decides a case, and *obiter dicta* is defined as non-binding remarks made in the judgment, but which is not directly linked to the reasoning that determines the case.

In the continental European approach, there is not the same tradition of perceiving judgments as binding precedents.[2] Hans Kelsen, perhaps the best-known legal philosopher in the continental European legal tradition, largely did not theorize judgments as binding on later judgments, but instead linked the binding force of judgments to their legality. Judgments, for Kelsen, do not make binding law beyond the individual judgment that is binding for the parties only because (and if) the judgment is a correct application of pre-existing valid legal norms.[3]

In French law, there is even an outright prohibition against justifying a decision solely with reference to case law. There is generally an expectation that judgments are decided on the basis of statutory law – a practice that stems from a particular interpretation of the doctrine of distribution of power and which is based on a fear that the courts will move away from the law and create its own regime of law through precedents and therefore beyond democratic control.[4]

The notion, role, and use of precedent therefore varies significantly across jurisdictions and, on top of this, the role of precedents within the law is theorized in different ways across different approaches to general jurisprudence. To illustrate: Raimo Siltala sets up no less than 16 different models for precedent use divided into 8 different precedent ideologies.[5] Still Siltala's work captures only the main strands of legal theory that has been developed up through the 20th century. His work therefore does not

---

2 See further Kodek, 'Precedents in Private Law – A Civil Law Perspective', in this volume.

3 See Kelsen, *Pure Theory of Law* (1967).

4 This practice in the French state and its relation to algorithmic decision-making is discussed in Palmer Olsen et al., 'What's in the Box? The Legal Requirement of Explainability in Computationally Aided Decision-Making in Public Administration' (2019) 162 *iCourts Working Paper Series*.

5 Siltala, *A Theory of Precedent: From Analytical Positivism to a Post-Analytical Philosophy of Law* (2000).

capture the role of the European courts, which especially at the very end of the 20th century and up through the beginning of 21st have emerged as very active courts with an active use of citation of its own practice. Since this paper focuses on network analysis applied to the practice of ECtHR, it is important to briefly introduce how precedent is perceived in this context.

In a 2013 article, Jan Komárek shows why the European Court of Justice's precedent practice must be understood in a different way than the US Supreme Court's precedent practice.[6] Komárek points out in particular that the case law of the European Court of Justice is largely more focused on quoting general principles and thus repeating specific textual passages through several successive judgments than on the more factual approach to precedents that characterize American common law (the *stare decisis* tradition). In the case law of the European Court of Justice, the use of precedents is more a matter of repeating and applying the same legal principles to the same type of legal question than of settling cases that have similar facts in exactly the same way.[7] In other words, the focus is not on *ratio decidendi*, but rather on the retention of more abstract legal principles over time (Textual precedent). In our view, Komárek's analysis of the case law of the Court of Justice of the European Union is also relevant to understanding the case law of the European Court of Human Rights. Thus, one cannot directly apply the understanding of precedent practice developed in American-oriented research (typically with the precedent practice of the Federal American Supreme Court as the subject). The understanding of what the precedent value is for the international courts must instead be drawn from the courts' own case law, and not only understood analogously to national legal traditions.

There is a large amount of recent literature which describes and theorizes the international precedent practice as it exists both in the individual

---

6 Komárek, 'Reasoning with Previous Decisions: Beyond the Doctrine of Precedent' (2013) *61 American Journal of Comparative Law*, 149. Komárek's observation is important because most of the early literature on network analysis in law had USSC case law (drawn from the Spaeth database: <http://scdb.wustl.edu/> accessed 8 June 2021) as its object of analysis.

7 See also Ridi, '"Mirages of an Intellectual Dreamland"? Ratio, Obiter and the Textualization of International Precedent' (2019) 10 *Journal of International Dispute Settlement*, 361, 377. Studying the practice of the International Court of Justice, World Trade Organization Appellate Body and ICSID tribunals, Ridi finds no consistent understanding of the ratio decidendi / obiter dictum distinction. 'Textualist precedent' should not be confused with 'Textualism', the formalist legal theory.

international courts and between them.[8] Komárek, for example, puts forward a theory which breaks down Siltala's various categories to two more basic models, which he describes as the "case-bound" and the "legislative" model respectively.[9]

The case-bound method Komárek associates with the common law (he also calls this "The Common Law notion of Precedent", and he describes this method via an article by John Gardner, in which he (Gardner) explains precedent as a rule, which can be inferred from a legal decision.[10] The rule that a case stands for is closely associated to the facts of the decided case. The key to precedent in the common law system, therefore, is that the *ratio decidendi* – the rationale that determined the decision – is a composite unit of fact and rule which after its rendering becomes part of the legal system.

The legislative model of precedent is different. It is characterized by focusing more on the formulation of a general principle of law. Komárek identifies this model in the case law of the CJEU. That court's *modus operandi* is characterized by being predominantly concerned with assuring that EU law is correctly implemented in member state jurisdictions. The cases that come before it, therefore, are decided by considering how EU-law should be applied. Since its decisions will have an impact in many jurisdictions (CJEU's rulings are considered a source of law (precedent) also for those EU member states who are not party to the dispute), it will formulate its decisions in a more principled way, being very careful about the exact wording of their decisions and relying on that wording in future decisions. The legislative model, then, is more focused on text than on the composite "fact-rule" found in the common law.[11]

We agree overall with Komárek in his analysis of the different models of precedent, but our aim in this paper is not to discuss models of precedent. Our aim is instead to address the question of operationalization. The

---

8 See e.g. N. Miller, 'An International Jurisprudence? The Operation of "Precedent" Across International Tribunals' (2002) 15 Leiden Journal of International Law, 483; von Bogdandy and Venzke, *International Judicial Lawmaking: On Public Authority and Democratic Legitimation in Global Governance* (2012); Shahabuddeen, *Precedent in the World Court* (Cambridge University Press 2007); Ridi, 'The Shape and Structure of the "Usable Past": An Empirical Analysis of the Use of Precedent in International Adjudication' (2019) 10 *Journal of International Dispute Settlement*, 200.

9 Komárek (n 6), 151.

10 See Gardner, 'Some Types of Law', in Edlin (ed), *Common law theory*, (2007) 51.

11 See also Ridi (n 7) where the same textualization phenomenon is empirically studied in a number of international courts.

problem we address more specifically is the problem of how one can find and identify precedent. This is a problem that occurs when the amount of case law that has to be digested in order to create an overview over the law in some field numbers in the 100s or 1000s. How do we find out which of these many cases are usable precedents? And how do we find out what they are precedent for?

B. Operationalizing precedent

Classic doctrinal theory focuses on analysis of the individual case one by one. It operates on the idea that one seeks out (usually without saying how this seeking out is supposed to take place) a case and then subjects this case to qualitative scrutiny (analysis) in order to determine what – if any – the rule or principle is in that case – i.e. what it is precedent for. Many textbooks are produced in this way.[12] Since the aim of these books is to help give an overview of the law in some field, usually aimed at law students, methodological issues are not dealt with (but left to jurisprudence classes to handle). Handbooks for practitioners are usually dealt with in the same way.

Presuming that one has a specific litigation interest this may be a plausible way of going about looking for precedent. For practicing lawyers who seek to promote the interest of their clients, seeking out precedent that support a view of what the law is on some point may not be all that difficult provided that one has ample research assistants on hand who knows how to use the legal information retrieval services that are available on the market and who have access to relevant textbooks and other legal literature in the field. Furthermore, in litigation, argumentative practice prevails, and it is legitimate to promote the client's interest.

Legal researchers are in a different position. The aim of legal research is not to promote some clients interest, but to present what the law is in some more objective and neutral way. Although objectivity may not be fully achievable and although the researcher may not be able to isolate his or her values completely from the object of study, research methodologies are introduced precisely with the purpose of advancing more objectivity, neutrality and comprehensiveness to the process of research. This is done

---

12 Three French, German and English textbooks are analyzed in Frese and Olsen, 'Citing Case Law: A Comparative Study of Legal Textbooks on European Human Rights Law' (2019) 11 *European Journal of Legal Studies*, 41.

with the aim of creating a public and transparent way of validating knowledge that supersedes what can be gained from everyday interest driven practices that may be less stringent in obtaining and analysing data.

In this paper we introduce a new approach to case selection and case law analysis – one that is more empirical and which to some extent may be seen as challenging the classical view of precedent analysis. The examples used to introduce this approach are taken from research projects done on the ECtHR and its comprehensive human rights case law. With respect for differing legal traditions and aware that an international court like the ECtHR is placed in a very different position from domestic courts, we aim to show that the role of precedent in legal analysis might be made a little more transparent than it has been traditionally. This may be done by temporarily shifting the focus away from inspecting the individual case in isolation and towards a focus on how cases have in fact been used in the courts reasoning. In doing so one studies precedent through the way a court (in this case the ECtHR) itself uses precedent when deciding new cases. Through studying the practice of the court, one takes on a perspective of precedent that does not try to be omniscient, but is rather relative to what the court itself does.

For the ECtHR, the precedential practice serves a number of purposes.[13] A primary purposes is finding the precedents that can best be utilized to create a coherent jurisprudence, carried forward by general principles and an identifiable and legitimized course for new decisions. The ECtHR has relied on this construction of its own precedent since its early cases, necessitated by the fact that the ECHR is a vague human rights document.[14] The precedential practice is therefore worth understanding as it has a large role to play in the workings of the court.

Understanding this practice can be done empirically and comprehensively by leveraging computational methods that allows to extract information from case law databases and applying network analysis to this data. In the case of the ECtHR, by collecting the full text of judgments and decisions ever rendered by the court, it will be possible to track every

13 See Lupu and Voeten, 'Precedent in International Courts: A Network Analysis of Case Citations by the European Court of Human Rights' (2012) 42 *British Journal of Political Science*, 413.

14 For how the ECtHR built general principles from a selection of cases in the period between 1975–1980, see Madsen, 'The Challenging Authority of the European Court of Human Rights: From Cold War Legal Diplomacy to the Brighton Declaration and Backlash' (2016) 79 *Law & Contemp. Probs.*, 141, 152.

citation the court has ever made to its own case law.[15] Once these citations has been retrieved, various network analysis techniques can be performed on the data. Applying such a data science approach, one can achieve an empirically grounded base of information that will serve to complement and enhance the quality of research results that may otherwise be achieved via a more classical doctrinal approach in which individual cases are found manually (often through undisclosed methods) and studied in isolation from other judgments that for some reason or another were not selected for inclusion.

B.I. Network analysis applied to the study of precedent

Because the ECtHR regularly and extensively relies on, and cites, its own case law when deciding new cases, the entire set of cases from the court can be seen to be connected via these citations. Furthermore, since the court almost always cites its own previous case law in favour of the new decision it makes, case citations can generally be taken as a strong indicator for precedent use[16] in the sense of textual precedents.[17] Hence the network that is created by case-to-case citations can be seen to constitute the universe of explicit precedent use.[18] This allows some simple inferences to be drawn from the network.

As a starting point one may easily find out which cases are cited, and which are not, what cases they are cited by, when they have been cited, how many times they have been cited and so on. Using this citation information, alone or together with the metadata available for the different judgments, one can also identify various citation patterns in such a network.[19] One can for example identify whether some cases are often cited together, and one can identify whether groups of cases tend to cite

15 This data is available on HUDOC, the ECtHR's database. See HUDOC, <https://hudoc.echr.coe.int/> accessed 8 June 2021.

16 Sometimes, of course, cases are cited negatively, but that is rare. It is therefore of little numerical relevance and will be picked up during subsequent qualitative analysis if it is significant.

17 Komárek (n 6); Ridi (n 7).

18 See Panagis et al., 'Giving Every Case Its (Legal) Due: The Contribution of Citation Networks and Text Similarity Techniques to Legal Studies of European Union Law' in Casini and Wyner (ed), *Legal Knowledge and Information Systems JURIX 2017* (2017).

19 Both HUDOC, the ECtHR's online database, and CURIA, CJEU's online database have significant metadata attached to the individual judgments.

the same cases. Such patterns can lead to the identification of clusters within the network – thereby indicating (but not affirming) that these cases share some of the same characteristics.[20] This could be an overlap in regard to their legal and/or factual content, but could also relate to cases originating from the same respondent state or something else. One could also identify a network centrality score, or authority score, for each case in the network. These metrics can be used to assess the importance of particular cases relative to the network.[21] There is, in other words, a variety of empirical parameters that could be used to analyse the role of case citation (precedent) in the court's practice.[22] All this considered, it seems relevant to ask whether this data-driven approach to precedent does present valuable new knowledge about the law? In answering this question, we shall evaluate it from two perspectives: 1) is it compatible with a doctrinal approach to identifying what valid law is? 2) What are the strength and weaknesses of network analysis approaches compared to more traditional doctrinal approaches? We shall now briefly examine these two questions.

1) While the network analysis approach described above may at first seem alien to legal research and analysis, there are at closer inspection some obvious similarities. Citation network analysis and doctrinal legal analysis share the overarching view that information must be presented as belonging to a coherent web or pattern.[23] There is, in other words, a structural similarity in the way these two types of analysis operate. In seeking more interaction between the two types of analysis (citation network

---

20 Alschner and Charlotin, 'The Growing Complexity of the International Court of Justice's Self-Citation Network' (2018) 29 *European Journal of International Law*, 83, 90–91.

21 Centrality and Authority measures are two prominent examples of computational metrics that assign a relative value to the individual nodes based on their connections within the network. See e.g. Kleinberg, 'Authoritative Sources in a Hyperlinked Environment' (1999) 46 *Journal of the ACM (JACM)*, 604.

22 A number of different metrics are explored in Derlén and Lindholm, 'Goodbye van Gend En Loos, Hello Bosman? Using Network Analysis to Measure the Importance of Individual CJEU Judgments' (2014) 20 *European Law Journal*, 667.

23 The idea of law as a seamless web originates with F.W. Maitland in 1898. It has later been applied to a number of legal citation network analyses. See Maitland, 'Prologue to a History of English Law' (1898) 14 *Law Quarterly Review*, 13; and Bommarito et al., 'Law As a Seamless Web?: Comparison of Various Network Representations of the United States Supreme Court Corpus (1791–2005)', in Association for Computing Machinery (ed), *Proceedings of the 12th International Conference on Artificial Intelligence and Law, ICAIL '09 (2009);* T. Smith, 'The Web of Law' (2007) 44 *San Diego Law Review*, 309.

analysis and manual doctrinal analysis), it will be helpful to rely on a theory of law that has as one of its key factors, the analysis of case law and adjudication. Ronald Dworkins theory of law is such a theory. Dworkins theory of law revolves around the idea of an ever-evolving chain of legal normativity that is constantly being interpreted and reinterpreted in order to find the most optimal balance between fit and justification. The best interpretation should both fit and justify the legal material being studied.[24] It will be useful therefore to take a closer look at Dworkins description of the interpretive process that is responsible for generating the insight into what the law is.

Dworkin identifies three stages in the process of legal interpretation: (1) a pre- interpretive stage in which the lawyer collects all the rules and standards that as a whole make up the law on some given point or issue; (2) an interpretive stage in which those rules and standards are assembled into a coherent and justified whole; and (3) a post- interpretive stage in which the underlying justification identified in (2) is used to revisit the original rules and standards identified in (1) and to possibly adjust one's initial understanding of what these rules and standards are.[25]

Our point is now that case citation network analysis renders – in Dworkin's language – a more complete mapping of the pre-interpretive stage of legal interpretation; that is, the stage at which one has to identify all the relevant legal material that becomes a part of the interpretive process. By identifying, through a case-to-case citation network, which cases the court itself uses, how often and when, one gets a more complete understanding of the role of precedent (case citation) in actual court practice. Presenting these as a network makes it possible to more easily navigate the relevant sources (cases) and decide on the relevance of inclusion or exclusion.

Moreover, not only may more traditional approaches based on manual reading of cases be either inefficient or outright impossible to achieve, but it should also be noted that even the most careful and capable of readers could miss connections between cases. The human eye and mind may not absorb all the relevant legal details set out in these texts and may not be tuned into performing the kind of computations that a machine can easily do. Thus, without a comprehensive overview of relationships between cases through a systematic and exhaustive case-to-case citation analysis, legal scholars working only with manual reading of judgements may neither

24 Dworkin, *Law's Empire* (1986) 228–238.

25 Ibid 65–69.

be able to provide a complete account of what the law is nor empirically test the accuracy of their assumptions about how the body of law under scrutiny is organized. While network analysis on its own may not be able to do so either, coupled to more traditional qualitative doctrinal analysis, it can provide a base of verifiable information about how the court itself uses its own case law when issuing judgments.

Furthermore, the categories and concepts used by previous doctrinal scholarship (which often serve as a platform for new doctrinal scholarship/textbooks) may turn out to give a less accurate or less complete representation of the law as it is today. With a steady increase in the number of judgements from a court, it is possible that not all dimensions of these developments would be fully and accurately described by a manual approach. This is especially relevant for the study of the case law generated by very active courts, where precedent and judicial practice are often the main drivers of legal development.[26]

There are thus important and unexplored methodological advantages in marrying citation network analysis to qualitative legal analysis. Both methods target the content of judicial decisions, albeit in different ways and different aspects of that content. Citation network analysis and doctrinal legal studies share, as mentioned before, the idea of webs and patterns. Just as citation network analysis connects cases through their citations and orders the network in clusters, so too the doctrinal scholar organizes legal sources in a conceptual and systematic order, where different cases belong to different parts of the system. Most importantly, when used in a complementary manner legal analysis and citation network analysis can efficiently address the methodological shortcomings of each discrete method, offering new and advanced possibilities for both. On this background we conclude that network analysis of case-law citations is indeed compatible with doctrinal approaches to identifying what valid law is.

2) There are certain strengths and weaknesses to the network approach to a legal analysis compared to a doctrinal approach. The doctrinal approaches are often focused on legal problems, which occur in a single case or in a small group of cases. Especially in the continental European tradition, legal commentary orders individual legal events (cases) according to more general rules and principles and often structured around a

26 This practice is particularly apparent among international courts, see Alschner and Charlotin (n 20); Charlotin, 'The Place of Investment Awards and WTO Decisions in International Law: A Citation Analysis' (2017) 20 *Journal of International Economic Law*, 279; Ridi (n 8).

statutory law's logic. Its aim is to seek and ensure the logic and coherence of law, frequently relying on prior systematizations and established legal categories. This method poses the risk that inquiry will be disproportionately shaped by predefined categories and that therefore, cases which do not fit into these categories will be either left out as irrelevant or misrepresented.[27] Furthermore, the accounts of the case law will most likely not be based on exhaustive reading of all potentially relevant cases, or on research into all possible connections between these cases. Consequently, some cases that play a role in legal practice risk being overlooked by researchers. It is not uncommon that some cases are perceived as almost canonical by textbook authors and are therefore repeatedly used as examples or illustrations of some legal point even though those cases may not be very important in contemporary litigation. It may also be that some cases receive a lot of attention at the time of writing and that it is therefore extensively covered in a textbook. Only, such a case may not necessarily be an important case in future case law. If the Court decides not to give it any importance in their future decisions, then it could be said to be a case that created a lot of fuss for nothing.

By comparison, computer-assisted analysis of legal networks is not only comprehensive (with the limitation that what it represents (citations) is more superficial than what can be synthesized from qualitative analysis) but it can also expand beyond network analysis and into computational linguistic analysis, thereby revealing more about the citation practice than can be gleaned from the simple citations themselves. Using Natural Language Processing, the legal text that are cited as well as the text that surrounds citations can reveal more about the legal content of those citations and hence move closer towards a qualitative doctrinal analysis, while still being quantitatively comprehensive. This allows for increased flexibility in research approaches: It would be possible to – for example – investigate the language of a part of the corpus (defined for example by a specific citation cluster) and compare it with the language of the rest of the corpus.[28] Another approach would be to compare the language of courts across different time periods in order to detect change that reflects legal development over time. Alternatively, one can look for concepts or phrases

27 See Frese and Olsen (n 12).

28 Panagis et al. (n 18); Panagis et al., 'On Top of Topics: Leveraging Topic Modeling to Study the Dynamic Case-Law of International Courts.', in Bex and Villata (eds), *Legal Knowledge and Information Systems JURIX 2016* (2016).

that indicate departure from existing case law in order to investigate how the court introduces new law.

The strength of the traditional doctrinal approaches is conceptual richness and attention to detail in identifying distinguishing features between cases. Its weakness is mirrored in these strengths: It is difficult to create an overview over the entire and continually evolving case-law, excessive focus on detail can overshadow the larger picture, conceptual rigidity can hinder uptake of empirical data etc. Network analysis and computational methods more generally are limited by their quantitative nature. Citations can be identified and counted; words can be mathematically processed in NLP etc; implicit citations can be identified via verbatim repetition of phrases or use of very similar language, but ultimately these methods cannot be used to describe the law. To do so requires that this information is contextualised through legal theory (doctrine). Its strength, on the other hand is that these methods allows for analytic processing of much larger sets of data, is operational as empirical research and allows for much faster information processing than what can be achieved through manual reading.

B.II. The contributions of network analysis.

Network analysis can contribute to legal research in a number of different ways. Here is a couple of illustrations:

A recent study compared three different textbooks in three different languages on European Human Rights Law (each textbook is well acknowledged in their own language community: German, English and French). The study focused on what cases the textbooks cited in their chapters the discrimination prohibition (art. 14 in ECHR).[29] The finding was that not only did the authors cite different cases in support of their presentation of what the law is, they also (to some extent) cited different cases than the ones that were (most) cited by the court itself. Scrutinizing these findings closer using a qualitative approach (doctrinal analysis) the authors find that the empirical method added information about the court's practice that would have been difficult to obtain without using quantitative studies.[30] Furthermore, none of the leading textbooks were explicit about which methods they had used in selecting the cases they cited. It was

29 Frese and Olsen (n 12).
30 Ibid 131.

therefore impossible to ascertain whether the differences in the selection of cases used as the basis for describing European non-discrimination law was due to the use of different methodologies across the three textbooks or whether the differences could be explained in some other way.

Another slightly earlier study found that the so-called rich-get-richer effect applies to the way in which cases from ECtHR accumulates citations.[31] What this means is that citations to a case will tend to grow exponentially: the more it gets cited, the more likely it is that it will attract even more citations. In this study, the occurrence of the rich-get-richer effect is interpreted as an indication that the Court focuses on selected specific cases and uses these as fix-points in giving direction to the way the case law develops – much like Komárek has described in regards to the CJEU. The finding furthermore indicates that the Court – presumably the registry – deliberately chooses some citations over others. This in turn implies that not all precedents are given equal weight by the court – some have more weight than others because they are selected to represent the interpretations applied by the court to give meaning to the treaty text.

A final illustration of how network analysis can be used is found in a paper that uses a bi-partite network to identify which convention article a case is precedent for.[32] Judgments rendered by the ECtHR not only cite previous cases they also cite convention articles. A case-to-case network can therefore be enriched by adding information about case-to-article citations, thereby creating a bi-partite network (a graph containing two disjointed and independent set of nodes). This allows for information about what articles are cited by those cases that cite a former case. This can give a better indication of what a case is cited for. For example: Assume a case A deals with articles 9 (Freedom of thought, conscience and religion), 10 (Freedom of expression) and 11 (Freedom of assembly and association). Assume furthermore that this case is cited by, say, 25 subsequent cases. The question is now, what is it cited for? The answer to this question is not necessarily clear – A may be cited for different things by different cases. Yet it might also be possible that it is indeed cited for the same thing many times. One way of moving a bit closer towards a possible answer to this question would be by investigating what *articles* the citing cases cite. If say, 22 cases cite article 9 and none or only a few cites article 11, it is likely that

31 Leitão et al., 'Quantifying Long-Term Impact of Court Decisions' (2019) 4 *Applied Network Science*, 1.

32 Christensen et al., 'Identification of Case Content with Quantitative Network Analysis: An Example from the ECtHR' in Bex and Villata (eds), *Legal Knowledge and Information Systems JURIX 2016* (2016).

A is mostly cited for its contribution to the law on religious freedom.[33] In other words, *tell me who cites you, and I will tell you who you are.*

In a follow-up article, Olsen and Esmark[34] used the same bi-partite network to search for judgments that were cited more broadly across the entire network. In other words, where the above-mentioned article attempted to identify those judgments that were cited for specific article related content, this new article attempted the opposite: to identify judgments that were cited for more generalised principles of law. Dividing the network into subnetworks based on the Main-In score and computing two centrality scores (Pagerank) for each judgment – one score for its centrality in the subnetwork and one for its centrality in the overall network – the authors hypothesize that if a judgment is more central in the overall network than in its own network, then it is precedent for a legal principle that is relevant not only to the interpretation of the substantial rights provision that defines which sub-network it belongs to (its calculated MainIn), but to a range of cases that cut across the different rights provisions in the convention.

The advantage of a computational approach is precisely that it can be used to operationalize a metric that can show citation behaviour, which in turn can be interpreted as perceived value in practical use: the more a case is used (cited) the more value it has (relative, of course, to what it is used for). If the assumption is broadly correct, that citation behaviour is deliberate and a reflection of what case law is considered relevant and important in practice, then this information can also be used to predict what citations are likely to be used in which (future) cases, and can then be translated into recommender systems for the purpose of decision support etc.[35] The technology, when further developed, thus hold opportunities to enhance both efficiency and stringency in legal practice.

---

33 Ibid 51.

34 Olsen and Esmark, 'Needles in a Haystack: Using Network Analysis to Identify Cases That Are Cited for General Principles of Law by the European Court of Human Rights', in Wahlen (ed), *Computational Legal Studies* (2020).

35 The distribution within legal networks show that the distribution is far from random, but rather follows the characteristics of other scale-free networks. Smith (n 23), 313; Barabási and Albert, 'Emergence of Scaling in Random Networks' (1999) 286 *Science*, 509.

C. *Quantitative and qualitative approaches to precedent – stronger together*

To return to Dworkin's theory of interpretation as a model for generating legal knowledge: if the material selected at the pre-interpretive stage is incomplete, randomly selected or biased, then these deficiencies will influence the two next – interpretive and post-interpretive – stages of interpretation. The result of this will be a representation of legal reality that could become unreliable because it would not properly reflect (Dworkin would say "fit") the court's practice. It would be like a map that does not properly describe the territory.

Now, one does not have to subscribe *en bloc* to Dworkin's theory of law to see that legal interpretation can never be better than the pre-interpretive materials allow. If the pool of cases selected to become part of the process of legal interpretation during the pre-interpretive phase is either incomplete or inaccurate, then the subsequent interpretation will likely be affected by this bias. This may result in an inaccurate and, in the worst case, misleading rendering of what the law (in practice) really is. Using computational technology at the pre-interpretive stage, can assist the interpretive exercise by making it more complete and helping the interpreter find a more accurate balance point between 'fit' and 'justification', and thereby identify the best possible answers to legal questions. Moreover, citation network analysis may also aid the legal scholar in identifying otherwise hidden patterns in the citation network, potentially revealing facts in or about the case law that may have implications for our understanding of the law. Ultimately, to use a Dworkinian metaphor, computational analysis can help to make legal scholars more Herculean. But these new methods and approaches cannot replace qualitative legal analysis – they can only add to and qualify the use of such qualitative analysis.

Citation network analysis orders the documents (cases) into a structure based on the objective fact of case citation (a link between two cases), and it identifies cases that are central to this structure. It does not, however, uncover why they are central to this structure legally speaking (i.e. why case A cites case B). The content of citations and the reasons behind citations remain obscure. Moreover, citation network analysis gives a static image of a dynamic process: in reality law is not a perfect spider web, but more like an ongoing Scrabble game (Dworkin uses the analogy of chain novel), constantly evolving. Doctrinal analysis adds qualitative legal insight and meaning to the findings of the quantitative citation inquiry.

Citation network analysis could be complemented with more linguistic computational approaches, such as for example corpus linguistic analysis. This can further enhance insights at the pre-interpretive stage. Yet such analysis does not provide any conclusive answers as to the legal importance and relevance of individual texts either. Nor does it distinguish between more and less important cases or between more and less legally relevant concepts. Often, the software does not structure the documents historically but weighs and orders them by linguistic similarity. It looks for linguistic patterns in the case law but not at its legal structure. To answer any questions about why specific patterns occur, the findings must be interpreted in light of law's history and with the specialized knowledge of lawyers.

C.I. Finding Relevant Precedent

Authority is an implied or explicit part of most definitions of precedent.[36] Precedents must in some way prompt the respect of future decision-makers.[37] This paper has highlighted an operationalized conception of precedent that uses empirical methods to pin-point *relevant* precedents within the larger practice of courts. In this sense the operationalization is to aid in the selection of precedents, not in discovering what is behind the authority of the precedent. Rather, it is the working hypothesis behind the operationalization that the practice of a court is indicative of their precedential preferences, and it is these preferences that can be found using the methods highlighted. The methods find the authorities that authority cites.[38]

The use of these methods is not only for scholars who want an accurate picture of the practice of a court but also for lawyers who want to align their legal argumentation. Regarding the ECtHR this is imperative also for national courts because of the ECtHR's use of the principle of *res interpretata.* Contracting states are required to take the full body of relevant ECtHR case law into account when performing their obligations under the ECHR.[39] The trick is then to figure out *which* case law to take into account.

36 See Schauer, 'Authority and Authorities' (2008) *Virginia Law Review*, 1931; Duxbury, *The Nature and Authority of Precedent* (2008).

37 See Ridi (n 7), 364–365 for four models of how decisions can prompt respect.

38 See the title of the first empirical citation study John Henry Merryman, 'The Authority of Authority' (1954) 6 *Stanford Law Review*, 62.

39 See Arnardóttir, 'Res Interpretata, Erga Omnes Effect and the Role of the Margin of Appreciation in Giving Domestic Effect to the Judgments of the European Court of Human Rights' (2017) 28 *European Journal of International Law*, 819.

As an example of the network analysis being utilized by lawyers arguing in front of a national court, we can mention a Danish Supreme Court case on disenfranchisement of individuals under guardianship.[40] Such disenfranchisement is legal under the Danish constitution but was now being challenged as being in violation of ECHR, Protocol 1, art. 3. In defence of the existing disenfranchisement practice, the attorney the Danish State argued that the correct line to follow would be the general principle found in *Hirst v. United Kingdom;* that the right to vote is not absolute and that the state is allowed a margin of appreciation.[41] The *Hirst* case dealt with voting rights for convicted criminals and not individuals under guardianship. But *Hirst* is the most cited judgment in cases on voting rights and contains the main principles for interpreting the right to vote. The applicant instead relied on *Alajos Kiss v. Hungary*. This case dealt with disenfranchisement of a person under partial guardianship and in the judgment, this was considered disproportionate to Article 3 of Protocol 1 of the ECHR.[42] But *Kiss* is not much cited in subsequent case-law. In the Danish case, the attorney for the state presented a citation network analysis which showed that the general principle of *Hirst* was a more integrated, and more cited,[43] part of the ECtHR's practice, whereas *Kiss* (and other judgments) were more marginal. Relatedly the attorney also presented an analysis which showed the increasing emphasis in ECtHR's case law on the role of margin of appreciation, a principle that (according to *Hirst*) is of high relevance and importance in voting rights cases. The Danish case ended by the Supreme Court finding the constitutional provision proportional and in line with their commitments under the ECHR.[44] In the subsequent

---

40 See *Stemmeretssagen*, Danish Supreme Court Judgment of 18 January, 2018, case 159/2017, published in U.2018.1460H.

41 See *Hirst v. United Kingdom*, App. No. 74025/01 (06/10/2005).

42 See *Alajos Kiss v. Hungary*, App. No. 38832/06 (20/05/2010).

43 As of 3rd November 2020 *Hirst* is cited in 88 subsequent judgments, *Kiss* is cited in 17 subsequent judgments. The same numbers as of 22 June 2017 was *Hirst*: 81, *Kiss*: 14.

44 See *Stemmeretssagen*, U.2018.1460H, analysing *Hirst v. United Kingdom, Zdanoka v. Latvia no. 58278/00 (2006), Scoppola v. Italy (no. 3) No. 126/05 (2012) and Alajos Kiss v. Hungary.* For a discussion on the relevance of citation analysis in general as well as specifically in relation to the Danish stemmeretssagen, see: Bogetoft, 'Er end om et bedre præjudikat, hvis den har flere citationer? Om netværksanalyser baseret på citationstal' (2020) 2 *Tidsskrift for Rettsvitenskap*, 133. For a reply, see: Olsen and Christensen, 'Præjudikatsbrug og netværksanalyse' (2020) 5 *Tidsskrift for Rettsvitenskap*, 133.

judgment of the ECtHR,[45] the Court stresses the importance of *Hirst*, and cites extensively from that ruling.[46] The Court immediately thereafter stresses the importance of the principle of subsidiarity and margin of appreciation.[47] Most importantly, *Hirst* is also cited for the principle that it is not a requirement for depriving a person of their right to vote that a specific and individual assessment of their voting capacity has been carried out.[48] *Kiss*, which was again relied upon by the disenfranchised applicant is also mentioned by the Court in its judgment, but it seems clear from the language used by the court that this judgments is viewed as an exception because of its wide ranging blanket character. The situation in Hungary, thus, was significantly different from the situation in Denmark.[49] While it would be a mistake to conclude that *Kiss* was not afforded any weight in the ruling – the Court pointed out that the Danish Supreme Court's analysis of *Kiss* was a sign that it had conducted a thorough analysis of the case, which in turn supported that its decision should be respected, in our view, the result of the network analysis corresponds well with the qualitative analysis: *Hirst* was, and still is, the most important precedent in this area because it continues to define the main framework for deciding on the legality of limiting the right to vote.

C.II. Possibilities and Limitations

The first networks in the context of legal research were built on case-to-case citations.[50] Much subsequent research has been done on case-to-case citation networks, so far culminating in the development of machine learning techniques used to analyse how different features impact on the predictability of citations.[51]

Complex data science methods have been developed to create more nuanced forms of analysis. For example, one method identifies the most

45 *Strøbye and Rosenlind v. Denmark*, Apps. Nos. 25802/18 and 27338/18 (02/02/2021).

46 Ibid para. 91

47 Ibid para. 92–93

48 Ibid para. 114

49 Ibid para. 107.

50 Lupu and Voeten (n 13); James H Fowler and Sangick Jeon, 'The Authority of Supreme Court Precedent' (2008) 30 *Social Networks*, 16; Smith (n 23).

51 Enys Mones and others, 'Emergence of Network Effects and Predictability in the Judicial System' (2021) 11 *Scientific Reports*, 2740. In this article the authors also show how a recommender system for case law citations may be construed.

prevalent legal content that a case is cited for. Using bi-partite network analysis one can identify not only case-to-case relations, but also case-to-article relations, thereby identifying which articles in the ECHR are more relevant in the case-to-case relationship.[52] Another method has been developed to build case-to-paragraph networks, thereby identifying not only the cited cases, but the precise part of the case that is cited.[53] This allows for more accurate identification of the wording that are relied on as precedent, both for individual citations, groups of citations (clusters) and overall. Building in a time component can show how the courts language change over time. Still, the rougher approach of case-to-case network analysis also reveals some structural characteristics pertaining to what cases are used as precedent, and how citation structure evolves.

Another obstacle is that citations are sometimes imprecise or missing. Citations can be unclear or indirect, leaving the reader guessing what exact precedent is relied upon. Linguistic data science methods have been developed to identify the "indirect" precedent in these cases, as for example when a new case use language from a former case verbatim.[54]. There may still be some work to do in producing algorithms that can trace all such "indirect" precedents, but this seems well within reach in light of the latest advancements in NLP.

A bigger problem is perhaps the fact that the data science approaches are necessarily "historical". If one infers precedent only from the courts' (direct or indirect) citation practices, one can only identify cases as precedent once they have been applied by the court. But what about cases that have not been cited by the court so far – are they really all devoid of precedent value? Or what about cases that have been cited only once or twice because they have been decided recently and therefore have not had much time to be cited?

Some cases are considered by lawyers to be relevant and significant almost the same day they have been decided by the court.[55] Are there good reasons why they should not be considered relevant as precedent when setting out descriptions of valid law even though they have not yet had time to be cited? Or what about cases that decide issues in rare areas of law, where new cases come about only infrequently. Many would think

52 Christensen, Olsen and Tarissan (n 32).

53 Panagis, Sadl and Tarissan (n 18).

54 Ibid.

55 See Antoine Vauchez, 'EU Law Classics in the Making: Methodological Notes on Grands Arrêts at the European Court of Justice' in Fernanda Nicola and Bill Davies (eds), *EU Law Stories* (2017).

that judgments in areas of law where cases are rare would be relevant when new cases arise even though these judgments have been issued several years ago and never been cited. In such scenarios would it not be misleading to rely on court citations as a proxy for precedent?

Indeed, this is a weakness: when focusing exclusively on actual use, latent precedent will not be part of an analysis. This would be quite unusual and most legal scholars would find it wrong not to include the most recent case law in some field simply because those cases have not yet been cited.

On the other hand, it could be argued that there will be some degree of uncertainty associated with whether a new judgement will have such a forceful effect that it normatively changes the existing law in the field. A new decision is after all only one event in a long series of events. Going back to Ronald Dworkins legal theory (again without having to necessarily endorse his entire theoretical framework) a new judgment is just one new element in the Chain of law. Whether this new element should be read as giving the story so far a new twist or whether it should be seen as a mistaken turn of events to be corrected in subsequent judgments is an open question – legal interpretation would most often allow for both options. From a scholarly point of view, therefore, it will be difficult to ascertain the precedential effect of such a new judgment before it impacts normatively on the way the court perceives the law in the field – which in turn means that the new case is authoritatively cited by the Court (explicitly or at the least implicitly, which may also be open to interpretation).

Thus, if it is argued that there must be some empirical basis for identifying whether a given judgement has precedent value, one must wait to see the subsequent case law before one can measure whether the significance attributed to the case will be what commentators have predicted on the ground of their assessment of its importance. Conversely, in relation to the need for practitioners to keep up to date with the latest developments of the law, it is clear that this (data science driven) method is inadequate as it cannot be used to evaluate the significance of a new judgement *here and now*. Here the choice lies between either guessing (interpreting) the importance of the new case and its use in legal argument, or refraining from relying on the new case on the ground that its value as a precedent is uncertain – a choice that will presumably always be influenced by the intended purpose of a given analysis. Data science approaches may, have a tendency to "freeze" the view of law because it focuses on facts that are necessarily belonging to the past – thereby neglecting a more normatively dynamic approach familiar from doctrinal approaches embedded in the more interpretive oriented tradition of legal science.

D. Conclusion – What is precedent?

We have introduced a new way of looking at precedent, or more accurately looking *for* precedent. A way that is more data driven than the classical doctrinal method proposes. This approach is not without its weaknesses, but it also has several strengths. One of its main strengths is that it renders inquiries into legal practice more transparent and reproducible. Thus, these new approaches advances legal science in regards to its pursuit of answers to the main question that drives most legal doctrinal inquiry, i.e. "what is valid law?" Furthermore, our findings on the ECtHR case law suggest that the model of legislative precedent proposed by Komárek has good explanatory value for the data sets we have explored. This further indicates that the Court seeks to uphold consistency in its very large set of case law by systematically citing broadly the same set of case paragraphs when deciding what they perceive are similar from a legal point view even though factual situations differ. The cited paragraphs are micro-units of legal normativity used to structure and legitimize new decisions under the same Convention provision. Using our empirical approach, it will be possible to map all the micro-units and explore how the landscape of precedents evolves and changes over time. In our view, this constitutes the present forefront of network analysis approaches to legal research.

E. Bibliography

Wolfgang Alschner, and Damien Charlotin, 'The Growing Complexity of the International Court of Justice's Self-Citation Network' (2018) 29(1) *European Journal of International Law*, 83–112 <https://doi.org/10.1093/ejil/chy002>

Oddný Mjöll Arnardóttir, 'Res Interpretata, Erga Omnes Effect and the Role of the Margin of Appreciation in Giving Domestic Effect to the Judgments of the European Court of Human Rights' (2017) 28 *European Journal of International Law*, 819–43 <https://doi.org/10.1093/ejil/chx045>

Albert-László Barabási, and Réka Albert, 'Emergence of Scaling in Random Networks' (1999) 286 *Science*, 509–12 <https://doi.org/10.1126/science.286.5439.509>

Rasmus Arler Bogetoft, 'Er en dom et bedre præjudikat, hvis den har flere citationer? Om netværksanalyser baseret på citationstal.' (2020) 133 *Tidsskrift for Rettsvitenskap*, 217–260. <https://doi.org/10.18261/issn.1504-3096-2020-02-03-01>

Armin von Bogdandy, and Ingo Venzke, *International Judicial Lawmaking: On Public Authority and Democratic Legitimation in Global Governance* (Springer, Berlin, Heidelberg 2012)

Michael J., II Bommarito, Daniel Katz, and Jon Zelner, 'Law As a Seamless Web?: Comparison of Various Network Representations of the United States Supreme Court Corpus (1791–2005)', in Association for Computing Machinery (ed), *Proceedings of the 12th International Conference on Artificial Intelligence and Law, ICAIL '09* (ACM, New York 2009), 234–235 <https://doi.org/10.1145/1568234.1568270>

Damien Charlotin, 'The Place of Investment Awards and WTO Decisions in International Law: A Citation Analysis' (2017) 20 *Journal of International Economic Law*, 279–99 <https://doi.org/10.1093/jiel/jgx010>

Martin Lolle Christensen, Henrik Palmer Olsen, and Fabien Tarissan, 'Identification of Case Content with Quantitative Network Analysis: An Example from the ECtHR', in Floris Bex and Serena Villata (eds), *Legal Knowledge and Information Systems JURIX 2016* (IOS Press, Amsterdam, Berlin, Washington 2016) <https://doi.org/10.3233/978-1-61499-726-9-53>

Mattias Derlén, and Johan Lindholm, 'Goodbye van Gend En Loos, Hello Bosman? Using Network Analysis to Measure the Importance of Individual CJEU Judgments' (2014) 20 *European Law Journal*, 667–87 <https://doi.org/10.1111/eulj.12077>

Neil Duxbury, *The Nature and Authority of Precedent* (Cambridge University Press, Cambridge 2008)

Ronald Dworkin, *Law's Empire* (Belknap Press, Cambridge, Massachusetts 1986)

James H. Fowler, and Sangick Jeon, 'The Authority of Supreme Court Precedent' (2008) 30 *Social Networks*, 16–30 <https://doi.org/10.1016/j.socnet.2007.05.001>

Amalie Frese and Henrik Palmer Olsen, 'Citing Case Law: A Comparative Study of Legal Textbooks on European Human Rights Law' (2019) 11 *European Journal of Legal Studies*, 41

John Gardner, 'Some Types of Law', in Douglas E Edlin (ed), *Common Law Theory* (Cambridge University Press, Cambridge 2007) 51–72

Hans Kelsen, *Pure Theory of Law* (University of California Press, Berkeley 1967)

Jon M, Kleinberg, 'Authoritative Sources in a Hyperlinked Environment' (1999) 46 *Journal of the ACM (JACM)*, 604–32

Jan Komárek, 'Reasoning with Previous Decisions: Beyond the Doctrine of Precedent' (2013) 61 *American Journal of Comparative Law*, 149–71 <https://doi.org/10.5131/AJCL.2012.0013>

Jorge C. Leitão, Sune Lehmann, and Henrik Palmer Olsen, 'Quantifying Long-Term Impact of Court Decisions' (2019) 4 *Applied Network Science*, 1–15 <https://doi.org/10.1007/s41109-018-0110-3>

Yonatan Lupu, and Erik Voeten, 'Precedent in International Courts: A Network Analysis of Case Citations by the European Court of Human Rights' (2012) 42 *British Journal of Political Science*, 413–39 <https://doi.org/10.1017/S0007123411000433>

Mikael Rask Madsen, 'The Challenging Authority of the European Court of Human Rights: From Cold War Legal Diplomacy to the Brighton Declaration and Backlash' (2016) 79 *Law & Contemp. Probs.*, 141

Frederic William Maitland, 'Prologue to a History of English Law' (1898) 14 *Law Quarterly Review*, 13

John Henry Merryman, 'The Authority of Authority' (1954) 6 *Stanford Law Review*, 613

Nathan Miller, 'An International Jurisprudence? The Operation of "Precedent" Across International Tribunals' (2002) 15 *Leiden Journal of International Law*, 483–526 <https://doi.org/10.1017/S0922156502000249>

Enys Mones, Piotr Sapieżyński, Simon Thordal, Henrik Palmer Olsen, and Sune Lehmann, 'Emergence of Network Effects and Predictability in the Judicial System' (2021) 11 *Scientific Reports*, 1 <https://doi.org/10.1038/s41598-021-82430-x> accessed 8 June 2021

Henrik Palmer Olsen and Martin Lolle Christensen, 'Præjudikatsbrug og netværksanalyse – Svar til Bogetoft' (2020) 133 *Tidsskrift for Rettsvitenskap*, 691–713 <https://doi.org/10.18261/issn.1504-3096-2020-05-04>

Henrik Palmer Olsen, and Magnus Esmark, 'Needles in a Haystack: Using Network Analysis to Identify Cases That Are Cited for General Principles of Law by the European Court of Human Rights', in Ryan Whalen (ed), *Computational Legal Studies* (Edward Elgar Publishing, Cheltenham 2020)

Henrik Palmer Olsen, Jacob Livingston Slosser, Thomas Troels Hildebrandt, and Cornelius Wiesener, 'What's in the Box? The Legal Requirement of Explainability in Computationally Aided Decision-Making in Public Administration' (2019) 162 *iCourts Working Paper Series* <https://doi.org/10.2139/ssrn.3402974>

Yannis Panagis, Martin Lolle Christensen, and Urska Sadl, 'On Top of Topics: Leveraging Topic Modeling to Study the Dynamic Case-Law of International Courts.', in Floris Bex and Serena Villata (eds), *Legal Knowledge and Information Systems JURIX 2016* (IOS Press, Amsterdam, Berlin, Washington 2016) 161–66

Yannis Panagis, Urska Sadl, and Fabien Tarissan, 'Giving Every Case Its (Legal) Due The Contribution of Citation Networks and Text Similarity Techniques to Legal Studies of European Union Law', in Adam Wyner and Giovanni Casini (eds), *Legal Knowledge and Information Systems JURIX 2017* (IOS Press, Luxembourg 2017) 59–68 <https://doi.org/10.3233/978-1-61499-838-9-59>

Niccolò Ridi '"Mirages of an Intellectual Dreamland"? Ratio, Obiter and the Textualization of International Precedent' (2019) 10 *Journal of International Dispute Settlement*, 361–95

———, 'The Shape and Structure of the "Usable Past": An Empirical Analysis of the Use of Precedent in International Adjudication' (2019) 10 *Journal of International Dispute Settlement*, 200–247 <https://doi.org/10.1093/jnlids/idz007>

Frederick Schauer, 'Authority and Authorities' (2008) 94 *Virginia Law Review*, 1931–61

Mohamed Shahabuddeen, *Precedent in the World Court* (Cambridge University Press, Cambridge 2007)

Raimo Siltala, *A Theory of Precedent: From Analytical Positivism to a Post-Analytical Philosophy of Law* (Hart Publishing, Oxford 2000)

Thomas A. Smith, 'The Web of Law' (2007) 44 *San Diego Law Review*, 309–54

Antoine Vauchez, 'EU Law Classics in the Making: Methodological Notes on Grands Arrêts at the European Court of Justice', in Fernanda Nicola and Bill Davies (eds), *EU Law Stories* (Cambridge University Press, Cambridge 2017), 21–34 <https://doi.org/10.1017/9781316340479.002>

The Practical Construction of Precedent in the Jurisprudence of the European Court of Human Rights

Amalie Frese

I Introduction

One of the key actors in the development of European human rights law is the European Court of Human Rights (ECtHR and the Court)[1]. In guarding the Convention by ensuring that the contracting states respects the rights enshrined in the Convention, the Court is a pivotal actor in clarifying the scope and meaning of the Convention. Consequently, the case law of the Court is a crucial source of law in the area of human rights in Europe. As the Court resolves questions of legal uncertainty in the cases brought to the Court, it concurrently sets a precedent for how to resolve other similar cases that may reach the Court in the future. Comprehensive accounts of European human rights law are only possible by reference to the case law of ECtHR. However, the endeavour of selecting which cases that are authoritative and have status as precedents gives rise to a number of further questions relating to how we assess case law authority and what the practice of precedents for the ECtHR is.

This chapter addresses one of the basic questions related to the role of precedent and case law in European human rights law by asking *how* the European Court of Human Rights rely on past cases. This is achieved by answering the questions of 1) Which cases become judicial precedents? And 2) Which content does the Court use from these cases in later cases?

To answer this question I use a case law citation network, which maps the references and citations between judgments of the Court, in order to gain insight into how the Court is using its own past cases in its decision-making. I thus focus on the way the past cases' content are recycled in later cases.

The advantage of perceiving the explicit citations and references in a network is that this method can facilitate identification of the varying

1 *See generally* Madsen, 'The Challenging Authority of The European Court of Human Rights: From Cold War Legal Diplomacy to the Brighton Declaration and Backlash' (2016) 79 *Law and Contemporary Problems*, 141.

degrees of authority, which the Court attributes to the cases measured by how frequently the cases are used, i.e. cited or referred to in later case law. Citations and references are consequently assumed to represent precedential authority.

The study utilizes a network technology, which allows for shifting the viewpoint of case importance from the legal scholarly point of view of what precedent consists in, to the point of view of the Court itself and thus provides insight into which cases that have authority seen from the perspective of the bench.

I combine the quantitative network approach with a qualitative analysis of the most cited paragraphs in the most cited cases of the ECtHR. For this purpose I select a smaller sample of cases in the area concerned with the ECHR's prohibition against discrimination (Article 14). It is helpful for the study to focus on one legal area, since such focus makes it possible to explore the development of the specific legal domain over time by detecting principles and rules specific to this legal domain, which are repeatedly referred to or cited in past cases.

This chapter shows that precedent citation is a versatile practice in the jurisprudence of the European Court of Human Rights.

Firstly, it is not cases as such that serves as precedents, but rather arguments, principles and rules within past cases, which are referred to and cited in later cases as building blocks for constructing the overall conclusion of the relevant case. As a consequence, the use of past cases in judicial decision-making develops the law forwardly.

Secondly, rather than observing a single, uniform type of precedent from the case law citations, the study finds that there exist more than one type of judicial precedents in the case law of the ECtHR. On this basis I argue that precedent should be understood as a broadly conceived legal tool in judicial decision-making particularly in the international sphere, where it allows a court to develop the meaning and clarifications of the legal basis according to its own jurisprudence. As a consequence, case-based reasoning and precedent is context-dependent and court-dependent. This means that there is not a one-size-fit-all type of precedent, defining its meaning across all contexts and its role in all courts.

Finally, this chapter shares its objective and methodology with other chapters in the anthology for example William Byrne's chapter *Reconstructing Scholarly Authority in International Law* on the construction of authority as entry point to exploring precedent. Moreover, Henrik Palmer Olsen's and Martin Lolle Christensen's chapter *The Weight of Precedent: From Abstract Theorizing to Concrete Application: The case of ECtHR* explores for the technologies which are employed in this chapter and provides an overview of how network analysis can be used in legal research and in particular with respect to studies of precedent.

The chapter proceeds as follows. In section two I account for the theoretical framework, the relevant conceptualisation of precedent, the ECtHR as a case law driven court and network analysis as a tool for studying the construction of precedent. I section three I conduct the case law citation network in two steps: I select a subset of cases based on these being cited most frequently in the network, i.e. their mathematical authority, and subsequently analyse the content of these cases qualitatively based on a paragraph-to-paragraph network. I section five I conclude the chapter on the practical construction of precedent in the case law of ECtHR.

II Precedent in theory and practice

In international law there is no binding doctrine of precedent. However, this of course does not mean that international courts cannot refer to their own past case law, and in fact, it takes very little insight to confirm that they do so. Therefore, in light of the importance of case law for the clarification of the European Convention of Human Rights and the general acceptance of this central role of the case law, a scrutiny of the characteristics of the case law system of the European Court of Human Rights is in order.

Scholarship has to a very large extent focussed on the dichotomy between binding versus non-binding precedent. Properly binding precedents is claimed to prevail in the common law system and to develop law from lower courts.[2] Inversely, non-binding precedents are claimed to only be guiding in nature and that such type of precedent is predominantly used in civil law systems. The attention has therefore been on the absence of *stare decisis* in civil law systems in defining a difference between the common and civil law system, frequently leading to the assumption that there either is no precedent in civil law systems or that precedent is an inadequate imitation of a common law precedent. These a priori assumptions about precedent in civil and common law systems unfortunately divert the focus away from the practical importance and actual effects of the use of

2 Mathias Siems, *Comparative Law* (2018) 53–55.

case law.[3] Indeed the practical influence of a past case can be significant on later judgments even if the doctrine of precedent does not follow the rules of *stare decisis* and past cases used are not per se binding later decision-makers. In other words, acknowledging the existence in practice of different types and degrees of constraint or authority does not equal denying that precedents sometimes do in fact constrain, but the recognition of different types of precedent allows for fruitful scientific inquiries based on the precedential practice rather than predefined concepts.

I thus propose to operate with pluralism in relation to the concept of precedent. I build upon several studies, which abandon a narrow version of precedent and the common versus civil law dichotomy, and instead turn to the practical importance, which reasoning with past case law can have.

Jan Komárek has for example been a proponent of a plurality of precedent by proposing to distinguish between a case-bound model of precedent and a legislative model of precedent, where adherence in the former model is to the cases as such and the latter characterises a use of precedents, as exemplified by CJEU, where judgments are written as legislative texts, and in the later use of these judgments, as precedents the later court (or member states' courts) searches for rule-pronouncement by the higher court.[4]

Similarly, Marc Jacob scrutinised the versatile modes of precedent in the CJEU's decision-making form and its role in judicial law-making and maps different modes in which the CJEU uses precedent.[5]

Mattias Derlén and Johan Lindholm have also thoroughly examined the CJEU's use of precedents in several studies. They find that the Court does not exercise any strict adherence to its past cases, yet, there is a system of citing which is neither random nor confused, but a system that reflects the CJEU as a constitutional court, providing guidance to the member states in regard to EU's primary and secondary law.[6]

These studies demonstrate that a concept of a plurality of precedent, where the function and role of precedent is not deducted from theory and

---

3 Derlén & Lindholm, 'Peek-A-Boo, It's a Case Law System!: Comparing the European Court of Justice and the United States Supreme Court from a Network Perspective' (2017) 18 GERMAN L.J., 647, 649.

4 See Komárek, 'Reasoning with Previous Decisions: Beyond the Doctrine of Precedent' (2013) 61 AM. J. COMP. L., 149.

5 See Marc Jacob, *Precedents and Case-based Reasoning in the European Court of Justice: Unfinished Business* (2014).

6 Derlén & Lindholm, 'Characteristics of Precedent: The Case Law of the European Court of Justice in Three Dimensions' (2015) 16 GERMAN L.J., 1073.

its binding force is not pre-defined, allows for inquiries where the practical importance and effects are the research interests.

I employ this version of precedent and demonstrate in the case law of ECtHR precedent is a practice different from, and with much more variety than precedent as the version of *stare decisis* captures. In this chapter, I take precedent in the jurisprudence of the ECtHR, to mean 'whatever the Court uses it for'. In other words, I do not take precedent to only mean those cases, which the court uses for a specific purpose and I do not assume that precedent citation implies one particular normative force. This does not entail that I deny that precedent can constrain, but I assume that cases can exercise different types and degrees of authority on cases adjudicated later in time. Concretely, I assume that cases achieve their authority through the Court's frequent use—i.e. citations and references to a case is a reflection of the case's importance and authority. The main inquiry of the chapter is not whether precedents constrain, but how the ECtHR, through its use of past case law itself, practically constructs precedents.

Lastly, the study in this chapter is concerned with self-precedent or what can be called horizontal precedent. In other words, it is the ECtHR's use of its own past cases in its later adjudication that is the object of study, rather than, for example, a lower court using case law from a higher court as is traditionally the understanding from a common law system and which could be called vertical precedent.

A. *The role of case law at ECtHR*

The role of case law for the European Convention of Human Rights should be explored in light of the institutional characteristics of the European Court of Human Right and its internal practices of decision-making as well as the considerations of how these variables influence the practices of precedent citation.

The ECtHR is the supreme interpreter of the European Convention of Human Rights. Individuals and institutions of contracting states to the Convention may send applications to the Court for assessment of whether a contracting state has violated the rights enshrined in the Convention. As the supreme interpreter of the Convention, the ECtHR has a *review* role, which essentially means that it is a control organization. This review role entails the judicial power to ensure that decisions by domestic courts are made in coherence with the law that the decisions are justified and procedurally approved legislative acts are in concordance with the relevant higher order laws, i.e. the European Convention of Human Rights[7]. Opposite dispute settlement, which entails settling disputes between parties and means *ruling on facts*, review functions like that of the ECtHR means *ruling on law* as the Court interprets the legal instruments with which it was set up and as such it is similar to an appeal court or a court of cassation.

Additionally, the fact that the Convention is written with a very sparse use of words makes it advantageous to use past cases in the decision-making. Due to formulation of the rights in the Convention as general principles, pre-existing interpretations of these from previously delivered cases is both a heuristic and a pragmatic tool.

Moreover, the informal practices of decision-making at the ECtHR also play important roles beyond the formal organisation of the Court. In this regard three aspects are of significance; the law clerks' drafting practices, the role of submissions by parties to a case and the internal citation guidelines.

Firstly, the law clerks at the Court are the first to receive the case material in the chambers. The initial stage of drafting a judgment is thus conducted by the law clerks, who begins the drafting process by searching the ECtHR's database for similar past cases, which can be relevant. This research stage of the judgment drafting is important because it has potential to provide the law clerk with a broader range of potential precedents than what may be within the pre-existing knowledge of the drafting lawyer.

Secondly, ECtHR is not a court embedded in any nation state. Its legal culture is pluralistic as it is staffed with 47 different nationalities with different legal educations, experience, roles and outlook. Such diversity in the working environment is likely to also be a conducive factor for diversity in the way of using past cases as well as variety in which cases that are perceived as important. The judgment drafting is therefore organised so as to incorporate a number of quality checks and streamlining, which is intended to ensure a common ground and takes the form of both templates for the drafting and informal conversations among the clerks and judges in the chambers.

Thirdly, citation guidelines have recently been introduced at ECtHR also with the purpose of guaranteeing uniformity in the use of past cases. The citation guidelines require the drafting lawyers (or judges) to refer

---

7 On these aspects of judicial governance see for example: Sweet, *Governing with Judges, Constitutional Politics in Europe* (2000); Alter, 'The Multiple Roles of International Courts and Tribunals' in Dunoff and Pollack (eds), *Interdisciplinary Perspectives on International Law and International Relations: The State of the Art* (2013) 345.

to the temporally first relevant case, the most recent relevant case and then cases 'in between'. The law clerks describe these citation guidelines as formalizing a practice, which was already internalized in their work of judgment drafting and as such is uncontroversial. From a scholarly point of view, however, particularly the choice of which cases 'in between' that are considered authoritative and deserving of a reference in a later judgment is of interest.

These factors in the ECtHR's formal and external roles and informal and internal practices, can support the Court's use of its own case law and furthermore show that self-citation form part of a larger purposeful practice as well as be indicative of the Court's own perception of case law authority and which cases that best justify its later decisions.

B. Case law citation network analysis

Case law can be perceived as a bundle of cases delivered by a court independently of each other at different points in time. This is often the impression one gets when reading legal textbooks, where the cases that are discussed, as landmark cases seem to be handpicked according to which of the cases the author and legal expert subjectively perceives as most representative of the relevant legal area.

However, case law also implies a whole or a corpus of judgments. An entire corpus of cases require some kind of processing in order to empirically explore which of the cases that carry more authority than the rest. As such case law can also be perceived through the optics of a network.

James Fowler was among the first to introduce network analysis in legal scholarship with two articles applying the approach to studies of precedent in the US Supreme Court.[8] Similarly, Yonatan Lupo and Erik Voeten used network analysis to study case citations and precedent in the case law of the European Court of Human Rights.[9]

I also draw inspiration for this study from several previously conducted studies on the CJEU. Mattias Derlén and Johan Lindholm have been using network analysis and similar methods to conduct research on the charac-

---

8 Fowler et al., 'Network Analysis and the Law: Measuring the Legal Importance of Precedents at the U.S. Supreme Court' (2007) 15 *Pol. Analysis*, 324; Fowler & Jeon 'The Authority of Supreme Court Precedent' (2008) 30 *Soc. Networks*, 16.

9 Lupu & Voeten, 'Precedent in International Courts: A Network Analysis of Case Citations by The European Court of Human Rights' (2012) 42, *British J. Pol. Sci.*, 413.

teristics of the CJEU's precedent system and comparing it the US Supreme Court.[10]

This is not an exhaustive overview of relevant scholarship, but it shows that what these studies have in common is the use of case law citation networks to measure importance of individual cases and on that basis achieve an empirical basis for analyses of legal importance in the jurisprudence, legal decision-making, and legal development.

While I in this chapter use the network analysis approach in the studies mentioned above, I furthermore supplement the analysis by selecting a smaller sample of cases, connecting their cited *paragraphs* in a paragraph-to-paragraph network. This analytical supplement allows me to explore the content of the most cited cases and their judicial authority.

All network studies are essentially charting links or relationships between entities, here, legal cases. This network analysis therefore evolves around nodes that are judgments, and links constituted by citations and references. Hence, beyond simply mapping the connections between the entities in the network, a network analysis will also entail measures of authority. This level of a network analysis, as a 'case-to-case citation network' where the judgments are linked together through references and citations, displays mathematical authorities. The authorities are mathematical in the sense that they are calculated on the basis of their ingoing citations and references. Yet, in what way does mathematical authority correspond to judicial or legal authority? In order to answer this question we need to ask what citations are and what they mean.

Citations and references to past cases is a common legal decision-making tool and used by a court to draw from past cases that are relevant for the present case. References and citations may take place for a number of purposes, e.g. if cases represents similar legal issues or similar factual circumstances that justifies a similar ruling, or that it is similar in certain aspects but differs in other respects and thus justifies a ruling that departs from the ruling in the past case. Importantly, a reference does not necessarily mean complete endorsement of the past case, but recognition of some element of relevance. To put it bluntly, a court does not refer to a past case that is completely irrelevant and unimportant for the present case of adjudication.

10 *See e.g.* Derlén & Lindholm, 'Characteristics of Precedent: The Case Law of the European Court of Justice in Three Dimensions' (2015) 16 *German L.J.*, 1073; Derlén & Lindholm 'Goodbye van Gen den Loos, Hello Bosman? Using Network Analysis to Measure the importance of Individual CJEU Judgments' (2014) 20 *Eur. L.J.*, 667.

A few significant limitations to the approach ought also to be mentioned here. Firstly, the most significant limitation to a network approach to case law and judicial authority is what may be termed 'tacit precedents' in the sense that courts may use past cases without directly referring to or citing them. Such practice cannot be captured by a citation network and it cannot be ruled out that the use of tacit precedents is integrated into drafting practices at ECtHR. Nonetheless, while the network approach cannot capture tacit precedents and the use of the approach does not convey a courts perception of its case law in an exhaustive manner, it is clear that explicit references and citations constitute a solid practice in the drafting process at ECtHR.

This connects with a general challenge for network approaches to case law at the quantitative level, is that it is not possible to see exactly what the citations, i.e. the ties in the network, are directed at. A citation in a network simply points to a past case as a whole. It is therefore necessary to supplement the quantitative network analysis with analyses of the content of the relevant ties in the network as will be the object of the following analysis.

III. The ECtHR case law citation network

A case-to-case network was built with cases delivered by the ECtHR. The network consists of cases from the beginning of the Court's judicial activity in 1960 to end of 2013.

The entire citation network of judgments of the ECtHR contains 16263 judgments and 57691 citations and consists of judgments only and thus not of admissibility decisions. All the judgments in the network are thus delivered by Chambers or Grand Chamber.

The network can be illustrated with the graph below. The graph exemplifies the judgments as nodes in the network and their ties as citations or references between them. Authority is represented by the size of the node which means that the larger the node the more references the judgment, which the node represents, receives.

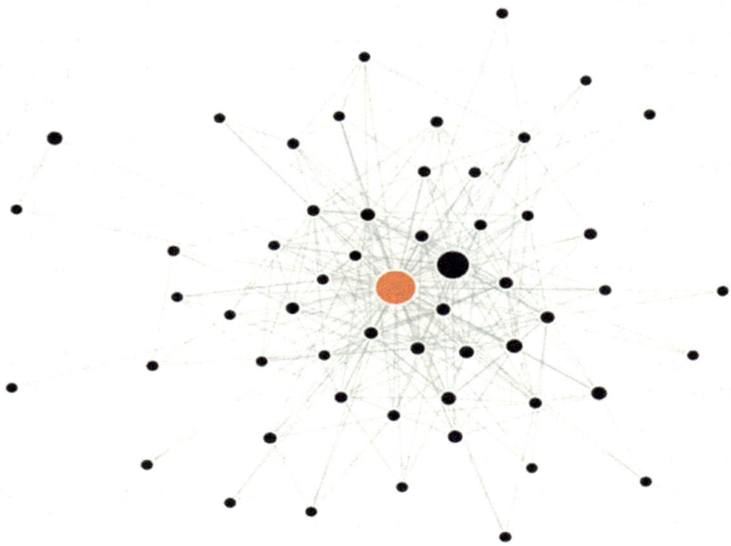

Figure 1: representation of case law citation network.

As accounted for above, for a network of communication, which a case-law citation network essentially constitutes, a metric of centrality is necessary for measuring authority. In this study degree-centrality is used as metric for case authority. Degree-centrality illustrates the number of citations of a particular judgment by counting the citations, which a judgment receives overall from all other judgments in the networks. The interest is whether some judgments receive a high number of citations.[11] Degree-centrality is the simplest metric for measuring authority in a network.[12]

The case of *Frydlender v France*[13] has the highest in-degree score of 1173 while it is only itself citing 6 other cases. Six judgments have an in-degree score over 500 equivalent of only 0,04% of all the judgments in the network. The judgments which receive over 500 citations, all concern Article 6 of the Convention, which guarantees the right to a fair trial. The remaining distribution is 122 judgments, equivalent of 0,8%, receiving between

11 *See* Freeman, 'Centrality in Social Networks Conceptual Clarification' (1978) 1 *SOC. Networks*, 215.

12 *See e.g.* Kleinberg 'Authoritative Sources in a Hyperlinked Environment' (1999) 46 *J. ACM*, 604.

13 *Case 30979/96 Frydlender V France*,(2000).

100–500 citations, 236 judgments receiving between 50–100 citations or equivalent of 1,45%, 6020 judgments receiving between 1 and 50 citations equivalent of 37%. Finally, 9873 judgments do not receive any citations, which constitutes 60,7% of the judgments in the citation network. The average in-degree score is 5.9 and this is also the average out-degree.

Very few judgments cite more than 100 other judgments, 0,02%, also a minority of the cases cited between 50–100 judgments equivalent of 0,5%, while the majority, 54,3 %, cite between 1–50 judgments and another significant part of the entire number of judgments cite none, i.e. 45,2%.

It is clear that there is a great variety as regards the number of ingoing citations and references which cases in the network receive. As such some cases constitute authorities seen from a quantitative network perspective. What is not clear at this point is what the authoritative quality is constituted by. In other words, at the quantitative network level it is not possible to identify for what a case is cited frequently and why it becomes a authority.

A. Selection of subset cases

For the purpose of a exploring what the authoritative quality of the highly cited cases consist in, a selection of a smaller number of cases is necessary. In other words, some focus cases are required to gain insight into what the references and citations are constituted by. For this purpose 8 focus cases from the courts' case law citation network were chosen, which are listed in the table below.

Case ID	**Title**	**Year**	**Out-going citation**	**In-going citation**
1474/62	Belgian Linguistics	1967	0	55
5493/72	Handyside v The United Kingdom	1976	9	175
6833/74	Marckx v Belgium	1979	8	159
6289/73	Airey v Ireland	1981	9	198
9697/82	Johnston and others v Ireland	1986	11	75
34369/97	Thlimmenos v Greece	2000	7	73
57325/00	DH and other v Czech Republic	2006	36	59
13378/05	Burden and Burden v The United Kingdom	2008	24	52

Figure 2: list of sample cases

The cases were selected on the basis of three parameters. Firstly, they are authoritative nodes in the sense that among all judgments the focus judgments receive a high number of ingoing citations in the overall network.

As a second parameter for the selection of the subset cases was the frequency of occurrence of the words 'discrimination' and 'Article 14' in the content of the cases. When conducting a subject-matter search in HUDOC for cases related to 'discrimination'[14] a very high number of cases are listed. However, upon reading a these cases I discovered that many of them do not concern discrimination as a subject-matter of the case. Rather, the case may merely mention the term once, and the court has assigned the case the label 'discrimination' without the case directly ruling on the matter. Therefore, to ensure that the cases, being the outset for detecting the development of legal principles of discrimination, did in fact adjudicate on the matter, they were chosen among the judgments with the highest in-degree score and authority score in the overall network, on the basis of having the highest frequency of the word 'discrimination' in their text content.

Thirdly, the cases were chosen by their time of delivery. Several cases met the first and second criterion; yet, besides centrality in the citation network and actual subject-matter relevance, it is of interest that the cases are delivered at different times to detect the development of the cited content over time. Hence, the subset cases were delivered over a period of approximately 40 years, from the 1960'ies to 2010.

B. *From numerical to judicial authority*

While the subset cases immediately appear to be authorities in the case law citation network, in order to qualify what their numerical authority, which they gave gained through receiving a high number of citation, is constituted by is a paragraph-to-paragraph level of analysis. The paragraph-to-paragraph network of a subset of the numerically authoritative cases can reveal the content of the authorities by following citations starting from one paragraph in a citing judgment aimed at a paragraph in the cited judgment. This will allow for detecting the most frequently cited paragraphs in the focus cases and subsequently which specific content that attracts the citations in the paragraphs.

The figure below shows the most frequently cited paragraphs in the cases of ECtHR. The charts are constructed on the basis of a paragraph-

14 The subject-matter search can be on 'discrimination', 'anti-discrimination', 'non-discrimination' etc. The point above is valid for all possible search entries in HUDOC.

to-paragraph network. Thus, the case-to-case networks, which the quantitative network analysis is based on, is particularized into a paragraph-to-paragraph network created from the content of all the judgments in the initial networks.

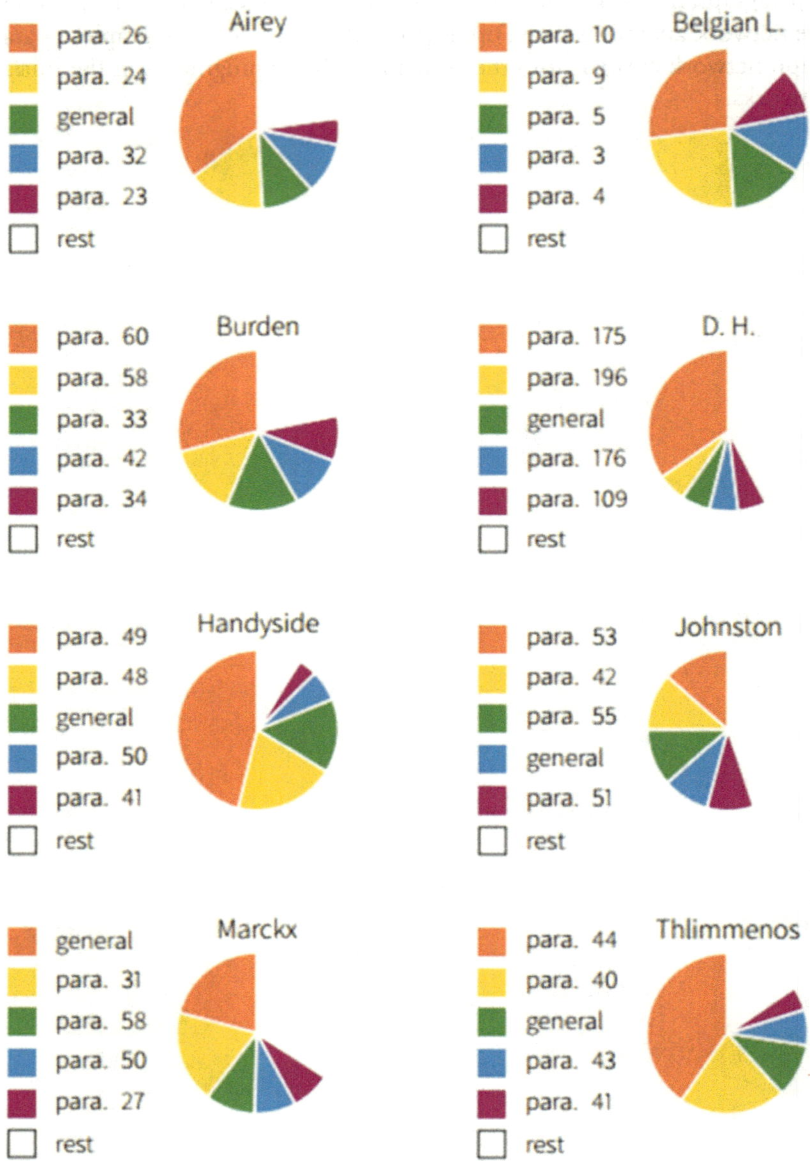

Figure 3: distribution of citations of paragraphs in sample cases

The research interest in the distribution of citations to paragraphs is what the authorities are receiving their citations for, in others words; what content works as precedents by being used by later judgments?

In the following I analyse the content of the most cited paragraphs, which immediately appear as numerical authorities and explore the content for which these cases have been cited and how they can be considered judicial authorities and precedents. As it appears on the circle diagrams above of the distribution of citations to the paragraphs in the cases, there is not an even distribution. Instead, one or two paragraphs tend to receive the majority of the in-going citations or references. For the scope of this chapter and the purpose of understanding the judicial authority and case law status as precedent, I will concentrate the following analysis on the content of the paragraphs that by far receive the highest number of ingoing citations and references.

Belgian Linguistics' most frequently cited paragraphs are paragraph 9 and 10 in its section 'The interpretation adopted by the Court'. They are the only cited paragraphs in the judgment that concern Article 14 and discrimination. Paragraph 9 and 10 together receive more than half of all the citations, 34 citations out of 55 altogether. Paragraph 9 in *Belgian Linguistics* clarifies the role of Article 14 in the Convention and how prohibition against discrimination constitutes an obligation for the Contracting States. Here the Court explains that Article 14 forms an integral part of all other articles in the Convention and even when a State fulfils the obligations thereto it can still be found to do so in a discriminatory way if unequal treatment takes place. Paragraph 10 supplements paragraph 9 by clarifying the wording of Article 14 and unfolding that Article 14 does not prohibit every difference in treatment, some of which in fact correct factual inequalities, and the paragraph is very often cited for stating that the principle of equality of treatment is violated if the distinction has no objective and reasonable justification. Hence, Belgian Linguistics seems to be a precedent, in particular, with regard to the assessment criteria with which discriminatory treatment should be interpreted and adjudicated by the Court.

Belgian Linguistics

§ 9 While it is true that this guarantee has ***no independent existence*** *in the sense that under the terms of Article 14 (art. 14) it relates solely to "rights and freedoms set forth in the Convention",* ***a measure which in itself is in conformity with the requirements of the Article enshrining the right or freedom in question may however infringe this Article when read in conjunction with Article*** *14* ***(art.*** *14****) for the reason that it is of a discriminatory nature****. Thus, persons subject to the jurisdiction of a Contracting State cannot draw from Article 2 of the Protocol (P1–2) the right to obtain from the public authorities the creation of a particular kind of educational establishment; nevertheless, a State which had set up such an establishment could not, in laying down en-*

> *trance requirements, take discriminatory measures within the meaning of Article 14 (art. 14). To recall a further example, cited in the course of the proceedings, Article 6 (art. 6) of* ***the Convention does not compel States to institute a system of appeal courts. A State which does set up such courts consequently goes beyond its obligations under Article 6 (art. 6). However it would violate that Article, read in conjunction with Article 14 (art. 14+6), were it to debar certain persons from these remedies without a legitimate reason while making them available to others in respect of the same type of actions.*** *In such cases there would be a violation of a guaranteed right or freedom as it is proclaimed by the relevant Article read in conjunction with Article 14 (art. 14).* ***It is as though the latter formed an integral part of each of the Articles laying down rights and freedoms.*** *No distinctions should be made in this respect according to the nature of these rights and freedoms and of their correlative obligations, and for instance as to whether the respect due to the right concerned implies positive action or mere abstention. This is, moreover, clearly shown by the very general nature of the terms employed in Article 14 (art. 14): "the enjoyment of the rights and freedoms set forth in this Convention shall be secured".*
>
> *§ 10 In spite of the very general wording of the French version ("sans distinction aucune"),* ***Article 14 (art. 14) does not forbid every difference in treatment in the exercise of the rights and freedoms recognised.*** *This version must be read in the light of the more restrictive text of the English version ("without discrimination"). In addition, and in particular, one would reach absurd results were one to give Article 14 (art. 14) an interpretation as wide as that which the French version seems to imply. One would, in effect, be led to judge as contrary to the Convention every one of the many legal or administrative provisions which do not secure to everyone complete equality of treatment in the enjoyment of the rights and freedoms recognised. The competent national authorities are frequently confronted with situations and problems which, on account of differences inherent therein, call for different legal solutions; moreover,* ***certain legal inequalities tend only to correct factual inequalities.***
> *The extensive interpretation mentioned above cannot consequently be accepted. It is important, then, to look for the criteria which enable a determination to be made as to whether or not a given difference in treatment, concerning of course the exercise of one of the rights and freedoms set forth, contravenes Article 14 (art. 14). On this question the Court, following the principles which may be extracted from the legal practice of a large number of democratic States, holds that* ***the principle of equality of treatment is violated if the distinction has no objective and reasonable justification.*** *The existence of such a justification must be assessed in relation to the aim and effects of the measure under consideration, regard being had to the principles which normally prevail in democratic societies.*
> ***A difference of treatment in the exercise of a right laid down in the Convention must not only pursue a legitimate aim: Article 14 (art. 14) is likewise violated when it is clearly established that there is no reasonable relationship of proportionality between the means employed and the aim sought to be realised.*** *In attempting to find out in a given case, whether or not there has been an arbitrary distinction, the Court cannot disregard those legal and factual features which characterise the life of the society in the State which, as a Contracting Party, has to answer for the measure in dispute. In so doing it cannot assume the rôle of the competent national authorities, for it would thereby lose sight of the subsidiary nature of the international machinery of collective enforcement established by the Convention.* ***The national authorities remain free to choose the measures, which they consider appropriate in those matters which are governed by the Convention.*** *Review by the Court concerns only the conformity of these measures with the requirements of the Convention.*

The case of *Thlimmenos v Greece* concerned the rejection of a Mr. Thlimmenos, who was a Jehovah's Witness, as chartered accountant on the basis of his criminal records, which consisted in his refusal to join the military due to his religious beliefs. The case thus dealt with discrimination on the ground of religion and the Court found that Greece had failed to treat Thlimmenos different from others with a criminal record as his was based on his exercising his right to freedom of religion.

The judgment in *Thlimmenos v Greece* receives the majority of its citations to paragraphs that concern issues related to discriminatory treatment. Paragraph 44 receives a third of all ingoing citations. The judgment dealt with the discrimination on the grounds of religion as Mr. Thlimmenos alleged violation of Article 14 in conjunction with Article 9. Paragraph 44 forms part of the Court's assessment of these exact claims.

Thlimmenos v Greece

§ 44. The Court has so far considered that the right under Article 14 not to be discriminated against in the enjoyment of the rights guaranteed under the Convention is violated when States treat differently persons in analogous situations without providing an objective and reasonable justification (see the Inze judgment cited above, p. 18, § 41). However, the Court considers that this is not the only facet of the prohibition of discrimination in Article 14. ***The right not to be discriminated against in the enjoyment of the rights guaranteed under the Convention is also violated when States without an objective and reasonable justification fail to treat differently persons whose situations are significantly different.***

In *Thlimmenos* the Court firstly affirms its criteria of assessment of Article 14 as put forward in previous case law. It is, however, the articulation of the principle that Article 14 can be violated when a state without an objective and reasonable justification fails to treat people who are in significantly different situations differently, which is cited or referred to extensively by following judgments. Hence, the judgment in the case of *Thlimmenos* must be considered to be a precedent for a doctrine of more substantive equality in the sense that equality requires not only equal treatment, but that the relevant authorities take peoples actual situations into account and treat them accordingly and even differently when their different situations demand so in in order to ensure an substantive and not just formal equality.

In the judgment *D.H. & Others v Czech Republic*, which concerned allocation of children of Roma ethnicity to special schools in the Czech Republic, the most cited paragraph among all the paragraphs is 175, which receives a third of all citations. The paragraph firstly summarizes the Court's practice in the domain of Article 14, as set out in previous judgments – and secondly defines indirect discrimination. From the citations it appears that the most cited content (i.e. principles which are not already articulated in previous judgments) of this paragraph is the formulations asserting that a failure to attempt to correct inequality through differential treatment may in itself give rise to a breach of Article 14 and that a general policy or measure that has disproportionately prejudicial effects on a particular group may be considered discriminatory, i.e. indirect discrimination.

D.H. & Others v Czech Republic

§ 175 The Court has established in its case-law that discrimination means treating differently, without an objective and reasonable justification, persons in relevantly similar situations (see Willis v. the United Kingdom, no. 36042/97, § 48, ECHR 2002-IV, and Okpisz v. Germany, no. 59140/00, § 33, 25 October 2005). However, Article 14 does not prohibit a member State from treating groups differently in order to correct "factual inequalities" between them; indeed ***in certain circumstances a failure to attempt to correct inequality through different treatment may in itself give rise to a breach of the Article*** *(see Case "relating to certain aspects of the laws on the use of languages in education in Belgium" v. Belgium (merits), 23 July 1968, p. 34, § 10, Series A no. 6; Thlimmenos v. Greece [GC], no. 34369/97, § 44, ECHR 2000-IV; and Stec and Others v. the United Kingdom [GC], no. 65731/01, § 51, ECHR 2006-VI). The Court has also accepted that* ***a general policy or measure that has disproportionately prejudicial effects on a particular group may be considered discriminatory*** *notwithstanding that it is not specifically aimed at that group (see Hugh Jordan, cited above, and Hoogendijk, cited above), and that discrimination potentially contrary to the Convention may result from a de facto situation (see Zarb Adami, cited above).*

One of the more recent judgments, *Burden and Burden v the United Kingdom* from 2008, concerned two co-habiting sisters, who also co-owned property and claimed to be discriminated against (Article 14 in conjunction with P1–1) as each one of them upon the other's death would not be exempted from inheritance tax as would a married couple or couples living in civil partnerships.

The citations are spread across paragraphs related to the assessment of discrimination allegations, but two of these paragraphs receives a substantial number of citations. The most cited paragraph in *Burden* is paragraph 60 which is primarily cited for its assertion that the Contracting States enjoy a margin of appreciation in assessing which differences in treatment are justifiable and that this margin is usually wide when the issue of a case concerns economic and social strategies in the Contracting state. In the judgment the Grand Chamber assessed the alleged violation of Article 14 in conjunction with Article 1 of Protocol 1 paragraph 58 to 66 and found that there had been no violation of Article 14 with P1–1 as the Court did not find that sisters were in a relevantly similar situation to married couples or couples living in civil partnership. It is however, paragraph 60 and its assertion of the margin of appreciation doctrine, which seems to constitute the precedent value in *Burden.*

Burden and Burden v the United Kingdom

§ 60 The Court has established in its case-law that in order for an issue to arise under Article 14 there must be a difference in the treatment of persons in relevantly similar situations (see D.H. and Others v. the Czech Republic [GC], no. 57325/00, § 175, ECHR 2007-IV). Such a difference of treatment is discriminatory if it has no objective and reasonable justification; in other words, if it does not pursue a legitimate aim or if there is not a reasonable relationship of proportionality between the means employed and the aimsought to be realised. ***The Contracting State enjoys a margin of appreciation***

> ***in assessing whether and to what extent differences in otherwise similar situations justify a different treatment, and this margin is usually wide when it comes to general measures of economic or social strategy*** *(see Stec and Others v. the United Kingdom [GC], nos. 65731/01 and 65900/01, §§ 51–52, ECHR 2006-VI).*

The citations to the judgment of *Marckx v Belgium* are spread across a wide range of paragraphs. The case concerned the comparison between conditions of legitimate versus illegitimate families and their succession rights. Paula Marckx, Belgian national, unmarried and a journalist by profession, gave birth to Alexandra Marckx in 1973. Under Belgian law at the time of the judgment, no legal bond between an unmarried mother and her child resulted from the mere fact of birth. Hence, the applicant had to officially recognize her daughter as her child. The applicant alleged that the distinction in the legislation between 'legitimate' and 'illegitimate' children and between unmarried and married mothers constituted discrimination within the meaning of Article 14 taken in conjunction with Article 8 (art. 14+8) and that the Belgian legislation allowed that any man could recognize an 'illegitimate' child, even if he is not the father, was a breach of Articles 3, 8 and 14 constituting a discriminatory legislation on the basis of sex between men and women.

It appears that the case is mostly referred to in a general manner, in the sense that there is no reference to a specific paragraph in the *Marckx* judgment from the referring judgments. These types of references seem to use the *Marckx* judgment as an exemplification of a legal topic, rather than using specific legal content in specific paragraphs.

Paragraph 31 in the judgment consists first of the Court's reasoning concerning the definition of family life according to Article 8 of the Convention and whether the Article covers the 'illegitimate' family as well as the 'legitimate' family and what type of obligation that bestows upon the State to protect family and private life according to the Convention. Moreover, the other highly cited paragraphs in the judgment do explicitly display content relating to discrimination or equal treatment between the legitimate and illegitimate family. Yet, as allegations of a breach of Article 14 together with Article 8 due to a distinction between legitimate and 'illegitimate' families and married and unmarried mothers in regards to, among other things, succession rights are at the centre of the judgment, paragraphs which contains deliberations about these allegations are cited by later judgments. These paragraphs are 32 and 33, 40 and 54. The first two clarify the criteria with which Article 14 is assessed in the adjudication of the Court repeating to some degree criteria which were already put forward in *Belgian Linguistics*. Paragraph 40 and 54 discusses the protection of the illegitimate family under Article 8 and affirms its equal protection compared to the legitimate family actualizing Article 14. The Marckx judgment is therefore to some degree cited for its content relating to the application of Article 14 and the assessment of the allegations under Article 14, even if the paragraphs which contain the deliberations are not the most frequently cited.

Marckx v Belgium

§ 32. Article 14 (art. 14) provides:"The enjoyment of the rights and freedoms set forth in this Convention shall be secured without discrimination on any ground such as sex, race, colour, language, religion, political or other opinion, national or social origin, association with a national minority, property, birth or other status. "The Court's case-law shows that, ***although Article 14 (art. 14) has no independent existence, it may play an important autonomous role by complementing the other normative provisions of the Convention and the Protocols. Article 14 (art. 14) safeguards individuals, placed in similar situations, from any discrimination in the enjoyment of the rights and freedoms set forth in those other provisions.*** *A measure which, although in itself in conformity with the requirements of the Article of the Convention or the Protocols enshrining a given right or freedom, is of a discriminatory nature incompatible with Article 14 (art. 14) therefore violates those two Articles taken in conjunction. It is as though Article 14 (art. 14) formed an integral part of each of the provisions laying down rights and freedoms (judgment of 23 July 1968 in the "Belgian Linguistic" case, Series A no. 6, pp. 33–34, para. 9; National Union of Belgian Police judgment of 27 October 1975, Series A no. 19, p. 19, para. 44). Accordingly, and since Article 8 (art. 8) is relevant to the present case (see paragraph 31 above), it is necessary also to take into account Article 14 in conjunction with Article 8 (art. 14+8).*

§ 33. According to the Court's established case-law, a distinction is discriminatory if it "has no objective and reasonable justification", that is, if it does not pursue a "legitimate aim" or if there is not a "reasonable relationship of proportionality between the means employed and the aim sought to be realised" (see, inter alia, the above-cited judgment of 23 July 1968, p. 34, para. 10).

§ 40. The Government do not deny that the present law favours the traditional family, but they maintain that the law aims at ensuring that family's full development and is thereby founded on objective and reasonable grounds relating to morals and public order (ordre public). The Court recognises that support and encouragement of the traditional family is in itself legitimate or even praiseworthy. However, in the achievement of this end recourse must not be had to measures whose object or result is, as in the present case, to prejudice the "illegitimate" family; ***the members of the "illegitimate" family enjoy the guarantees of Article 8 (art. 8) on an equal footing with the members of the traditional family.***

§ 54. On the other hand, ***the distinction made in these two respects between "illegitimate" and "legitimate" children does raise an issue under Articles 14 and 8 (art. 14+8) when they are taken in conjunction.***

The cases with the lowest judicial authority in relation to Article 14 ECHR are *Airey* and *Johnston*. The case from 1979 concerned the prohibition of divorce in Ireland and the lack of legal aid to obtain a divorce even in a violent marriage, which the applicant claimed infringed her rights under Article 6 and 8 as well as 14 in so far as those with financial means had better access to legal representation. A third of the ingoing citations directed at *Airey v Ireland* concern paragraph 26 which concerns how Article 6 must be interpreted with regards to the State's obligation to provide legal aid in matters relating to civil rights. A quarter of the ingoing citations are directed at paragraph 24 which states that *"The Convention is intended to guarantee not rights that are theoretical or illusory but rights that are practical and effective (...) This is particularly so of the right of access to the courts in view of the prominent place held in a democratic society by the right to a fair trial"*[15]. Clearly, paragraph 24 and 26 of the *Airey v Ireland* judgment are concerned with the right interpretation of Article 6 and the Convention in regards to Article 6. The cited principles are henceforth not specifically related to Article 14, but they are general principles about the interpretation of the Convention.

The Court's assessment of Article 14 appears in paragraphs 29 and 30. Paragraph 30 is cited four times and summarizes the criteria with which differential treatment is assessed in the Court's practice to decide whether a difference of treatment is discriminatory, as laid out in previous case law, for example as seen in *Belgian Linguistics.* However, since paragraph 30 is cited relatively few times compared to the 198 times *Airey* is cited altogether, the judicial authority cannot plausibly be held to stem from the judgment's deliberations concerned with discrimination.

Airey v Ireland

§ 30. Article 14 (art. 14) has no independent existence; it constitutes one particular element (non-discrimination) of each of the rights safeguarded by the Convention (see, inter alia, the above-mentioned Marckx judgment, pp. 15–16, para. 32). The Articles enshrining those rights may be violated alone and/or in conjunction with Article 14 (art. 14). ***If the Court does not find a separate breach of one of those Articles that has been invoked both on its own and together with Article** 14 **(art.** 14**), it must also examine the case under the latter Article (art.*** *14). On the other hand, such an examination is not generally required when the Court finds a violation of the former Article (art. 6–1) taken alone.* ***The position is otherwise if a clear inequality of treatment in the enjoyment of the right in question is a fundamental aspect of the case*** *but this does not apply to the breach of Article 6 para. 1 (art. 6–1) found in the present proceedings; accordingly, the Court does not deem it necessary also to examine the case under Article 14 (art. 14).*

Johnston and Others v Ireland

§ 60. ***Article** 14 **(art.** 14**) safeguards persons who are "placed in analogous situations" against discriminatory differences of treatment in the exercise of the rights and freedoms recognised by the Convention*** *(see, as the most recent authority, the Lithgow and Others judgment of 8 July 1986, Series A no. 102, p. 66, § 177). The Court notes that under the general Irish rules of private international law foreign divorces will be recognised in Ireland only if they have been obtained by persons domiciled abroad (see paragraph 20 above). It does not find it to have been established that these rules are departed from in practice. In its view, the situations of such persons and of the first and second applicants cannot be regarded as analogous.*

Likewise, the judgment in the case of *Johnston & Others v Ireland,* delivered five years after *Airey* and which also concerned divorce as the applicants

15 *Case 6289/73 Airey v. Ireland* (1979). § 24.

claimed that the unconstitutional status of divorce in Ireland violated their rights to form a family anew and to be free of discrimination. The case receives few citations to its paragraphs that adjudicate on the allegation of discrimination contrary to Article 14. Overall, *Johnston & Others v Ireland* is cited equally for a range of paragraphs. The most cited paragraph is 53, which concerns the applicability of Article 12 of the Convention and deriving a right to divorce. Other cited paragraphs, for example paragraph 42, concerns the definition of being victim of a violation of a provision in the Convention.

The application included an allegation of discrimination contrary to Article 14 on the basis of financial means, which are dealt with in paragraph 59–61. Paragraph 60 is cited only 3 times. The paragraphs affirmed that *"Article 14 (art. 14) safeguards persons who are "placed in analogous situations" against discriminatory differences of treatment in the exercise of the rights and freedoms recognised by the Convention"*[16]. This is, however, a repetition of the principle pronounced in *Marckx*. As such the judicial authority of Johnston in the domain of discrimination law is low.

Finally, a complete lack of citations to paragraphs concerned with assessment of legal issues related to discrimination is seen in the Handyside judgment. The case concerned the publication in the UK of *The Little Red Schoolbook* containing a section of sexual education for school children, by Mr. Handyside who was later charged with having in his possession obscene books for publication for gain and who claimed that it violated his rights under the Convention including that he suffered discrimination in the enjoyment of his freedom of expression and his property rights. The most frequently cited paragraph in *Handyside v The United Kingdom* is paragraph 49, which describes the role of freedom of expression in a democratic society and the balance between the obligations of the State to respect freedom of expression of individuals and the obligation of the individual, who exercises freedom of expression. This paragraph serves a central role in the judgment as a whole considering the main allegation of Mr. Handyside claiming that his freedom of expression, guaranteed by Article 10, had been violated.

The allegations of a breach of Article 14 on the basis of political opinion are dealt with in the judgment on paragraphs 65 and 66. As it appears from the distribution of citation diagrams, these articles are not cited. According to a citation network analysis of the most paragraphs cited in *Handyside*, it can therefore be concluded that the judgment has not

16 *Case 9697/82 Johnston and Others v Ireland* (1986).§ 60.

attracted citations for the reasons of its content regarding equal treatment and discrimination. Despite *Handyside* fulfilling the criteria with which the focus judgments were chosen, i.e. high authority and in-degree score and high frequency of the term 'discrimination' or 'Article 14', upon moving from case-to-case analysis to paragraph-to-paragraph analysis, it appears that the authority of *Handyside* was in fact not attributed to its discrimination-related content. As network analysis as a method takes in-going citations as a proxy for authority, it can be ruled out that it is the content of the *Handyside* judgment, which has been attributed authority as there are no ingoing citations to this part of the judgment.

C. Preliminary conclusions

Even if this is not an exhaustive study of all cases' references in ECtHR jurisprudence, the paragraph-to-paragraph analysis shows a pattern concerning how judicial authorities in the case law can develop and how precedents are practically constructed. Most of the subset cases, which were selected on the basis of having mathematical authority, i.e. high authority as in-degree score, also have a relevant judicial authority. Most of these cases receive citations for at least one or more paragraphs which concern clarification or deliberation on aspects of Article 14 ECHR. Nonetheless, it is different contents in the rulings, which receive a high number of references. In other words, the quality of precedential authority is not uniform. It seems that there are at least two kinds of precedents, which can be identified in the subset cases. Some of the most cited paragraphs consist in elaborations of the assessment criteria for the Court when adjudicating the right to freedom from discrimination in Article 14. This was seen in *Belgian Linguistics,* which can be considered a precedent for asserting that Article 14 does not prohibit all differences in treatment and that with legitimate aim such treatment can be justified.

The *Burden* case similarly gained precedent status for asserting the margin of appreciation doctrine.

Other frequently cited paragraphs tend to concern the meaning and scope of Article 14 ECHR. *D.H.* gained precedent status for the principle that a failure to correct existing inequalities through differential treatment can violate Article 14 and moreover for the important doctrine of indirect discrimination as also covered by Article 14. Similarly in *Thlimmenos,* which has gained precedent status for articulating the principle that Article 14 can be violated if not treating people in significantly different situations differently.

However, not all of the most cited paragraphs concerned Article 14 and discrimination. Thus *Airey* and *Johnston* showed to have rather low judicial authority as Article 14 cases and *Handyside* was not at all cited for its paragraphs concerned with assessment of Article 14.

Interestingly, it is not the facts of the cases, which receive references or citations. This observation provides a corrective to the binding versus non-binding precedent dichotomy, according to which it is the similarity in the facts of a case, which binds the later case. A connected observation from the analysis of paragraph-to-paragraph network is that a reference to an authority appears to function as guiding in nature. This should probably be seen in connection to the fact that there are never two cases before the ECtHR which are identical as to the facts of the case, since admissibility criteria require that the legal issue has not been considered by the court before. Hence, there is not a single authority constituting the correct precedent, which decides a later case. On the contrary, past cases will as authorities be merged into the reasoning of the later case alongside other authoritative cases. The Court subsequently makes its decision based on a synthesis of analogies and distinctions to past cases' interpretations. Hence, the use of authorities is not as binding precedents, but as guiding authorities that, depending on the precedent and the context, can be more or less constraining and offer more or less scope for changing the line of case law.[17]

IV. Conclusion

This study demonstrated the practical construction of precedent citation by applying a case law citation network to the analysis of the corpus of case law of the ECtHR. Supplementing the case-to-case network with a sample of cases in a paragraph-to-paragraph network, allowed for reading the *cited* paragraphs together with the *citing* paragraphs and to filter in the content that essentially has the most authority and precedent value in the cited cases.

It is in the case law of the ECtHR that the most important doctrines of the Convention have been developed. These doctrines become authorities

17 A finding confirmed in Derlén & Lindholm 'Characteristics of Precedent: The Case Law of the European Court of Justice in Three Dimensions' (2015) 16 *German L.J.*, 1073.

as they are repeated in later cases decided by the ECtHR, which cite and refer to these principles.

An important finding in this study is that as precedents the cases are primarily cited for their clarification of the principles in the Convention. In fact, the most cited paragraphs were often those, which concerned assessment criteria (e.g. *Belgian Linguistics*) for Article 14 and clarifications of the scope and meaning of Article 14 (e.g. *D.H. and Thlimmenos*). Contrary to what often is expected based on theories of precedent, it is not the facts of the cases and the similarity between these which attract citations and references.

Considering the role of the ECtHR as a court ruling on law and not on facts, contextualises the court´s use of precedents. The institutional features of ECtHR showed that the use of past case law through references and citations are consciously a part of the practice of decision-making at the court. The utilization of case law network analysis as a metric for case authority overall seems to correspond to the importance which the Court attributes to its case law. The network approach thus assists du in refining the concept of precedent, from a uniform concept to a conceptualisation of precedents which acknowledges its pluralistic form..

Bibliography

Karen Alter, 'The Multiple Roles of International Courts and Tribunals' in Dunoff & Pollack (eds.), *Interdisciplinary Perspectives on International Law and International Relations: The State of the Art* (Cambridge University Press, Cambridge 2013), 345.

Mattias Derlén & Johan Lindholm,'Peek-A-Boo, It's a Case Law System!: Comparing the European Court of Justice and the United States Supreme Court from a Network Perspective' (2017) 18 *German L.J.*, 647.

Mattias Derlén & Johan Lindholm, 'Characteristics of Precedent: The Case Law of the European Court of Justice in Three Dimensions' (2015) 16 *German L.J.*, 1073.

Mattias Derlén & Johan Lindholm, 'Goodbye van Gen den Loos, Hello Bosman? Using Network Analysis to Measure the importance of Individual CJEU Judgments' (2014) 20 *Eur. L.J.*, 667.

James H. Fowler et al., 'Network Analysis and the Law: Measuring the Legal Importance of Precedents at the U.S. Supreme Court' (2007) 15 *Pol. Analysis*, 324.

James H. Fowler & Sangick Jeon, 'The Authority of Supreme Court Precedent' (2008) 30 *Soc. Networks*, 16.

Linton C. Freeman, 'Centrality in Social Networks Conceptual Clarification' (1978) 1, SOC. Networks, 215.

Marc Jacob, *Precedents and Case-based Reasoning in the European Court of Justice': Unfinished Business* (Cambridge University Press, Cambridge 2014).

Jan Komárek, 'Reasoning with Previous Decisions: Beyond the Doctrine of Precedent' (2013) 61 *Am. J. Comp. L.*, 149.

Jon M. Kleinberg, 'Authoritative Sources in a Hyperlinked Environment' (1999) 46 *J. ACM*, 604.

Tobias Lock, *The European Court of Justice and International Courts* (Oxford University Press, Oxford 2015).

Yonatan Lupu & Erik Voeten, 'Precedent in International Courts: A Network Analysis of Case Citations by The European Court of Human Rights' (2012) 42 *British J. Pol. Sci.*, 413.

Mikael Rask Madsen, 'The Challenging Authority of The European Court of Human Rights: From Cold War Legal Diplomacy to the Brighton Declaration and Backlash' (2016) 79 *Law and Contemporary Problems*, 141.

Mathias Siems, *Comparative Law* (2nd edn, Cambridge University Press, Cambridge 2018).

Alec Stone Sweet, *Governing with Judges, Constitutional Politics in Europe* (Oxford University Press, Oxford 2000)

Reconstructing Scholarly Authority in International Law

William Hamilton Byrne

The 'teachings' hold a special place in the sources and practices of international law. Article 38(1) of the *Statute of the International Court of Justice* instructs the Court to apply, in deciding disputes submitted to it in accordance with international law, 'judicial decisions' and 'the teachings of the most highly qualified publicists' as 'subsidiary means for the determination of rules of law'. The sensibility of international lawyers instructs that the term 'subsidiary' here can be something of a misnomer, as legal scholarship can perform the role of advisor, counsellor, consigliere, or even master. Legal scholarship may provide the theoretical framework which creates system from international legal norms, or even a decisive point for the decision of a court. The 'teachings of the most highly qualified publicists' thus seem to be associated with some kind of legal authority in this exalted position where it sits alongside 'judicial decisions' as a source of law for the World Court.

This is a curious positioning in light of the traditional distinction drawn of theory and practice in law. However, legal precedent and legal scholarship share more in common than is often supposed. Legal precedent as a source of legal authority is a product of socio-cultural communities that endow the vessels of the legal past with authority for the purposes it can serve in the present legal context. Legal scholarship also captures the past but appears to perform a different role to legal precedent as a type of theoretical rather than practical authority – it does not demand action in adjudication, but rather guides a hypothetical course of conduct for the law applying authority as a source of legal knowledge. Legal scholarship and legal precedent may both hold argumentative authority but it is distinct in the way it is performed, as theory as a set of principles of general application does not connotate the sense of legal pedigree that arises from delegated authority and institutional validation by a court.

What can be taken to explain the special position enjoyed by legal scholarship in international law? The reasons are partly historical. The historiography of international law has tended to associate the systematization of international law with the work of naturalist scholars who blended accounts of state practice with theological lessons in a hermeneutic reconstruction of the past with the present[1]. The jurisprudence of early modern scholars is said to mark the emergence of international law as an independent discipline with its own set of rules[2]. Grotius is spoken of as a forefather of public international law with his concept of an international society of states that laid the intellectual foundations for the Treaty of Westphalia in 1648[3]. Vattel's *The Law of Nations* is evoked as a turning point for the emergence of a positive body of law with an authority derived from the consent of its subjects[4]. This foundational role arose in the absence of constraint from central governance.

Yet, by the end of the twentieth century the role of theory in international law seemed to be changing, as national diplomats began to replace legal scholars as catalysts of international law making.[5] The ravages of the world wars accelerated this development as international law came to increasingly take shape through a vast network of treaty arrangements with symbolic order emanating from the United Nations.[6] The style of international legal discourse moved in tandem - from historicity and iteration, to a kind of 'craftsmanship' geared for practice in the multilateral institutional architecture[7]. International law has since undergone a profound process of judicialization, as international courts have expanded in number and scope and produced a tremendous output of decisions and judgments[8]. However, some things are still largely the same. International law remains

---

1 Brett, 'Sources in the Scholastic Legacy: the Reconstruction of the Ius Gentium in the Second Scholastic' in d'Aspremont and Besson (eds) *The Oxford Handbook of the Sources of International Law* (2017) 67

2 Verosta, 'History of International Law, 1648 to 1815' in Wolfrum (ed) *Max Planck Encyclopaedia of Public International Law* (2007).

3 Bull, 'The Importance of Grotius in the Study of International Relations' in Bull, Kingsbury, and Roberts (eds) *Hugo Grotius and International Relations* (1992) 63.

4 Parry, *The Sources and Evidences of International Law* (1955) 32.

5 Orakhelashvili, 'The Relevance of Theory and History – the Essence and Origins of International Law' A Orakhelashvili, (ed) *Research Handbook on the Theory and History of International Law* (2008) 4.

6 Onuf, 'Lawmaking and the Global Community' in Onuf (ed) *International Legal Theory: Essays and Engagements 1966–2006* (2008) 94.

7 See for example, Jenks, 'Craftsmanship and International Law' (1956) 50 American Journal of International Law, 32

8 See further Olsen and Toddington, 'The End of an Era: Static and Dynamic Interpretation in International Courts' (2004) 14 International Criminal Law Review, 920.

a non-hierarchical and decentralized body of legal norms, with no central legislature or mechanisms for enforcement[9].

The structural characteristics of the international legal order creates common problems for international courts. Firstly, international courts are instructed to decide disputes according to the settled law before that specific court[10]. Secondly, and despite juridification, international legal orders remain less materially developed than national legal orders, creating the need for constant factual engagement and legal transformation[11]. Thirdly, international courts lack formal rules for legal precedent and authoritative sources, with no formally shared criteria outside of their constitutive treaties and documents[12]. Fourthly, their unique constituency extends the burden of persuasion from the state parties of the instant case to a wider *erga omnes* international audience[13]. Finally, there is what might be called the 'invisible college' problem – the sociological field of international lawyers is typified by cross-institutional allegiances and role swapping between judicial, academic, and policy functions[14].

In light of these quandaries, is recourse to legal scholarship by an international judge a rule, recourse or an act of last resort? Legal scholarship, like legal precedent, forms part of practices of judicial decision-making, even where it might not be expected to play a role[15]. But what even is precedent in international law? International legal scholarship has mostly focused on analysing the decisions of international courts as de-facto systems of legal precedent by borrowing from common law concepts such

---

9 Hernández, 'The Activist Academic in International Law,' European Society of International Law Reflections Series, 2013, 1, 3, See further Collins, *The Institutional Problem in Modern International Law* (2016).

10 See, for example, Hernández, *The International Court of Justice and the Judicial Function* (2014).

11 On the transformational aspect of law as a technology that mediates social conflict, see especially Olsen and Toddington, 'The Scandanavian Roots of a New Approach to Legal Knowledge' (2012) 34 Retfærd 57.

12 Cf. d'Aspremont, *Formalism and the Sources of International Law* (2012).

13 On audiences of international courts see Alter, *The New Terrain of International Law: Courts, Politics, Rights* (2013).

14 Schachter, 'The Invisible College of International Lawyers,' (1977–1978) Northwestern University Law Review 217, and also Villalpando, 'The "Invisible College of International Lawyers" Forty Years Later,' European Society of International Law Conference Paper Series No. 5/2013.

15 See the Editors Introduction in this volume.

as persuasiveness and bindingness, and often with rich empirical results[16]. However, less attention in legal scholarship has been afforded what authority means more broadly in this context[17]. Further traction must be gained in light of the prominent, yet variable role played by legal scholarship in the practice of international courts[18]. To follow a rule, as Taylor wrote, requires an element of know-how, '(u)nderstanding is always against a background of what is taken for granted, just relied on.'[19] What kind of authority then is the authority of legal scholarship before international courts?

This Chapter will sketch the outline for a reinvigoration of a hermeneutic understanding of scholarly authority before international courts. To arrive at this point, it will take a brief *tour d'horizon* through some of the more prominent explanations for the authority of legal sources in international law. Firstly, legal formalism, which holds that legal authority may only arise from settled sources of law. Secondly, naturalist theories, which hold the authority of scholarship can be equated with some other type of authority. Thirdly, sociological accounts, which explain authority in terms of the expertise of the scholar, legitimation of the court, or as generated by interactions of participants in a legal system. Finally, hermeneutical philosophy, which locates authority in the cultural traditions of the interpreter. The Chapter will conclude with some reflections on what we can

16 For a critical assessment of the literature see Ridi, 'Rule of Precedent and Rules on Precedent' in de Branderbare et al (eds.) *Comparative Procedure in State-to-State Disputes* (forthcoming, 2021).

17 See for example, Schauer, 'Authority and Authorities,' (2008) 94(8) Virginia Journal of International Law, 1931; Zarbiyev, 'Saying Credibly What the Law Is: On Marks of Authority in International Law,' (2018) 9(2) Journal of International Dispute Settlement, 291; Venzke, 'Semantic Authority' in d'Aspremont and Singh, *Fundamental Concepts for International Law: Contributions to Disciplinary Thought* (2019) 815.

18 See, for example, Helmersen, 'The Application of Teachings by the International Tribunal for the Law of the Sea' (2020) 11 Journal of International Dispute Settlement, 11; Helmersen, 'Finding 'the Most Highly Qualified Publicists': Lessons from the International Court of Justice' (2019) 30(2) European Journal of International Law, 509; Helmersen, 'The Use of Scholarship by the WTO Appellate Body,' (2016) Goettingen Journal of International Law, 309; Stappert, 'A New Influence of Legal Scholars? The Use of Academic Writings at International Criminal Courts and Tribunals,' (2018) 31(4) Leiden Journal of International Law 963; Cole, 'Non-Binding Documents and Literature,' in Gazinni and de Brabandere (eds.) *International Investment Law: Sources of Rights and Obligations* (2010) 289.

19 Taylor, *Philosophical Arguments* (1995) 167.

take from a turn hermeneutics in making sense of precedents as rules and practices as vessels of the past in service of the present in international law.

A. *Legal doctrinal orthodoxy*

Formalist accounts of the authority of legal scholarship are associated with source based legal reasoning and mark a line between theoretical and practical authority. For instance, Hobbes spoke of a distinction between counsel and command. Of command, Hobbes says, 'do this ...without expecting other reason than the will of him that says it.' Of counsel, in contrast, do this 'but the anticipated reason for action is 'the benefit that ariveth to him and to whom he saith it.' In both instances, the speech is imperative, but in the latter a person acts not due to the content of the advice and not due to the imposition of the will of the State[20]. Theoretical authority is based on the content of the advice given, which the receiver of the advice is free to accept or reject on his or her own accord. Practical authority, in contrast, arises from the source or the 'command' of the claim of the authority of law.

The constitutive treaties of international courts and tribunals provides concrete expression of this point. Article 38(1)(d) of the *Statute of the International Court of Justice* assigns a subsidiary role to the 'teachings of the most highly qualified publicists' in the list sources of international law that the Court may consider in a case before it[21]. The general doctrinal consensus on the meaning of the term 'subsidiary' is that teachings do not qualify as a source of law, but rather, as evidence of law that can be found in the formal sources of treaties, custom, and general principles of law[22]. The treaties of a number of representative international courts and tribunals are less clear on what is deemed as prescribed sources of law: the *European*

20 Harrison, *Hobbes, Locke and Confusion's Masterpiece* (2013) 81–82.

21 On the drafting history of the provision see Peil, 'Scholarly Writings as a Source of Law: A Survey of the Use of Doctrine by the International Court of Justice' (2012) 1(3) Cambridge Journal of International and Comparative Law, 136, 140, noting that the 'intentionally ambiguous language' reflected the scope of disagreement on the role of doctrine

22 See, for example, Wood, 'Teachings of the Most Highly Qualified Publicists (Art. 38 (1) ICJ Statute)' in *Max Planck Encyclopedia of Public International Law* (Online, 2016); Thirlway, *The Sources of International Law* (2013) 8; Pellet 'Article 38,' in Zimmermann, Tomuschat, and Oellers-Frahm (eds), *The Statute of the International Court of Justice: A Commentary* (2006) 784.

Convention on Human Rights does not mention sources of law[23], the *Rome Statute of the International Criminal Court* lists a number of sources but makes no reference to legal scholarship[24], whilst the *ICSID Convention* refers to 'such rules of international law as may be applicable'[25]. Looking at the law would seem to suggest that legal scholarship holds no authority in the practice of international adjudication as it is not a formal source of international law.

Can this really be the end point? A standard view of legal authority deriving from the legal positivist jurisprudence of Hart suggests that this may be so. On this view, legal authority arises from a formal legal source and provides content independent reasons for action[26]. Most conceptions authority in international law similarly refer to the authority that arises from positive norms through the legally binding quality of state consent to international law[27]. The authority of legal scholarship is based on its ability to provide an objective frame of the positive law: legal scholarship 'purports to examine controversial legal issues from a neutral, value free perspective'.[28] Law provides content-independent reasons for action, in contrast to the content dependent authority of legal scholarship. Legal scholarship derives its authority from its role in providing a frame for the application of positive law, which is the task of law-applying authority, such as an international court.

This line of reasoning has been further developed within the theory of international legal positivism. Kammerhofer's revival of Kelsen's *Pure Theory of Law*[29] propounds a theory of international law as a separate normative order that is created and ordered by sources of international law. Kammerhofer posits that no norm of positive international law grants legal scholars the power to make international law, therefore, '(l)aw-making by scholarship is by definition not possible, because 'legal scholarship' is

---

23 *European Convention on Human Rights as amended by Protocols Nos. 11 and 14 and supplemented by Protocols Nos. 1, 4, 6, 7, 12, 13 and 16.*

24 *Rome Statute of the International Criminal Court,* Article 21.

25 *Convention on the Settlement of Investment Disputes between States and Nationals of Other States,* Art. 42(1).

26 See generally, Green, 'Legal Obligations and Authority' in the *Stanford Encyclopedia of Philosophy* (Online).

27 Çali, *The Authority of International Law: Obedience, Respect, and Rebuttal* (2015) 22.

28 Bard, 'Advocacy Masquerading as Scholarship; or, Why Legal Scholars Cannot be Trusted' (1989) 55 Brooklyn Law Review 853–862, cited in Hernández, 'The Activist Academic in International Law,' (2013) European Society of International law Reflections Series 1, 3.

29 Kelsen, *Pure Theory of Law* (1967).

defined as the cognition of law, not as law-making. That the same human being may exercise the functions of scholar and law-maker does not make his or her task, in making law, an exercise in scholarship'[30]. d'Aspremont arrives at a similar point through a revitalization of Hart's thesis of the rule of recognition, whereby legal validity is derived from the social practice of 'legal officials' with an 'internal point of view'[31]. d'Aspremont thus holds that legal scholars 'do not themselves yield social practice,' but the 'law-ascertainment carved out and polished by legal scholars can be conducive to the shaping of practice of law-applying authorities'[32]. In effect, legal scholars perform the function of a 'grammarian' who systematizes the distinction between law and non-law[33].

However, there remains questions over whether the legal positivist theory of legal scholarship adequately reflects the actual use of legal scholarship within practices of law. Schecaira argues that legal scholarship constitutes a source of law with reference to its use by national courts[34]. Schecaira develops Hart's thesis to draw an analogy between statutes, judicial decisions, and official customs, from which norms can be derived by courts. As domestic courts use legal scholarship to document rules and practices, it provides content independent reasons for action and is therefore a source of law[35]. Yet, there are difficulties in transposing Hart's theory to international law[36]. Authority in international law is shaped by the structure of the legal system, which is different to national law primarily because it draws a less firm distinction between the legal official and the legal subject.[37] The international judge faces a less determinate legal tradition

30 Kammerhofer, 'Law-Making by Scholars' in Brölmann and Radi (eds) *Research Handbook on the Theory and Practice of International Law-Making* (2015) 305, 324.

31 Hart, *The Concept of Law* (2012).

32 d'Aspremont (fn12) 209.

33 Ibid, 212. The metaphor of scholars as a 'grammarian' has been a prominent feature of the discourse on this topic, see especially Hernández, 'The Responsibility of the International Legal Academic: Situating the Grammarian Within the "Invisible College"' in d'Aspremont et al (eds), *International Law as a Profession* (2017) 160.

34 Shecaira, *Legal Scholarship as a Source of Law* (2013); See also Duxbury, *Jurists and Judges: an Essay on Influence* (2001) for a summation of the empirical evidence of citation practices of courts in France, the UK and USA.

35 Ibid, 9–60.

36 Hart himself thought international law was law but its laws did not constitute a legal system as such.

37 See especially Collins, 'The Problematic Concept of the International Legal Official' (2016) 6 Transnational Legal Theory 608, Collins and Bohm, 'International

than the national judge, caught between state sovereignty and the lack of centralized authority that is typically characteristic of state polities.

The authority of legal scholarship in international law must be taken for analysis on its own qualities. On this note, it is increasingly thought that the doctrine of sources of international law is outmoded 'because it omits important sources of international law while misrepresenting the nature and weight of others'[38]. There is an emerging doctrinal consensus that 'judicial decisions' can hold normative effects that goes beyond their formal role of evidence of law found in formal sources[39]. In this light, it might be better to speak of the authority of the 'formal' and 'informal' sources of international law[40]. Formal norm change occurs as a matter of the doctrine of sources, but international law also changes when the meaning of texts shift over time through the interpretation of legal norms[41]. States remain central to norm creation, but much legal change occurs outside of diplomatic forums. This designation is better attuned to the path of normative development in international law, which often occurs outside of formal channels – in particular, through adjudication by international courts[42].

This helps to cast a different light on the distinction between precedent and scholarship as sources of law. Firstly, legal scholarship advises but does not demand a course of action; it is for the role of counsel rather than command that it is mostly appreciated for in law. Secondly, however, the structural characteristics of international law arising from a lack of central legislative mechanisms elevates the cognitive role of legal scholarship in advising the law applier what *is* international law. As Berman notes, this

Law as a Professional Practice: Crafting the Autonomy of International Law' in d'Aspremont et. al. (eds) *International Law as a Profession* (2017) 67.

38 Roberts and Sivukamaran, 'The Theory and Reality of the Sources of International Law' in Evans (ed) *International Law* (2018) 89.

39 For a discussion of the literature see Hernández, 'International Judicial Law-Making' in Brölmann and Radi (eds.) *Research Handbook on the Theory and Practice of International Law-Making* (2015) 200.

40 The notion of informal sources is now commonly accepted as a phenomenon, irrespective of their theoretical consequences. Relatedly, see Pauwelyn, Wessel, and Wouters (eds) *Informal International Lawmaking* (2012).

41 Kleinlein, 'Matters of Interpretation: How to Conceptualize and Evaluate Change of Norms and Values in the International Legal Order' KFG Working Paper Series, No. 24 (2018). See further and in particular Venzke, *How Interpretation Makes International Law: on Semantic Change and Normative Twists* (2012).

42 Ibid, See also Olsen and Toddington, 'The End of an Era: Static and Dynamic Interpretation in International Courts' (2004) 14 International Criminal Law Review, 920 for a fuller account of the consequences of this shift.

can be seen in Article 38(1)(d) of the *Statute of the International Court of Justice*, which imposes no formal hierarchy between judicial decisions and teachings of publicists, considered in light of Article 59, which provides that a decision is binding on the parties to litigation.[43] This construction seems to imply that '(w)ithout central authority, authoritativeness in international law must always be earned (though decisions are more likely to fulfil the criteria of authoritativeness.)'[44] The authority of legal scholarship therefore emerges as *sui generis*, functionally distinct from formal sources of international law that command assent through consent to their terms.

This realisation sheds light on why international courts cite legal scholarship often, and sometimes in an almost equal breath to legal precedent, notwithstanding differences in their formal competence. But it also helps to show why the transposition of the common law dichotomy between 'binding' and 'persuasive' authority is mostly unpersuasive in the context of international adjudication, if it could ever even be taken as the reality of adjudication before common law courts. Put simply, the characteristic of being binding is mostly as misleading as that of persuasive: binding authority sometimes seems non-obligatory, and persuasive authority sometimes seems to be obliging[45]. Precedent as system of 'rules' and a body of accepted 'practice' tend to diffuse in the absence of a central institutional authority for demarcating the appropriate extent of both concepts. The authority of legal scholarship is contextual, sitting between blind obedience and the internalization of norms by its subjects. Some scholars have sought to resolve this quandary by appealing to an authority that is anterior or within law in order to explain the authority of legal scholarship in international law.

B. *Naturalism revisited*

Naturalist accounts of the authority of legal scholarship measure authority against normative concepts such as legitimacy, democracy, and the rule of

---

43 Note that the lack of formal rules of precedent is common amongst international courts, see Borda, 'A Formal Approach to Article 38(1)(d) of the ICJ Statute from the Perspective of the International Criminal Courts and Tribunals' (2013) European Journal of International Law, 649. But see also Ridi (n16) for a more qualified view.

44 Berman, 'Authority in International Law,' KFG Working Paper Series, No. 22 (2018) 12.

45 Schauer, *Thinking like a lawyer: a new introduction to legal reasoning* (2009) 67–77.

law. Carty traces the lineage of this association as arising from the Roman legal tradition, which allowed jurists to freely resort to concepts of justice and equity in their scholastic prescription for legal obligations. An element of legal doctrine was that 'it is supposed to have authority… not as a source of law as such but as a freely and spontaneously held opinion which is likely to be accepted'[46]. This concept of scholarly authority based on universal morality has now mostly been replaced by reference to values said to arise from the nature of law.

One strand of literature builds from Raz's service conception and the normal justification thesis, whereby the authority of official claim is justified if by following it one is more likely to conform to that reason than one's own judgment[47]. It has been said that this helps to explain our sense of deference to experts, such as the authority of a doctor as patient[48], or 'the kind that governments claim to have over their subjects, parents over their children, and so on[49]'. Besson offers extension of Razian theory to the authority of legal scholarship on an assumption of law as a kind of moral normativity that remains distinct from theoretical authority[50]. Besson maintains that legal scholarship 'facilitates…normative reasoning…(but)…remains distinct from practice as it does not enact and enforce legal norms for lack of (public) authority to do so'[51]. Besson's theory thus derives the authority of legal scholarship as persuasive on the basis of principles derived from public law[52]. It is surely correct that the authority of legal scholarship is distinct from the kind of authority that is exercised through practice, such as state consent to treaty or a judgment of an international court. However, questions remain on the appropriate line is to be drawn when these practices merge. How can

46 Carty, *Philosophy of international law* (2009) 1–2.

47 See Raz, *The Authority of Law* (2009).

48 Green, 'Legal Obligations and Authority' in the *Stanford Encyclopedia of Philosophy* (Online).

49 Star and Delmas, 'Three Conceptions of Practical Authority' (2011) 2(1) Jurisprudence 143, 145.

50 Besson, 'International Legal Theory Qua Practice of International Law' in d'Aspremont et al (eds.) *International Law as a Profession* (2017) 343, See also more generally Besson 'Theorizing the Sources of International Law' in Besson and Tasioulas (eds) *The Philosophy of International Law* (2010) 163 for further elaboration of her thesis on sources.

51 Ibid, 347.

52 On legal scholarship as merely of persuasive value only see also Rubin, 'What does prescriptive legal scholarship say and who is listening to it? A reply to Dan Cohen' (1992) 63 University of Colorado Law Review, 731.

theory be separate from practice when it is applied in the daily practice of international courts? Contrariwise, do international courts not project their own concepts of law through their case law? To adopt a common but fitting trope – is there nothing more practical than a good theory after all?

Peters offers a similar thesis from the perspective of constitutionalist theories of international law: 'scholars cannot and should not 'make' international law in the same sense as governments, because they lack the legitimizing factors of representativity, participation, publicity, and accountability. The authority of scholars is not an institutional, procedural, or social one, but purely an epistemic one'[53]. The distinction invokes Plato's 'philosopher king' and the legitimate authority of right process[54]. Peters rightly respects that the authority of legal scholarship is based on its ability to provide knowledge. However, this thesis adopts an assumption characteristic of normative approaches to law: conflating abstract notions of political legitimacy with concrete signs of legal authority, the former (and latter) of which can ultimately be identified or even analysed empirically as distinct concepts[55]. International courts appear to endow legal scholarship with some kind of authority outside of its formal status and quite apart from the potential risk of anointing a 'philosopher king' within the law[56]. Who can be the true philosopher king in a college that is invisible and affirms no reigning monarch? What makes the 'public' in international law in a legal system that is decentralized and dialogical?

Brunnée and Toope have answered this question to some degree by building on Fuller's natural law to posit a theory of international law based on legitimate interactions between international legal actors. The authors conceive scholarly authority as a component of norm creation through its capacity to transmit shared understandings of legality in international law-making communities of practice[57]. Yet, they do so only by affirming prescriptive criteria for a desired legal process governed by the rule of law, and largely assess legal scholarship as failing to exercise authority

---

53 Peters, 'Realizing Utopia as a Scholarly Endeavour' (2013) 24(2) European Journal of International Law, 347, see also Peters, *Beyond Human Rights: The Legal Status of the Individual in International Law* (2018) 298.

54 Lang, *International Political Theory: an Introduction* (2015) 22.

55 For similar claims see also Madsen, Helfer, and Alter (eds) *International Court Authority* (2018).

56 On epistemic responsibility see also Jan Smits, *The Mind and Method of the Legal Academic* (2012).

57 Brunée and Toope, *Legitimacy and Legality in International Law: An Interactional Account* (2010).

in their many examples[58]. But the rule of law is not an *a priori* construct, it represents an ideal to which legal systems typically aspire to, and at worst, appropriates an idea of substance as a 'feeling' that is amenable to politics[59]. Simply put, the (international) rule of law is not empirical fact but an essentially contested concept[60]. Furthermore, an assessment of authority from a global perspective is not tailored judicial contexts. The authority of legal scholarship as it arises before international courts draws on context specific practices, norms, and discourses which are specific to the practice of adjudication of law.

Theories that draw on moral concepts to explain the authority of legal scholarship draw dichotomies between theory and practice that might bode well in legal argument but are unsuited to understanding the nature of law. As Paulus rightly notes, '(t)he reality of human society is too rich and concrete to be captured by rules and principles of a general nature'[61]. But complete uncertainty need not amount to radical scepticism[62]. From the counter post, to say that legal scholarship is the handmaiden of politics[63], or an abstraction that is detached from the *real* business of lawyers[64] is undesirable to the extent that it merely substitutes politics for morals in its analytical approach. Naturalist theories tend to suffer from a problem of 'interiority:' the attribution of an internal feature to legal system without explaining its actual existence or the basis of its normative force[65]. From a more qualitative point of view, a claim of a right to rule is less about deference and more about the quality of being authoritative. To say that someone is an expert is simply to say that they understand a subject

---

58 Ibid, 45, 247, 277–278, 342, 348.

59 Koskenniemi, 'Miserable Comforters: International Relations as New Natural Law' (2009) 15(3) European Journal of International Relations, 404, 408.

60 To borrow from Waldron, 'Is the Rule of Law an Essentially Contested Concept (In Florida)?' (2003) 21 Law and Philosophy, 137.

61 Paulus, 'International Law after Postmodernism: Towards Renewal or Decline of International Law?' (2001) 14(4) Leiden Journal of International Law, 727, 753.

62 See also Scobbie 'Towards the Elimination of International Law: Some Radical Scepticism about Sceptical Radicalism' (1990) 61(1) British Yearbook of International Law, 33.

63 Kennedy, 'Challenging Expert Rule: The Politics of Global Governance' (2005) 2 Sydney Law Review, 5, 7, Kennedy, *A World of Struggle: How Power, Law, and Expertise Shape Global Political Economy* (2016) 242.

64 Koskenniemi, *From Apology to Utopia: the Structure of International Legal Argument* (2006) 566–569.

65 See Reus-Smith, 'Obligation through Practice' (2011) 3(2) International Theory, 339, 340.

better than a non-expert[66] – authority is a situated relationship between interpretative subjects. Authority therein extends from subjective capacity to supra-individual knowledge[67]. The locus of authority this emerges as recognition *between* subjects[68]. This calls for deeper analysis of the sociological processes by which one argument comes to be accepted over another in the practice of international courts.

C. *The sociology of authority*

Sociological accounts hold that the authority of legal scholarship is generated in the social practice of relevant legal actors. These perspectives are naturally as diverse as sociology as a discipline. Weber's famous distinction between types of authority provides a useful starting point. Is the authority of legal scholarship traditional (cultural practice), charismatic (personal), or rational-legal (bureaucratic)?[69] Typically, it is neither one nor the other but a combination of these forms. Citation of scholarship is a legal-cultural practice, based at least in part on the credentials of the author, but also the historical function of legal scholarship in performing a role of legitimatizing the law. Three principal approaches to the authority of legal scholarship can be discerned from socio-legal scholarship: an agent-centric, an institutional-court focused, and an interaction-based perspective.

The agent-centric view focuses on the occupational expertise of the legal scholar. One aspect of this approach is to conceive authority as arising from the individual subject, for example, 'Holmes said so' is supposedly a more authoritative than 'Schauer said so' before a United States court[70]. Another is institutional affiliation: X scholar comes from Y institution and should be valued as a result. It might be possible to distinguish through format – for example, a monograph may be more authoritative than a journal article. Within this division, there may be forms of 'effort-based authority' (such as Oppenheim's work) and 'process-based authority' (such as

66 Duke, 'Gadamer and Political Authority,' (2013) 13(1) European Journal of Political Theory, 25, 27.

67 See also Sevel, 'Practical Authority as Self-Knowledge' in Green and Leiter (eds) *Oxford Studies in Philosophy of Law* (forthcoming, 2021).

68 Duke (fn66) 27.

69 Max Weber, 'Politics as a Vocation' in Owen and Strong (eds.) *Max Weber: the Vocation Lectures* (2004) 32.

70 Schauer, 'Authority of Legal Scholarship' (1991) 139 University of Pennsylvania Law Review, 1004, 1012.

the work of the International Law Association) and indeed subjective perceptions that recall the service conception, of the authority of doctor over patient[71]. This approach seems to assume that the judge will be less skilled at 'finding the law' than a legal scholar[72]. But also fails to encapsulate how the authority of legal scholarship can be both and indeed simultaneously based on the content of the advice but also and on the specific expertise of the legal scholar[73]. Put differently, legal scholarship can be persuasive due to its argument and that argument is persuasive due to its source. Moreover, what is the true source? The traditional doctrinal 'generalists' of public international law ground their expertise as *the* authorities on the wider corpus by moving between functional roles of the 'invisible college' as the author of leading textbooks, governmental lawyer, legal counsel, professor, or as an international arbitrator or judge[74].

An institutional approach similarly only offers a partial account. This type of argument is based on the assumption that international courts and judges act strategically in the exercise of judgment. This could extend to justification within a court; for example, in the greater use of legal scholarship in separate and dissenting opinions of international judges seeking to convince their fellow judges[75]. The more popular notion posits that citation is a sign of a process of legitimation by a court[76]. For instance, Lupu and Voeten argue that the European Court of Human Rights is more likely to embed its judgments in precedent when the expected value of persuading domestic court is highest[77]. Could such an approach extend to

---

71 See also Sivakumaran, 'The Influence of Teachings of Publicists on the Development of International Law' (2017) International and Comparative Law Quarterly, 1, 8 on the role of 'state empowered entities'.

72 Shecaira, 'Legal Arguments from Scholarly Authority' (2017) 30(3) Ratio Juris, 1, 9.

73 Schauer (fn70) 1017.

74 Generalist here refers to a specialism in no specific field but the wider body of public international law. See, for example, Kammerhofer, 'Orthodox Generalists and Political Activists in International Legal Scholarship' in Happold (ed) *International Law in a Multipolar World* (2010) 129 for a description of the use of these terms.

75 See especially Helmersen, *The Applications of Teachings by the International Court of Justice* (2021) for evidence of the use of legal scholarship in the separate and dissenting opinions of judges of the International Court of Justice.

76 See especially Merryman, 'The Authority of Authority: What the California Supreme Court Cited in 1950' (1954) 6 Stanford Law Review, 613.

77 See Lupu and Voeten, 'Precedent in International Courts: A Network Analysis of Case Citations by the European Court of Human Rights' (2012) 43(2) British Journal of Political Science, 413.

the practice of citation of scholarship by an international court? It could be assumed that citing some authority for a legal proposition is better than no authority at all. For example, a court may be more likely to cite legal scholarship when a legal decision is perceived as controversial- within the legal community[78], or amongst the public[79]. One study found that the US Supreme Court is more likely to cite 'rhetorical sources' such as the *Federalist Papers* when the perceived legitimacy of their decision is lower, such as when the Court moves to overturn a legal precedent[80]. Nevertheless, the study also found variance in the citation practice of individual benches and judges, and factors of efficiency effected the results as judges were less likely to cite 'rhetorical sources' in periods of higher workload[81]. An approach based on a judicial strategy could help to explain some of the citations of a court but cannot of itself explain the authority of legal scholarship.

The participatory approach offers a more comprehensive explanation through its focus on the way in which legal authority is generated through the interactions of participants in a legal system. Cohen's theory of international legal precedent proposes that international lawyers exploit their capital in the interpretation of law by affirming their ability to grasp the meaning of legal texts, and thereby generate the argumentative burden of precedents in an interpretive community through discourse[82]. It is significant to note that legal scholarship provides normative support to the legal precedents of international courts through its role in providing system and coherence to international law[83]. However, to present a legal claim by couching it within sources of law as answer that is 'correct' is

---

78 Squatrito, 'International Courts and the Politics of Legitimation and De-Legitimation' (2018) 33 Temple International Law and Comparative Law Journal, 298, 314–319.

79 See, for example Dothan, 'Judicial Deference Allows European Consensus to Emerge' (2018) 18(2) Chicago Journal of International Law, 393, 408.

80 Hume, 'The Use of Rhetorical Sources by the U.S. Supreme Court,' (2006) 40(4) Law and Society Review, 1, 18–20.

81 Ibid, 19.

82 See Harlan-Grant Cohen, The Sociology of International Precedent, in this volume.

83 See, for example, Hernández, 'A Divisible College?: Reflections on the International Legal Profession' (2018) 29(3) European Journal of International Law, 1003, Zidar, 'Interpretation and the International Legal Profession,' in Bianchi, Peat and Windsor (eds.) *Interpretation in International Law* (2015) 142, and more generally Edward Rubin, 'Legal Scholarship' in Dennis Patterson (ed.) *A Companion to Philosophy of Law and Legal Theory* (2010) 547.

the 'currency of the game' and does not in itself suggest that it will make those sources authoritative[84]. Moreover, from a sociological point of view, to argue from legal precedent connotates an expectant sense of social rule to refer to the relevant decisions of a court, and concomitantly, fear of sanction arising from a failure to abide by the norm of the group. Generally, however, lawyers are not expected to argue from legal scholarship as it is not a formal source of law. As Koskenniemi's 'culture of formalism' dictates, 'lawyers may want to cede ground to philosophers or novelists, but they can't themselves be poetic or philosophical without risking their reputation as competent professionals.'[85]

Put simply, the authority of legal scholarship as generated through interactions of relevant legal actors does not seem to be generated in the same way as the authority of precedent in international courts. The extent of any analogy that can be effectively drawn in this context is limited by the heterogeneity of legal scholarship and its distinct and principal function in providing a source of legal knowledge. Legal scholarship is characterized by diversity in terms of content, style, and form; it is multifarious and necessarily proliferates beyond immediate questions to be adjudicated by an international court. An international court is likely to adopt different texts in different situations, largely because legal scholarship is not hermetically sealed to the same extent as legal-institutional validation by a court. Legal scholarship and legal precedent share the same episteme, but it remains functionally and stylistically distinct in the way that it is performed, for example, on the scope of an interpretation of a legal norm, and on the policy reasons as to why such an interpretation should be inscribed into law. We are thus left with a conundrum: from a sociological perspective the authority of legal scholarship appears to be generated by interaction, but it is only likely to be determined in a specific context. This invites sharpened focus on the role of interpretation in constraining adjudicative choice – in other words, the hermeneutical frame by which scholarship becomes part of law in the practice of courts.

84 Venzke, 'Semantic Authority, Legal Change and the Dynamics of International Law' (2015) 12 No Foundations, 1.

85 Orford, 'A Journal of the Voyage from Apology to Utopia' (2006) 12 German Law Journal, 993, 1007.

D. Hermeneutic understanding

Hermeneutics is the theory, knowledge, and practice of interpretation. Law as hermeneutics resists strict definition due to the openness of the concepts. Legal hermeneutics has mostly focused on developing applied hermeneutics to find correct the methodology for legal interpretation[86]. Philosophical hermeneutics as a more general set of philosophical precepts projects that legal interpretation is just a special case of the way in which we interpret the world in general[87]. Hermeneutics sits between formalism and nihilism – it rejects that interpretation follows a rule bound procedure, yet posits that hermeneutics plays a critical role in the justification of our choices[88]. The hermeneutics that will be spoken for here is a theory of law informed by hermeneutical philosophy[89].

Philosophical hermeneutics based on Heidegger's theory of 'being' as the ontological condition of humankind provides a window into the problem at hand by conceiving interpretation as embedded in all social relationships. For Heidegger then, 'to be human is not primarily to be a rational animal, but first and foremost a self-interpreting animal'[90]. Gadamer – Heidegger's most famous student – extended Heidegger's ontological philosophy of 'being' to an ontology of 'understanding' by showing how history and culture are embedded in all acts of interpretation[91]. The 'historical tradition' is key to interpretation: every text is located in a particular time and place, but the meaning of the tradition may have to be 'discovered' in other sources. The process of understanding thus cannot be detached from the cultural location of the interpreter. Understanding takes place within 'effective history;' 'the operative force of the tradition over those that belong to it, so that in even rejecting or reacting to it they remain conditioned by it'[92]. Gadamer's concept of a 'fusion of horizons' describes a process whereby meaning is brought about through dialogical

---

86 See for example, Phelps and Pits, 'Questioning the Text: The Significance of Phenomenological Hermeneutics for Legal Interpretation' (1095) 29 St Louis University Law Journal, 353.

87 Mootz, 'The Ontological Basis of Legal Hermeneutics: A Proposed Model of Inquiry Based on the Work of Gadamer, Habermas and Ricoeur' (1988) 68 Boston University Law Review, 523.

88 Lehy, *Legal Hermeneutics, History, Theory and Practice* (1992) xii.

89 Sherman, 'Hermeneutics in Law' (1988) 51(3) Modern Law Review 386, 387.

90 Lafont, 'Heidegger's Hermeneutics' in Glanert and Girard (eds) *Law's Hermeneutics and Other Investigations* (2017) 11.

91 Blaikie, *Approaches to Social Enquiry: Advancing Knowledge* (2007) 151.

92 Warnke, *Gadamer: Hermeneutics, Tradition and Reason* (1987) 82.

exchange into the situation of the present – 'all reading involves application, so that a person reading a text is himself part of the meaning that he apprehends;' 'understanding is not reconstruction but mediation…it is an event.'[93]

Gadamer regarded legal interpretation as a paradigm case of hermeneutics – 'law does not exist in order to be understood historically, but to be concretized in its legal validity by being interpreted' – ascertaining the meaning of a legal text and discovering how to apply it to the immediate case are not distinct actions but one unitary process that anticipates unity of meaning between texts[94]. In effect, 'application is neither a subsequent nor merely an occasional part of the phenomenon of understanding but co-determines it as a whole from the beginning'[95]. Gadamer's ideal of the judge is thus required to apply a 'hermeneutic knowledge,' or the application of service to a thing, in contrast to 'knowledge as domination' that takes the form of objectified distance[96]. For Gadamer then, jurisprudence is a 'normative discipline that performs the necessary dogmatic function of supplementing the law, bridging the gap between the universality of settled law and the concreteness of the individual case'[97]. In contrast to Dworkin's Hercules that seeks to find one right answer, the Hermes of philosophical hermeneutics is 'wary of being more than an imperfect messenger who must recognize the need to place his own presuppositions at risk in response to the legal tradition'[98].

Hermeneutics allows us to confront the interpretative 'being' of the international legal professional: situated in a time and space, with a less firm distinction between the legal subject and legal official[99]. It might be objected that hermeneutics is concerned with the meaning of everyday people, and not scientific experts. That conclusion would be premature. Gadamer took hermeneutical philosophy as not so much a special method-

93 Linge, 'Editors Introduction' in Gadamer, *Philosophical Hermeneutics* (1976) xvi.

94 Gadamer, *Truth and Method* (2012) 309.

95 Ibid, 324.

96 Grodin, 'Gadamer's Interest for Legal Hermeneutics' in Glanert and Girard (eds) *Law's Hermeneutics and Other Investigations* (2017) 55.

97 Gadamer, 'Classical and Philosophical Hermeneutics' cited in Mootz (fn86) 357.

98 Mootz, 'Interpretation' in Sarat et al (eds.) *Law and the Humanities: An Introduction* (2010) 359, See Dworkin, *Law's Empire* (1986).

99 See also Burchardt, 'The Functions of Law and Their Challenges: The Differentiated Functionality of International Law' (2019) 20(4) German Law Journal, 409, 426 on the consequences of the interlinkage between law creating and law applying actors in the international legal system; chiefly, the strong role of law interpretation in such a sphere.

ology but a description of the way that we experience the world in general[100]. Hermeneutics is a 'practical philosophy;' as all theory starts from practice, 'theory is not so much the individual momentary act as ... a position and condition of openness.'[101] For Gadamer then, the 'myth of the ivory tower where theoretical people live is an unreal fantasy. We all stand in the middle of the social system'[102]. Hermeneutics helps to reveal the relationship between theory and practice in law as a productive tension. Some important work has been made in this direction by applying hermeneutical philosophy to the study of interpretation in international law[103]. For the purposes of the present endeavour, it is necessary to demarcate what we can take from a turn to hermeneutics. The first benefit is empirical, and the second arises from its theoretical consequent.

The empirical benefit can be seen through the application of hermeneutics as qualitative content analysis of legal texts, which reveals that the sources of international law are integrated and mutually dependent[104]. Take for example the development of the law of command responsibility under Article 28(a) of the *Rome Statute* by the International Criminal Court ('ICC.') Article 28(a) provides for responsibility of superiors for the crimes commited by those under his or her command. The interpretation of this provision was an important question in *Prosecutor v. Bemba*[105]. Pre-Trial Chamber II first took note of Sandoz' and Zimmerman's *ICRC Commentary on the Additional Protocols of 8 June 1977 to the Geneva Conventions of 12 Aug 1949* (ICRC, 1987) to hold that command responsibiliy differs from other modes of liability (Article 25) under the *Rome Statute* because it arises only in circumstances where a legal obligation is imposed

100 Blaikie (fn91) 153.

101 Gadamer, *Praise of Theory* (1998) cited in Mootz, 'A Future Foretold: Neo-Aristotelian Praise of Postmodern Legal Theory' (2003) 68(3) Brooklyn Law Review 683, 696

102 Cited in Ibid, 699.

103 Korhonen, *International Law Situated. An Analysis of the Lawyer's Stance Towards Culture, History and Community* (2000); Voyiakis, 'International Law, Interpretative Fidelity and the Hermeneutics of Hans-Georg Gadamer' (2011) 54 German Yearbook of International Law, 385, Kemmerer, 'Sources in the Meta-Theory of International Law: Hermeneutical Conversations' in d'Aspremont and Besson (eds) *The Oxford Handbook on the Sources of International Law* (2017) 469.

104 See Byrne, *Legal Scholarship at Work: An Empirical Analysis of the Use of Theory in the Practice of International Courts and Tribunals* (PhD Manuscript, University of Copenhagen, 2020).

105 For a contrasting analysis on the use of precedent in Bemba see also Nollez-Goldbach, The Precedent in the ICC Jurisprudence, in this volume.

on a commander to act[106]. The Chamber thereafter set out five requisite elements in order to prove criminal responsibility under Article 28(a) of the *Rome Statute* on the basis of the treaty, and addressed each element in turn. The Chamber relied heavily on legal scholarship in order to give meaning to to each of the elements[107]. In this process it made frequent reference to a chapter by Fenrick, 'Article 28' appearing in Triffterer (ed.), *Commentary on the Rome Statute of the International Criminal Court*, (1999.) This text is a collection of articles written by observers to the drafting of the *Rome Statute* and is frequently cited by the ICC as a kind of pre-interpretative, academic/historical context to the treaty terms.

Trial Chamber III returned the issue of command responsibility in the *Bemba* judgment. The Chamber cited a body of legal scholarship to note that 'there has been considerable debate' regarding the nature of the doctrine, and cited a number of texts, including Ambos, *Treatise on International Criminal Law* (2013), and Meloni, *Command Responsibility in International Criminal Law* (2010), which directly commented on the law of command responsibility as articulated by the Pre-Trial Chamber[108]. Trial Chamber III largely chose to concur on the requisite elements of the mode of liability, but in doing so, sought further confirmation of legal principles in the jurisprudence of the International Criminal Tribunal for the former Yugoslavia and the International Criminal Tribunal for Rwanda[109]. The Appeals Chamber subsequently disagreed with part of the Trial Chamber's decisions on the interpretation of Article 28. It found that the Trial Chamber took 'an unreasonably strict approach' on an element of command responsibility, and cited, Fenrick, 'Article 28' in Triffterer (ed.), *Commentary on the Rome Statute of the International Criminal Court* (1999), as well as a more specific text, G Mettraux, *The Law of Command*

106 *Prosecutor v. Jean Pierre Bemba Gombo,* Decision Pursuant to Article 61(7)(a) and (b) of the Rome Statute on the Charges of the Prosecutor Against Jean-Pierre Bemba Gombo, 15 June 2009, Pre-Trial Chamber II, ICC-01/05–01/08 (405).

107 *Prosecutor v. Jean Pierre Bemba Gombo,* Decision Pursuant to Article 61(7)(a) and (b) of the Rome Statute on the Charges of the Prosecutor Against Jean-Pierre Bemba Gombo, 15 June 2009, Pre-Trial Chamber II, ICC-01/05–01/08 (410–442).

108 *Prosecutor v. Jean Pierre Bemba Gombo*, 'Judgment pursuant to Article 74 of the Statute,' Trial Chamber III, 21 March 2016, ICC-01/05–01/08 (171).

109 *Prosecutor v. Jean Pierre Bemba Gombo*, 'Judgment pursuant to Article 74 of the Statute,' Trial Chamber III, 21 March 2016, ICC-01/05–01/08 (170–213).

Responsibility (2009) in order to further outline the principles of evidence which it had relied on in assessing whether the legal elements were met[110].

This is but one of many examples where the ICC practice of interpretation displays an exemplary hermeneutic: an act of conversation to seek the meaning of legal texts through the past and present. The ICC presents a fusion of horizons in its full scope that arises between the actors that forge international criminal law – the court itself, the ad-hoc tribunals, the drafters of the *Rome Statute*, legal practitioners, and legal academics. The ICC's relatively cautious approach indicates that its hermeneutic listens to the State parties that are its constituents, manifesting as a consensual outlook that is wary of potential criticism of judicial activism that plagued the ad-hocs tribunals[111]. The ICC manages and transfoms the legal traditions that comprise its competence – between the common and civil law, and procedural fairness and criminal punishment, for a more international sense of justice. Hermeneutics helps to show how legal scholarship not separate from the practice of law but integral to it. Legal scholarship as the theory of international law makes practice work in international courts.

From here it is possible to detail what we can further take from a turn to hermeneutics in making sense of sources of law as vessels of the past and present, or rules and practices in international law. This first benefit is to comprehend how every act of interpretation is little more than an act of understanding, but one here attuned to a specific context. It helps us to appreciate a world where law is seemingly everywhere[112] without lapsing into dreams (or nightmares) of global law[113], or reifying global governance on the *ex-ante* or *ex-post*[114]. The challenge that remains is 'the problem of the "definitional stop': where to draw the line between the legal and non-legal, whilst recognizing that law is a socially and culturally contingent concept[115]. The second advantage is greater appreciation that

110 *Prosecutor v. Jean Pierre Bemba Gombo*, 'Judgment on the appeal of Mr Jean-Pierre Bemba Gombo against Trial Chamber III's "Judgment pursuant to Article 74 of the Statute,"' Appeals Chamber, 8 June 2018, ICC-01/05–01/08 A (176).

111 On the desire to limit the power of judges see Hunt, 'The International Criminal Court High Hopes, 'Creative Ambiguity' and an Unfortunate Mistrust in International Judges' (2004) 2 Journal of International Criminal Justice, 56.

112 See Balkin, 'The Proliferation of Legal Truth' (2003) 26(1) Harvard Journal of Law and Public Policy, 5.

113 See, for example, Walker, *Intimations of Global Law* (2014).

114 See, for example, Krisch, 'Liquid authority in global governance' (2017) 9(2) International Theory, 237.

115 Twinning, 'General Jurisprudence' (2007) 15 University of Miami International and Comparative Law Review, 3, 43/46 (2007).

the sources of international law are of themselves 'reflexive spaces'[116], a product of the deeply dialectical nature of international law-making[117]. This understanding is better in line with the temporality of international law: its objects are in constant flux, and its subjects are created for a period of time, rarely tenured but only mandated[118]. A static vision of international law tends to ignore the subjective dimension as it is experienced by its interpreters[119]. The challenge that remains is to explain what sustains international law as a professional practice without lapsing into a view of social discipline as its principal determinant[120] or resurrecting an *a priori* sense of a virtue ethics[121].

The third benefit is greater appreciation of the 'textualism' of international adjudication: statements survive, whether decisive or not, by becoming malleable as text for advancing normative authority[122]. Legal scholarship therefore functions as a technology of international law, a medium for the translation or indeed refraction of forms of social conflict into a legally institutionalized form[123]. Put differently, theories of law 'do not offer subjective explanations of a reality that has a discrete and objective existence. They constitute the reality they intend to describe…'.[124] The challenge is to make the relationship theory and practice visible without lapsing into a view of law as mere empirical fact. The fourth benefit is recognizing the futility of drawing sharp lines between the *techne* and the

---

116 Kemmerer (fn103) 469.

117 This view is increasingly mainstream, see, for example, Roberts and Sivakumaran (fn38) 89.

118 See Ambrus and Wessel, 'Between Pragmatism and Predictability: Temporariness in International Law' (2014) 45 Netherlands Yearbook of International Law, 3.

119 Messenger, 'International Law, Perception, and the Problem of Time' in Pasquet et al (eds) *International Law and Time: Narratives and Techniques* (Forthcoming, 2021).

120 For instance, through the popular notion of interpretative communities, see Fish, *Is There a Text in This Class? The Authority of Interpretive Communities* (1990).

121 See, for example, Klabbers, 'Doing Justice? Bureaucracy, the Rule of Law and Virtue Ethics' (2017) 1 Rivista di filosofia del diritto, 27, See also Singh, The Potential of International Law: Fragmentation and Ethics' (2010) 24(1) Leiden Journal of International Law 23.

122 See also, for empirical support of this assessment, Ridi, ''Mirages of an Intellectual Dreamland'? Ratio, Obiter, and the Textualization of International Precedent' (2019) 10(3) Journal of International Dispute Settlement, 361.

123 Olsen and Toddington (fn11) 65.

124 Bianchi, *International Law Theories: an Inquiry into Different Ways of Thinking* (2016) 16.

episteme of international law as it plays out in the practices of international lawyers. In other words, the distinction between 'theoretical' and 'practical' authority as it can be extended, or a reason to believe in something as against a reason to act on it, dissolves on closer inspection. As Mootz explains: '(o)nce theory is reconceived as a disposition within practice—as an engagement in practice with a distinct comportment—its unavoidable significance becomes clear'[125]. The challenge that remains is to show how the theory of law is maintained over time as international legal doctrine.

E. Conclusion

Opening the black box of the authority of legal scholarship before international courts paves way for deeper engagement with the nature of the past as a vessel for the present in international law. Are precedents 'rules' or 'practices;' obligations, constraints, or strategic resource? The study of precedent often seems to be exhausted by the so-called internal and external approaches. Yet, hermeneutical philosophy helps us to see that they are ultimately two sides of the same coin. As Leyh reminds us, 'adopting a suspicious attitude toward authority is at the heart of hermeneutical discourse...it attempts to undermine...calm assurances transmitted by...legal orthodoxies'[126]. The rules and practices of international law are not given but contingent – a product of dialogue and consciousness. Authority is not just a legal construct but a phenomenon – as a social product that comes clothed in a specific historical, linguistic, and cultural form, it is interpretative and qualitative. There is, after all, many rules of precedent amongst international courts which shape the future present of international law[127]. As Taylor wrote, 'reason giving has a limit, and in the end must repose in another kind of understanding'[128]. To follow a rule requires an interpretation of what is required by the rule and that understanding is embodied. The rules, therefore, *lie in* the practice of international law. What we see is 'only islands in the sea of our unformulated practical grasp of the world'[129].

---

125 Mootz (fn101) 690.

126 See Lehy (fn88) xxi.

127 See further Ridi (fn16) 1 for insight into the contextual nature of rules of precedent of international courts.

128 Taylor (fn19) 170.

129 Ibid, 171.

Legal formalism projects that legal scholarship holds no formal authority because it is not a source of law – it cannot provide content independent reasons for use in the adjudicative practice of courts. The authority of legal scholarship must therefore arise outside of the doctrine of sources, as a form of counsel rather than command, which in the absence of formal hierarchy becomes more important. Naturalist theories equate legal authority with political authority and posit that legal scholarship holds no formal authority because it is not the product of a legitimate and due procedure or process. Yet, legal scholarship is not in and of itself a political construct, but the element of theory in a symbiotic process – its authority arises more from recognition and knowledge between interpretative subjects. The sociology of precedent helps to show that rule following is a practical phenomenon, but that must ultimately take place within context of specific interpretative framework that channels authority. Hermeneutics helps us to understand how lawyers are always situated in schemes of interpretation: legal interpretation is a special case of a process whereby we come to understand the world in general. The practice of a profession sustains international law as a dynamic between theory and practice.

Despite changes in recent decades, international law has remained a diverse but specifically legal body of norms, with decentralized characteristics that elevate the cognitive function of doctrine. Judicialization has coincided with rising challenges to the epistemological foundations of international law. We live with a kind of post-modern international law, where law is both an agent and an object of change, with complex relationships between legal subjects and legal forms[130]. Yet, in a world of competing legalities, the commitments of international law remain no less important[131]. International courts provide a focal point for a *praxis*, or an action orientated deliberation of norms[132]. The authority of legal scholarship arises from its role in supporting this *praxis* of international law which unfolds on an everyday basis in the activities of international courts. This Chapter could only provide a small glimpse into a hermeneutic universe that remains waiting to be explored.

130 Avbelj, 'Transnational law between modernity and post-modernity' (2016) 7(3) Transnational Legal Theory, 406.

131 Hakimi, 'Why Should We Care About International Law?' (2020) 118(6) Michigan Law Review, 1283.

132 Werner, 'Concluding Remarks' in d'Aspremont et al (eds.) *International Law as a Profession* (2017) 432

Bibliography

Karen Alter, *The New Terrain of International Law: Courts, Politics, Rights* (Princeton University Press, Princeton 2013)

Mónika Ambrus and Ramses Wessel, 'Between Pragmatism and Predictability: Temporariness in International Law' (2014) 45 Netherlands Yearbook of International Law 3

Matej Avbelj, 'Transnational law between modernity and post-modernity' (2016) 7(3) Transnational Legal Theory, 406

Sir Frank Berman, 'Authority in International Law,' KFG Working Paper Series, No. 22 (2018)

Samantha Besson 'Theorizing the Sources of International Law' In Samantha Besson and John Tasioulas (eds.) *The Philosophy of International Law* (Oxford University Press, Oxford 2010) 163

Samantha Besson, 'International Legal Theory Qua Practice of International Law' in Jean d'Aspremont et al (eds.) *International Law as a Profession* (Cambridge University Press, Cambridge 2017) 343

A Bianchi, *International Law Theories: an Inquiry into Different Ways of Thinking* (Oxford University Press, Oxford 2016)

Jack Balkin, 'The Proliferation of Legal Truth' (2003) 26(1) Harvard Journal of Law and Public Policy, 5

Norman Blaikie, *Approaches to Social Enquiry: Advancing Knowledge* (2nd edn. Polity Press, Malden 2007)

Aldo Zammit Borda, 'A Formal Approach to Article 38(1)(d) of the ICJ Statute from the Perspective of the International Criminal Courts and Tribunals' (2013) European Journal of International Law, 649

Jutta Brunée and Stephen Toope, *Legitimacy and Legality in International Law: An Interactional Account* (Cambridge University Press, Cambridge 2010)

Dana Burchardt, 'The Functions of Law and Their Challenges: The Differentiated Functionality of International Law' (2019) 20(4) German Law Journal 409

Annabel Brett, 'Sources in the Scholastic Legacy: the Reconstruction of the Ius Gentium in the Second Scholastic' in Jean d'Aspremont and Samantha Besson (eds) *The Oxford Handbook of the Sources of International Law* (Oxford University Press, Oxford 2017) 67

Hedley Bull, 'The Importance of Grotius in the Study of International Relations' in Hedley Bull, Benedict Kingsbury, and Adam Roberts (eds) *Hugo Grotius and International Relations* (Oxford University Press, Oxford 1992) 63

Anthony Carty, *Philosophy of international law* (Edinburgh University Press, Edinburgh 2009)

Basak Çali, *The Authority of International Law: Obedience, Respect, and Rebuttal* (Oxford University Press, Oxford 2015)

Tony Cole, 'Non-Binding Documents and Literature,' in Tarcisio Gazinni and Eric de Brabandere (eds.) *International Investment Law: Sources of Rights and Obligations* (Brill, Leiden 2010) 289

Richard Collins and Alexandra Bohm, 'International Law as a Professional Practice: Crafting the Autonomy of International Law' in Jean d'Aspremont et. al. (eds) *International Law as a Profession* (2017) 67

Richard Collins, 'The Problematic Concept of the International Legal Official' (2016) 6 Transnational Legal Theory 608

Richard Collins, *The Institutional Problem in Modern International Law* (Hart, Oxford 2016)

Jean d'Aspremont, *Formalism and the Sources of International Law* (Oxford University Press, Oxford 2012)

Shai Dothan, 'Judicial Deference Allows European Consensus to Emerge' (2018) 18(2) Chicago Journal of International Law, 393

George Duke, 'Gadamer and Political Authority,' (2013) 13(1) European Journal of Political Theory 25

Neil Duxbury, *Jurists and Judges: an Essay on Influence* (Hart, Oxford 2001)

Ronald Dworkin, *Law's Empire* (Harvard University Press, Cambridge 1986)

Stanley Fish, *Is There a Text in This Class? The Authority of Interpretive Communities* (Harvard University Press, Cambridge 1990)

Hans-Georg Gadamer, *Truth and Method* (Bloomsbury, London, 2012)

Leslie Green, 'Legal Obligations and Authority' in the *Stanford Encyclopedia of Philosophy* (Online)

Jean Grodin, 'Gadamer's Interest for Legal Hermeneutics' in Simone Glanert and Fabien Girard (eds) *Law's Hermeneutics and Other Investigations* (Routledge, Abingdon 2017) 55

Monica Hakimi, 'Why Should We Care About International Law?' (2020) 118(6) Michigan Law Review, 1283

Ross Harrison, *Hobbes, Locke and Confusion's Masterpiece* (Cambridge University Press, Cambridge 2013)

HLA Hart, *The Concept of Law* (3rd edn, Oxford University Press, Oxford 2012)

Sondre Torp Helmersen, 'Finding 'the Most Highly Qualified Publicists': Lessons from the International Court of Justice' (2019) 30(2) European Journal of International Law, 509

Sondre Torp Helmersen, 'The Application of Teachings by the International Tribunal for the Law of the Sea' (2020) 11 Journal of International Dispute Settlement, 11

Sondre Torp Helmersen, 'the Use of Scholarship by the WTO Appellate Body,' (2016) Goettingen Journal of International Law, 309

Sondre Torp Helmersen, *The Applications of Teachings by the International Court of Justice* (Cambridge University Press, Cambridge 2021)

Gleider Hernández, 'A Divisible College?: Reflections on the International Legal Profession' (2018) 29(3) European Journal of International Law 1003

Gleider Hernández, 'International Judicial Law-Making' in Catherine Brölmann and Yannick Radi (eds.) *Research Handbook on the Theory and Practice of International Law-Making* (Edward Elgar, Cheltenham 2015) 200

Gleider Hernández, 'The Activist Academic in International Law,' European Society of International Law Reflections Series, 2013

Gleider Hernández, 'The Responsibility of the International Legal Academic: Situating the Grammarian Within the "Invisible College"' in Jean d'Aspremont et al (eds), *International Law as a Profession* (Cambridge University Press, Cambridge 2017) 160

Gleider Hernández, *The International Court of Justice and the Judicial Function* (Oxford University Press, Oxford 2014)

Robert Hume, 'The Use of Rhetorical Sources by the U.S. Supreme Court,' (2006) 40(4) Law and Society Review, 1

Clarence Wilfred Jenks, 'Craftsmanship and International Law' (1956) 50 American Journal of International Law, 32

Jörg Kammerhofer, 'Law-Making by Scholars' in Catherine Brölmann and Yannick Radi (eds.) *Research Handbook on the Theory and Practice of International Law-Making* (Cheltenham, Edward Elgar 2015) 305

Jorg Kammerhofer, 'Orthodox Generalists and Political Activists in International Legal Scholarship' in Matthew Happold (ed) *International Law in a Multipolar World* (Routledge, Abingdon 2010) 129

Jörg Kammerhofer, *Uncertainty in International Law: a Kelsenian Perspective* (Routledge, Abingdon 2010)

Hans Kelsen, *Pure Theory of Law* (2nd edn, University of California Press, Berkeley 1967)

Alexandra Kemmerer, 'Sources in the Meta-Theory of International Law: Hermeneutical Conversations' in Jean d'Aspremont and Samantha Besson (ed.) *The Oxford Handbook on the Sources of International Law* (Oxford University Press, Oxford 2017) 469

David Kennedy, *A World of Struggle: How Power, Law, and Expertise Shape Global Political Economy* (Princeton University Press, Princeton 2016)

David Kennedy, 'Challenging Expert Rule: The Politics of Global Governance' (2005) 2 Sydney Law Review 5

Jan Klabbers, 'Doing Justice? Bureaucracy, the Rule of Law and Virtue Ethics' (2017) 1 Rivista di filosofia del diritto, 27

Thomas Kleinlein, 'Matters of Interpretation: How to Conceptualize and Evaluate Change of Norms and Values in the International Legal Order,' KFG Working Paper Series, No. 24 (2018)

Outi Korhonen, *International Law Situated. An Analysis of the Lawyer's Stance Towards Culture, History and Community* (Kluwer, Hague 2000)

Martti Koskenniemi, 'Miserable Comforters: International Relations as New Natural Law' (2009) 15(3) European Journal of International Relations 404

Martti Koskenniemi, *From Apology to Utopia: the Structure of International Legal Argument* (2nd edn, Cambridge University Press, Cambridge 2006)

Nico Krisch, 'Liquid authority in global governance' (2017) 9(2) International Theory, 237

Cristina Lafont, 'Heidegger's Hermeneutics' in Simone Glanert and Fabien Girard (eds) *Law's Hermeneutics and Other Investigations* (Routledge, Abingdon 2017)

Gregory Lehy, *Legal Hermeneutics, History, Theory and Practice* (University of California Press, Berkeley 1992)

Yonatan Lupu and Erik Voeten, 'Precedent in International Courts: A Network Analysis of Case Citations by the European Court of Human Rights' (2012) 43(2) British Journal of Political Science, 413

Mikael Rask Madsen, Laurence Helfer and Karen Alter (eds.) *International Court Authority* (Oxford University Press, Oxford 2018)

John Henry Merryman, 'The Authority of Authority: What the California Supreme Court Cited in 1950' (1954) 6 Stanford Law Review, 613

Gregory Messenger, 'International Law, Perception, and the Problem of Time' in L Pasquet et al. (eds) *International Law and Time: Narratives and Techniques* (Forthcoming, Springer, 2021)

Francis Mootz, 'A Future Foretold: Neo-Aristotelian Praise of Postmodern Legal Theory' (2003) 68(3) Brooklyn Law Review 683

Francis Mootz, 'Interpretation' in Austin Sarat et al (eds) *Law and the Humanities: an Introduction* (Cambridge University Press, Cambridge 2010) 359

Francis Mootz, 'The Ontological Basis of Legal Hermeneutics: A Proposed Model of Inquiry Based on the Work of Gadamer, Habermas and Ricoeur' (1988) 68 Boston University Law Review 523

Henrik Palmer Olsen and Stuart Toddington, 'The End of an Era: Static and Dynamic Interpretation in International Courts' (2004) 14 International Criminal Law Review, 920

Henrik Palmer Olsen and Stuart Toddington, 'The Scandanavian Roots of a New Approach to Legal Knowledge' (2012) 34 Retfærd, 57

Nicholas Onuf, 'Lawmaking and the Global Community' in Nicholas Onuf (ed.) *International Legal Theory: Essays and Engagements 1966–2006* (Routledge, Abingdon 2008) 94

Alexander Orakhelashvili, 'The Relevance of Theory and History – the Essence and Origins of International Law' in Alexander Orakhelashvili, (ed) *Research Handbook on the Theory and History of International Law* (Edward Elgar, Cheltenham 2008) 1

Anne Orford, 'A Journal of the Voyage from Apology to Utopia' (2006) 12 German Law Journal 993

Clive Parry, *The Sources and Evidences of International Law* (Manchester University Press, Manchester 1955)

Andreas Paulus, 'International Law after Postmodernism: Towards Renewal or Decline of International Law?' (2001) 14(4) Leiden Journal of International Law 727

Joost Pauwelyn, Ramses Wessel, and Jan Wouters (eds.) *Informal International Law-making* (Oxford University Press, Oxford 2012)

Michael Peil, 'Scholarly Writings as a Source of Law: A Survey of the Use of Doctrine by the International Court of Justice' (2012) 1(3) Cambridge Journal of International and Comparative Law, 136

Alain Pellet 'Article 38,' in Andreas Zimmermann, Christian Tomuschat, and Karin Oellers-Frahm (eds), *The Statute of the International Court of Justice: A Commentary* (Oxford University Press, Oxford 2006) 784

Anne Peters, 'Realizing Utopia as a Scholarly Endeavour' (2013) 24(2) European Journal of International Law, 347 Anne Peters, *Beyond Human Rights: The Legal Status of the Individual in International Law* (Cambridge University Press, Cambridge 2018) 298

Teresa Phelps and Jenny Pits, 'Questioning the Text: The Significance of Phenomenological Hermeneutics for Legal Interpretation' (1095) 29 St Louis University Law Journal, 353

Joseph Raz, *The Authority of Law* (Oxford University Press, Oxford 2009)

Christian Reus-Smith, 'Obligation through Practice' (2011) 3(2) International Theory 339

Nicollo Ridi, ''Mirages of an Intellectual Dreamland'? Ratio, Obiter, and the Textualization of International Precedent' (2019) 10(3) Journal of International Dispute Settlement, 361

Niccolo Ridi, 'Rule of Precedent and Rules on Precedent' in Eric de Branderbare et al (eds.) *Comparative Procedure in State to State Disputes* (Cambridge University Press, Cambridge forthcoming 2021)

Anthea Roberts and Sandesh Sivukamaran, 'The Theory and Reality of the Sources of International Law' in Malcolm Evans (ed.) *International Law* (5th edn, Oxford University Press, Oxford 2018) 89

Edward Rubin, 'Legal Scholarship' in Dennis Patterson (ed.) *A Companion to Philosophy of Law and Legal Theory* (2nd ed. Blackwell, Chichester 2010) 547

Edward Rubin, 'What does prescriptive legal scholarship say and who is listening to it? A reply to Dan Cohen' (1992) 63 University of Colorado Law Review, 731

Oscar Schachter, 'The Invisible College of International Lawyers,' (1977–1978) Northwestern University Law Review 217

Frederick Schauer, 'Authority and Authorities,' (2008) 94(8) Virginia Journal of International Law, 1931

Frederick Schauer, 'Authority of Legal Scholarship' (1991) 139 University of Pennsylvania Law Review 1004

Frederick Schauer, *Thinking like a lawyer: a new introduction to legal reasoning* (Harvard University Press, Harvard 2009)

Iain Scobbie 'Towards the Elimination of International Law: Some Radical Scepticism about Sceptical Radicalism' (1990) 61(1) British Yearbook of International Law 33

Michael Sevel, 'Practical Authority as Self-Knowledge' in Leslie Green and Brian Leiter (eds.) *Oxford Studies in Philosophy of Law* (Volume 4, forthcoming 2021)

Fábio Shecaira, *Legal Scholarship as a Source of Law* (Springer, London 2013)

Fábio Shecaira, 'Legal Arguments from Scholarly Authority' (2017) 30(3) Ratio Juris 1

Brad Sherman, 'Hermeneutics in Law' (1988) 51(3) Modern Law Review 386

Sahab Singh, The Potential of International Law: Fragmentation and Ethics' (2010) 24(1) Leiden Journal of International Law 23

Sandesh Sivakumaran, 'The Influence of Teachings of Publicists on the Development of International Law' (2017) International and Comparative Law Quarterly, 1

Jan Smits, *The Mind and Method of the Legal Academic* (Edward Elgar, Cheltenham 2012)

Theresa Squatrito, 'International Courts and the Politics of Legitimation and De-Legitimation' (2018) 33 Temple International Law and Comparative Law Journal, 298

Nora Stappert, 'A New Influence of Legal Scholars? The Use of Academic Writings at International Criminal Courts and Tribunals,' (2018) 31(4) Leiden Journal of International Law, 963

Daniel Star and Candice Delmas, 'Three Conceptions of Practical Authority' (2011) 2(1) Jurisprudence 143

Charles Taylor, *Philosophical Arguments* (Harvard University Press, Cambridge 1995)

Hugh Thirlway, *The Sources of International Law* (Oxford University Press, Oxford 2013)

William Twinning, 'General Jurisprudence' (2007) 15 University of Miami International and Comparative Law Review, 3, 43/46 (2007)

Ingo Venzke, *How Interpretation Makes International Law: on Semantic Change and Normative Twists* (Oxford University Press, Oxford 2012)

Ingo Venzke, 'Semantic Authority' in d'Aspremont and Singh, *Fundamental Concepts for International Law: Contributions to Disciplinary Thought* (2019) 815

Ingo Venzke, 'Semantic Authority, Legal Change and the Dynamics of International Law' (2015) 12 No Foundations, 1

Stephan Verosta, 'History of International Law, 1648 to 1815' in Rüdiger Wolfrum (ed.) *Max Planck Encyclopaedia of Public International Law* (2007) <https://opil.ouplaw.com/view/10.1093/law:epil/9780199231690/law-9780199231690-e707?prd=OPIL> accessed 8 June 2021

Santiago Villalpando, 'The "Invisible College of International Lawyers" Forty Years Later,' European Society of International Law Conference Paper Series No. 5/2013

Emmanuel Voyiakis, 'International Law, Interpretative Fidelity and the Hermeneutics of Hans-Georg Gadamer' (2011) 54 German Yearbook of International Law 385

Jeremy Waldron, 'Is the Rule of Law an Essentially Contested Concept (In Florida)?' (2003) 21 Law and Philosophy, 137

Neil Walker, *Intimations of Global Law* (Cambridge University Press, Cambridge 2014)

Georgia Warnke, *Gadamer: Hermeneutics, Tradition and Reason* (Polity, Cambridge, 1987)

Max Weber, 'Politics as a Vocation' in David Owen and Tracy Strong (eds.) *Max Weber: the Vocation Lectures* (Hackett, Indianapolis 2004)

Wouter Werner, 'Concluding Remarks' in Jean d'Aspremont et al (eds.) *International Law as a Profession* (Cambridge University Press, Cambridge 2017) 432

Michael Wood, 'Teachings of the Most Highly Qualified Publicists (Art. 38 (1) ICJ Statute)' in *Max Planck Encyclopedia of Public International Law* (2016) <https://opil.ouplaw.com/view/10.1093/law:epil/9780199231690/law-9780199231690-e1480> accessed 08 June 2021

Fuad Zarbiyev, 'Saying Credibly What the Law Is: On Marks of Authority in International Law,' (2018) 9(2) Journal of International Dispute Settlement, 291

Andraz Zidar, 'Interpretation and the International Legal Profession,' in Andrea Bianchi, Daniel Peat and Matthew Windsor (eds.) *Interpretation in International Law* (Oxford University Press, Oxford 2015) 142

Culture Clash: The Sociology of WTO Precedent

Harlan Grant Cohen[*]

A. *Introduction*

The question of precedent, as opposed to the value of particular precedents, rarely becomes a central issue in a diplomatic dispute. But there it was, front and center among the United States' complaints about the WTO Dispute Settlement system. In a statement to the WTO Dispute Settlement Body (DSB) on December 18, 2018, the United States complained that the WTO Appellate Body had been treating its reports as if they 'carry precedential weight, as if WTO Members had agreed in the DSU to a common law-like system of precedent.'[1] Over the course of 23 pages, the United States outlined its argument that the Appellate Body had erred when it announced that its prior interpretations should be followed absent 'cogent reasons,' and in so doing, had 'usurp[ed] the authority expressly reserved to Members'[2] to authoritatively interpret the WTO agreements.

These complaints, among others,[3] have led the United States to block all new appointments to the Appellate Body.[4] On December 10, 2019, the usual seven members had been reduced to one as the terms of two of the last three remaining members expired. As appeals must be heard by panels

* Gabriel M. Wilner/UGA Foundation Professor in International Law, University of Georgia School of Law. Thank you to Connor Harbin, Gamble Baffert II, Tahminehalsadat Madani, and Bailey Meyne for their invaluable research assistance.

1 U.S Mission to International Organizations in Geneva, 'Statements by the United States at the Meeting of the WTO Dispute Settlement Body Geneva' (18 December 2018), para. 10 <https://geneva.usmission.gov/wp-content/uploads/sites/290/Dec18.DSB_.Stmt_.as-deliv.fin_.public.pdf> accessed 17 October 2020.

2 Ibid para. 35.

3 USTR, *Report on the Appellate Body of the World Trade Organization* (February 2020) <https://ustr.gov/sites/default/files/Report_on_the_Appellate_Body_of_the_World_Trade_Organization.pdf> accessed 18 October 2020 (listing the most comprehensive accounting U.S. concerns); Lehne, *Crisis at the WTO: Is the Blocking of Appointments to the WTO Appellate Body by the United States Legally Justified?* (2019).

4 All appointments to the Appellate Body require consensus of all WTO members, allowing any single member to block an appointment.

of three, the Appellate Body lost its ability to function. Panel decisions appealed after that date are essentially left hanging, 'appealed into the void.' Partly over the proper role or rule of precedent, the United States has threatened the entire WTO dispute settlement system.

The Appellate Body fracas provides an interesting lens to examine how precedent operates at the international level. The United States' complaints are framed entirely in positivistic terms. Focused on the text of the treaties and arguments about customary international law, the United States argues that the Appellate Body has acted ultra vires in declaring the precedential effect of its own judgments. But the positivist account seems entirely unsatisfying. For one thing, it remains unclear both what role the Dispute Settlement Understanding (DSU) envisions for Appellate Body precedent and what role the Appellate Body has actually claimed.[5] While nothing in the DSU gives Appellate Body reports precedential authority, DSU Article 3.2 does describe the role of the WTO dispute settlement system as 'providing security and predictability to the multilateral trading system.' Whether predictability requires some adherence to prior interpretation is the essential question. For another, it's unclear how much any positive rule would actually matter to Appellate Body practice. Some observers have suggested that it might shift the cognitive bias regarding prior interpretation of WTO commitments, shifting the prior interpretation from a command to a suggestion.[6] From a different perspective, the U.S. position might actually make the Appellate Body's job more difficult, removing the cognitive/writing crutch of not having to justify or rationalize the interpretation of certain terms it already covered. Nor would it be able to so quickly dismiss a contrary panel interpretation. But would the judgments come out any differently? Would the AB members adopt a different approach to zeroing, or a different interpretation of state control for identification of a subsidy? Maybe.

But the United States' position can be read another way. The United States desires a particular outcome in WTO cases. It wants to win, but even more, it wants room to fight over the rules. Nor is this position surprising given, on the one hand, the United States' relative power compared to

5 WTO, 'Panels Established to Review Claims Against Trade Measures of Costa Rica, Russia, Saudi Arabia' (18 December 2018) <https://www.wto.org/english/news_e/news18_e/dsb_18dec18_e.htm> accessed 18 October 2020 ('[S]everal members questioned whether the Appellate Body was asserting such an authority').

6 Lester and Bacchus, 'Of Precedent and Persuasion: The Crucial Role of an Appeals Court in WTO Disputes' (12 September 2019) 74 *Free Trade Bulletin* <https://www.cato.org/sites/cato.org/files/2019-09/FTB_74.pdf> accessed 18 October 2020.

smaller WTO economies, and on the other, its increasing fear of a rising rival in China. Flexibility is an asset for the United States that it wouldn't be for others—for whom predictability is far more important—an asset which the United States fears losing. The Appellate Body too though, on this view, has a desired outcome. It wants its judgments to be authoritative and effective. Up until now, Appellate Body members might have calculated that that was best achieved by promoting both vertical stare decisis effect for its decisions on panels, and horizontal stare decisis to bind itself and future litigants before it. The United States' position might be seen a rational response to this rationalist analysis. By holding the Appellate Body hostage over the issue, it changes the calculus for supporters of an Appellate Body or whatever might replace it. Loosening control over interpretations might diminish the status or reputation of a reviewing body; its status or reputation matters little, though, if it ceases to exist entirely. If Appellate Body members and their supporters weren't considering a more conciliatory approach to precedent before December 10, 2019, one has to imagine that those considering a revival or replacement are now.

But even if this is the proper frame, it is unclear that such a victory would really give the United States what it wanted. In order to actually 'win' cases it might previously have lost, it needs more than a different Appellate Body position on precedent. It needs first to untie the hands of panelists, to free them from following Appellate Body jurisprudence with which they might disagree, and then second, to protect those favorable panel decisions from being overturned on review. The latter might be accomplished by eliminating review entirely (as is currently the case). If some sort of review is to reemerge, however, it would need to involve a more deferential stance towards panel opinions, including those that diverge from previous Appellate Body interpretations or its own views, a process more akin to annulment proceedings under the International Centre for Settlement of Investment Disputes (ICSID), in which arbitration decisions are annulled only when the panel 'manifestly exceeded its powers.' Even if the United States could achieve this through a treaty amendment or a decision by WTO members (using similar language to ICSID), it would only work with a shift in cultures regarding precedent at multiple points and levels—from panelists, to members of such a review mechanism, to member-state trade lawyers and policymakers. Here, the United States' complaints play a different role. Less demands for reform, they act as cultural signals, making arguments to and within the community of trade practice about acceptable approaches. By making the argument against precedential effect, the United States may free panelists to rethink Appellate Body jurisprudence, signaling that such a stance may have support in the community. It might also convince other members to make such arguments when they suit them. And it might convince those responsible for review that such an approach is not the end of its world (as U.S. continued opposition might be, at least for them). Precedent-talk—in this case, negative precedent-talk—might affect a subtle shift in community expectations and norms.

B. Three Frames

In previous work,[7] I have argued that precedent's force in international law can best be understood as a product of three overlapping, inter-dependent, and mutually constructed logics: (1) the jurisprudential, (2) the rational, and (3) the sociological. Much of the focus in the traditional literature on international courts and tribunal has been on the first two.

I. Jurisprudential

The jurisprudential account starts with the positive sources, much as the U.S. statement regarding the WTO Appellate Body does, asking what, if anything, the various agreements creating a particular body might say about the effect or weight of prior interpretation. This analysis rarely gets very far, though, as most international agreements are at best ambivalent about any weight precedent might have. To explain the ubiquity of practices of precedent across international law, the jurisprudential account has to go further and deeper, asking to what extent principles of law might require some reference or adherence to prior interpretations. Here, the focus is embedded ideas about avoiding arbitrariness, treating like cases alike, reason-giving, and reliance, all of which find some support in understandings of the rule-of-law or the concept of the law. These general principles thus create a legal argument or even legal obligation to give some weight to prior interpretations in arguments or decisions about the law's meaning and can help to explain the ubiquity of precedential arguments even in the absence of any specific mandate or permission.

The problem with this account, as highlighted by the U.S. statement, is that it can only go so far. While it might explain why prior interpretations

---

7 Cohen, 'Theorizing International Precedent' in Bianchi et al. (eds) *Interpretation in International Law* (2015).

cannot simply be ignored, it cannot, on its own, explain how much weight those interpretations should be given—whether, absent 'cogent reasons' to depart from them, they should be followed; whether they should be given persuasive authority; or whether they need merely be recognized in any argument. Nor can this account speak with much specificity about the weight of particular prior interpretations over others. Treating like cases alike and recognizing reasonable reliance brings analogical reasoning into play. Where a particular body has some unique authority to decide disputes or issue interpretations in an area and regularly does so, the analogies between new disputes and prior ones before that same body may seem obvious and most relevant. The WTO Appellate Body members might feel that rule-of-law norms require them to give some weight to their own prior interpretations. But even in those contexts (and certainly outside of them), drawing the proper analogies between a current dispute and prior ones may entirely be the question. Moreover, the number of sources of prior interpretations is vast, ranging from tribunals' decisions, the actions by international organization, rapporteurs' reports, the state interpretations and actions. The jurisprudential account gives little guidance as to which prior interpretations are most weighty either descriptively or normatively.

II. Rationalist

In the absence of much positive law guidance regarding the weight of precedent, many have turned to rationalist reasoning to explain the patterns of precedent observed in both arguments about the law and decisions by interpretive bodies. Under such an account, interpretations should be invoked or treated as precedent when doing so helps achieve various actors' broader goals. For a state actor, this may mean citing a prior interpretation that supports a position a state wants to take or that a court might predictably favor (for example, one of that court's own prior decisions). For the judge, it might mean citing a precedent from a court it is trying to convince or citing its own decisions to solidify its control over interpretation.

But such a rationalist account might also explain why states might support a broader system of precedent, even when doing so may not always favor their desired positions. To the extent that states are invested in a particular regime, predictability may be valuable enough for them to support precedent-based arguments generally. This is true whether the potential precedents are found in state actions or in judicial opinions. To the extent that third-party decisionmaking is capable of resolving difficult coordination problems, states may give a court or tribunal's decision precedential force in order to preserve that court or tribunal's authority in the regime. (Questioning that body's decisions too often might undermine that body's authority.) Moreover, treating prior decisions as precedential might add desirable clarity to the rules. To the extent that states value general clarity more highly than winning the cases precedent might cost them, states should support precedent.

Such rationalist accounts can be quite potent in explaining particular appeals to prior interpretations by advocates, parties, and judges. Two intertwined pieces, though, seem missing from these accounts. First, as I have described elsewhere, actors reference prior interpretations even when they do not seem to support the outcomes they desire.[8] For some reason, they seem to feel an obligation to reference and respond to those interpretations in order to make their case. Second, while appeals to prior interpretations supporting one's desired result may seem rational, they only make sense if we have some reason to believe they will carry weight with some decider. Both of these concerns point in the same direction—that the rationalist account lacks a theory of audience, that the account assumes that some audience is or can be convinced by precedential arguments and gives some amount of weight to analogical reasoning. In other words, audience, not just speaker, matters. Explaining that side of the equation, however, requires something more.

III. Sociological

This is where a sociological account becomes necessary. Appeals to precedent in international law are fundamentally an argumentative practice. They support a particular argument about the meaning of the law. But an argument to whom? An argument implies that there is someone to convince. And understanding the relationship between the citer of precedent, the particular precedent, and the audience for that precedent seems key to understanding the force that prior interpretations actually exert. More importantly, the identity of all three seem to be contingent and mutually constructed such that any change to one will produce different argumentative patterns—and, in turn, give international law in a particular area different meanings and content.

---

8 Cohen (n. 7).

C. *Practices of Precedent within Communities of Practice*

In my prior work, I have argued that precedent is best understood functionally. Precedent might best be understood as the burden that prior interpretations of a particular rule put on future arguments about the content or meaning of the rule.[9] In its weakest form, precedent simply supplies an argument that one must respond to; one cannot make an argument about the rule's meaning without some reference to why the prior decision is right, wrong, or distinguishable.[10] In its strongest form, precedent creates a strong presumption that the prior interpretation of the rule is in fact the rule. The question is not why actors do follow or do not follow precedent, but instead when and why prior interpretations place these burdens on arguments about the rule.

This means that fully understanding how and why interpretations take on weight as precedents requires understanding the process of legal argumentation and the practitioners who take part in it. Key to this understanding is an account of law as a product of a community of practice. As Emanuel Adler explains,[11] '[c]ommunities of practice "consist of people who are informally as well as contextually bound by a shared interest in learning and applying a common practice."'[12] Such a common practice, 'in turn, [is] sustained by a *repertoire of communal resources*, such as routines, words, tools, ways of doing things, stories, symbols, and discourse.'[13] One key in this description of community is that it does not require members to agree on everything—members may disagree sharply on substance and desired outcomes; instead, it requires only that members accept a set of common ground-rules for negotiation and contestation. Communities of practice can come in various shapes and sizes; their boundaries 'are determined by people's knowledge and identity and the discourse associated

---

9 Jacob, 'Precedents: Lawmaking through International Adjudication' (2011) 12 *German LJ*, 1005, 1019.

10 Ibid 1019 (suggesting that 'deliberately ignoring relevant prior decisions is so arbitrary and artificial a suggestion as to verge on farce').

11 Adler, *Communitarian International Relations: The Epistemic Foundations of International Relations* (2005).

12 Ibid 15 (quoting Snyder, 'Communities of Practice: Combining Organizational Learning and Strategy Insights to Create a Bridge to the 21st Century' (August 1997) *Community Intelligence Labs*, <http://www.co-i-l.com/coil/knowledge-garden/cop/cols.shtml> accessed 18 October 2020). Adler himself borrows the idea of communities of practice from the work of Jean Lave and Etienne Wenger on education and learning theory. Ibid 15 fn. 116.

13 Ibid 15.

with a specific practice.'[14] Some communities will be tightly organized, with small groups of practitioners who know each other well and engage with each other regularly on a defined set of issues.[15] Others will be much more diffuse, with members who never meet and are connected only by their shared practices—practices they apply to a broad range of activities.[16] Members may also have different relations to these communities. Some may be core members who actively work to develop its rules and norms, while others, farther from the core of the community of practice, may simply adopt, accept, or apply the results of that work.[17]

Law and legal discourse are particularly good examples of Adler's 'common practice,' and legal communities like particularly good examples of communities of practice.[18] Law provides a medium for debate and agreement, requiring actors to engage with each other in very specific fora, using very specific language and procedures. The legal community, in turn, is constituted by its members' shared acceptance of certain ground rules and their shared expectations about good and bad arguments. As Adler observes, '[i]t is as members of communities of practice that people exercise one of the highest forms of power: determining the meanings and discourses that produce social practices.'[19] The proposed structure of communities of practice, with concentric circles of core experts/practitioners and more peripheral adopters, helps conceptualize the relationship in a legal community between the expert lawyers who practice the law and the broader community of stakeholders whose influence and involvement are weaker, but whose broad acquiescence is still necessary.

Applied at the international level, such insights can begin to explain international actors and, in turn, the practice of international law. 'The closer we get to the level of practice, in fact, the more we can take the international system as a collection of communities of practice; for example communities of diplomats, of traders, of environmentalists, and of human-rights activists.'[20] Different areas of international law—international

---

14 Ibid 24.

15 Adler gives the example of U.N. weapons inspectors. Ibid 25.

16 Here, Adler uses the collective security community as an example. Ibid 24–25.

17 Ibid 24.

18 Cf. Brunnée and Toope, *Legitimacy and Legality in International Law: An Interactional Account* (2010) 13–16, 28.

19 Adler (n. 11) 25; cf. Anderson, 'The Rise of International Criminal Law: Intended and Unintended Consequences' (2009) 20 *EJIL*, 331 (349) (discussing 'communities of interpretation and authority').

20 Adler (n. 11) 15.

trade law, human rights law, international humanitarian law, international investment law, international criminal law—might each be conceptualized as a community of practice, in which a diverse, but specific, group of actors engage with each other over the rules of that field,[21] developing amongst themselves norms of proper argumentation and authority. Each involves different mixes of actors, with different assumptions and training, and we should not be surprised when these different groups coalesce around different norms of argumentation.

Imagining international law as a product of these communities of practice begins to unlock the mystery of precedent. Practices of precedent can be seen as products of second-person thinking. And whether approached as a rationalist or jurisprudential question, they require a theory of one's audience and that audience's expectations regarding good and bad arguments. But how does one develop such a theory or derive those expectations? They do so through interactions with and within the community of practice. In the United States, for example, *Korematsu*,[22] the notorious decision upholding the removal of Japanese-Americans from the coast during WWII, was well-understood to be a bad citation, even before its disavowal by the U.S. Supreme Court in *Trump v. Hawaii*.[23] But its companion case, *Hirabayashi*,[24] continues to be cited, and *Ex Parte Quirin*,[25] a case from the same period with all sorts of red-flags,[26] is cited regularly with authority and without embarrassment. How does one learn these patterns? To a certain extent, it can be learned from iterative practice—making arguments, citing sources, and seeing what happens. But in more developed fields, it will be buttressed by common education, practitioner links, etc.

This suggests looking for precedents' force and origins, not in particular arguments or decisions, but in the community of actors who make and respond to them. Different international law regimes—international trade law, international human rights law, international humanitarian

---

21 This conceptualization of areas of international law as communities of practice echoes Pierre Bourdieu's conceptualization of law as a "field." Bourdieu, 'The Force of Law: Toward a Sociology of the Juridical Field' (1987) 38 *Hastings LJ*, 805; Dezalay and Garth, *Dealing in Virtue: International Commercial Arbitration and the Construction of a Transnational Legal Order* (1998) (applying Bourdieu's insights and describing the 'field' of international commercial arbitration).

22 Korematsu v. United States, 323 U.S. 214 (1944).

23 *Trump v. Hawaii*, 138 S. Ct. 2392 (2018).

24 *Hirabayashi v. United States*, 320 U.S. 81 (1943).

25 *Ex parte Quirin*, 317 U.S. 1 (1942).

26 Cohen, 'Undead Wartime Cases' (2009) 15 *Tulane L. Rev.*, 957 (describing Quirin's shady story).

law, international investment law, or international criminal law—may involve different mixes of actors—advocates, political leaders, diplomats, military personnel, scientists, economists, international lawyers, and domestic lawyers. Each of these different actors will bring their own professional norms and biases to the debate, and different mixes of actors will agree on different norms and operating assumptions. Understanding the relative weight that different decisions by different bodies seem to carry in different contexts requires understanding the communities of actors who might perceive them that way.

The key is identifying the actors who practice in a particular area of law, both at the center of that practice, interacting regularly and intensely over the meaning rules, and at the periphery. Looking at these particular actors or groups of actors, we can begin to isolate characteristics, habits, biases, or incentives that might shape the international legal practice in which they engage.

Elsewhere, I have sought to catalogue the various potential sources of precedent in international law—the range of tribunal decisions, national court opinions, expert interpretations, and state actions that might be invoked as authoritative interpretations of international law—and the varied potential reasons any particular interpretation might be deemed more or less authoritative, ranging from the self-interested to the principled.[27] Focusing on the actors participating in international legal process helps us to see how they might interact with and understand these two factors.

We might, for example, focus on these actors' *professional training*, asking how training in law, economics, science, or soldiering might change or construct their views regarding particular sources. Based on their training, we might expect lawyers, particularly common-law lawyers, to be more familiar with judicial opinions and to find judicial opinions more easily accessible.[28] Given rule-of-law principles that suffuse their training, we might also expect them to weigh consistency with prior interpretation and adherence to the broader legal regime more heavily, and see judicial opinions that recognize these principles as more authoritative.[29] We might

27 Cohen (n. 7).

28 MacArthur, 'NAFTA Chapter 11: On an Environmental Collision Course with the World Bank' [2003] *Utah L. Rev.*, 913 (930) (commenting that it 'it is natural that lawyers and arbitrators trained in a common-law tradition would follow old habits in reasoning their way through these disputes').

29 Helfer and Slaughter, 'Toward a Theory of Effective Transnational Adjudication' (1997) 107 *Yale LJ*, 273; Voeten, 'Does a Professional Judiciary Induce More Compliance?: Evidence from the European Court of Human Rights' (27 March

expect military personnel to see sources differently, looking to pragmatic concerns of military effectiveness and looking to prior combat actions as more authoritative precedents.

Or we might look at look at the *epistemic communities* in which these actors operate, asking who they interact with on a regular basis. We might expect foreign ministry lawyers who deal regularly with diplomats to approach potential sources of precedent differently from military lawyers embedded within the military chain of command.[30] We might expect international criminal law lawyers with one foot in domestic criminal law to approach issues (often the same issues) differently from military lawyers.[31] And we might expect private commercial law lawyers, government lawyers, and public international lawyers to value different sources of authority in investment arbitration.[32]

Alternatively, we might want to look at different actors' *social and political capital* or incentives. How is success in their job defined and who defines it? Even if they are all trained as lawyers, politicians,[33] bureaucrats, NGO activists, judges, and military lawyers may all respond to different incentives and may look to different audiences for career or personal advancement. To the extent they work with other lawyers, particularly domestic lawyers, they may be expected to argue from judicial precedent. Failing to cite precedents that might seem relevant to other lawyers may even result in professional opprobrium or sanction. Within a legal organization, arguments that follow the professional script and reference judicial precedents will be rewarded. Arguments that seek to be overly creative or iconoclastic might not. And these effects should be compounded within subfields of international law, where specific sources—decisions of in-

---

2012), 4–6 <http://papers.ssrn.com/sol3/papers.cfm?abstract_id=2029786> (finding that decisions rendered by ECHR panels made up of majority professional judges were more likely to be complied with than decisions made by panels whose majority hailed from other areas and suggesting that this disparity might be explained by the relative importance of national judges as an audience for ECHR decisions and as compliance agents in enforcing those decisions at home).

30 Luban, 'Military Necessity and the Cultures of Military Law' (2013) 26 *Leiden J. Int'l L.*, 315 (318).

31 Anderson, 'The Rise of International Criminal Law: Intended and Unintended Consequences' (2009) 20 *EJIL*, 331 (describing divergence between epistemic communities attached to international criminal law and military law).

32 Roberts, 'Clash of Paradigms: Actors and Analogies Shaping the Investment Treaty System' (2013) 107 *AJIL*, 45.

33 Linos, *The Democratic Foundations of Policy Diffusion* (2013) (on why politician cite foreign models regarding health care and family policy).

ternational criminal tribunals, human-rights bodies, investment arbitral tribunals, national court opinions, International Committee of the Red Cross commentaries, UN Security Council resolutions—may be seen as particularly important or authoritative.

Working with non-lawyers, lawyers will face other considerations. In some cases, arguments from judicial precedent may enhance the lawyer's stature. Lawyers as a professional group have specific sources of political and social capital that they can use to maintain their importance and relevance in relation to other societal actors,[34] among which is lawyers' purported expertise in interpreting and applying certain legal sources. This expertise includes, among other things, stylized forms of analogical reasoning and the ability to parse legal opinions. Lawyers, seeking to maximize their own power and authority vis-à-vis other international actors, may want to emphasize the value of precedents and their unique ability to understand them. In other contexts, however, lawyers may fear being seen as irrelevant by other actors and too easily marginalized. Government lawyers often recount how precedent-strewn arguments made amongst lawyers are shorn of references to international decisions when made to political leaders who might perceive their authority differently (or in some cases, negatively).

Finally, we might group them according to their *function* and relationship to precedent: Are they advocating, judging, administering, or seeking guidance for action? Depending on the role they are playing, different actors may have different reasons to invoke a particular source as precedent. A court or tribunal may have very specific incentives different from those of other actors. It may want to cite high-prestige courts they might seek to convince or which may be seen as authoritative by other courts whose enforcement assistance it might need. It might want to cite other courts' precedent to hide its own creativity or shroud itself in another court's perceived legitimacy. It might cite its own decisions to enhance its authority over a particular set of rules. Actors performing other functions may have similarly idiosyncratic reasons to cite particular precedents.[35]

---

34 Bourdieu, 'The Force of Law: Toward a Sociology of the Juridical Field' (1987) 38 *Hastings LJ*, 805; Dezalay and Garth, *Dealing in Virtue: International Commercial Arbitration and the Construction of a Transnational Legal Order* (1998) (applying Bourdieu's insights and describing the 'field' of international commercial arbitration).

35 Importantly, we also need to look at these various actors as both actors and audiences. What we need to understand is not just why those who reference a precedent might find it weighty, authoritative, even binding, but also why the

D. *Revisiting the 'Crisis' of WTO Precedents*

Applying these three linked frames—the jurisprudential, the rationalist, and the sociological—to the United States' complaints about precedent at the WTO highlights the contingent and contextual nature of U.S. arguments, which, while drawing on text and based in self-interest, implicitly (and sometimes explicitly) play out against images of WTO culture.

I. *Respecting Formalities*

The Appellate Body's approach to precedent developed over a number of years. A new institution, a product of the 1994 agreements that brought the General Agreement on Tariffs and Trade into the new WTO, the Appellate Body's first concern was not with its own precedents, but with those of the GATT panels that predated the more formalized system laid out in the DSU. Recognizing both the practice and expectations of GATT/WTO members,[36] the Appellate Body announced in *Japan-Alcoholic Beverages II* that, while not binding on future parties in future cases, '[a]dopted GATT panel decisions reports are an important part of the GATT acquis. They are often considered by subsequent panels. They create legitimate expectations among WTO Members, and, therefore, should be taken into account where they are relevant to any dispute.'[37]

As the Appellate Body's own body of work began to grow, focus shifted to the weight of its own prior decisions. In *U.S.-Shrimp (Article 21.5 – Malaysia)*, the Appellate Body extended its reasoning regarding adopted GATT panel decisions to its own, observing that it would 'expect' panels to rely on its prior rulings.[38] The Appellate Body then reiterated this view in

---

audience that reference is aimed at might as well. In other words, we need to know why a lawyer assessing policy options or advocating a position might feel the need to cite a particular reference, as well as why her intended audience, policymakers, judges, opposing lawyers, might respond favorably to it.

36 Ridi, 'The Shape and Structure of the "Usable Past": An Empirical Analysis of the Use of Precedent in International Adjudication' (2019) 10 *JIDS*, 200 (on the practice of citing precedents in international trade law).

37 WTO, *Japan: Taxes on Alcholic Beverages – Report of the Appellate Body* (4 October 1996) WT/DS8/AB/R, WT/DS10/AB/R and WT/DS11/AB/R,14; Lehne (n. 3) 80–81.

38 WTO, *United States: Import Prohibition of Certain Shrimp and Shrimp Products (Article 21.5- Malaysia) – Report of the Appellate Body* (22 October 2001) WT/DS58/AB/RW, para. 107.

US – Oil Country Tubular Goods Sunset Reviews, in which it observed that 'following the Appellate Body's conclusions in earlier disputes is not only appropriate, but is what would be expected from panels, especially where the issues are the same.'[39]

But it was *US – Stainless Steel (Mexico)* that the Appellate Body formalized these expectations into a rule. Reviewing a panel decision that had disregarded prior Appellate Body pronouncements on the use of 'zeroing,' a controversial method for calculating anti-dumping duties, the Appellate Body formalized standards regarding both horizontal and vertical precedent. On the former, the Appellate Body observed that '[e]nsuring "security and predictability" in the dispute settlement system, as contemplated in Article 3.2 of the DSU, implies that, absent cogent reasons, an adjudicatory body will resolve the same legal question in the same way in a subsequent case.'[40] On the latter, the Appellate Body noted that 'the hierarchical structure contemplated in the DSU,' in which 'panels and the Appellate Body have distinct roles to play,' and observed that a panel's decision to disregard prior Appellate Body interpretations 'undermines the development of a coherent and predictable body of jurisprudence.'[41] Key to both observations was the Appellate Body's reading of DSU Article 3.2, which begins by recognizing that '[t]he dispute settlement system of the WTO is a central element in providing security and predictability to the multilateral trading system.' Notably, while announcing these expectations regarding practice, the Appellate Body has simultaneously disavowed a formal doctrine of stare decisis, observing that Appellate Body decisions are not formally binding beyond the parties to a particular dispute. Subsequent decisions by the Appellate Body confirmed the 'cogent reasons' standard for departing from prior rulings,[42] but aside from some dicta in panel reports, little more was done to articulate its meaning or application.

It is this 'cogent reasons' standard that has elicited the ire of the United States. As noted above, the arguments arrayed by the United States are facially positivistic, rooted in the language of the relevant treaties and the

---

39 WTO, *United States: Sunset Reviews of Anti-Dumping Measures on Oil Country Tubular Goods from Argentina- Report of the Appellate Body* (29 November 2004) WT/DS268/AB/R, para. 188.

40 WTO, *United States: Final Anti-Dumping Measures on Stainless Steel from Mexico – Report of the Appellate Body* (30 April 2008) WT/DS344/AB/R, para. 160.

41 Ibid para. 161.

42 As Lehne notes, it remains unclear whether the 'cogent reasons' is a standard just for the Appellate Body or one that panels can/should apply as well. Lehne (n. 3) 86.

revealed intent of WTO members. As the United States explains, nothing in the DSU gives precedential effect to prior Appellate Body decisions. On the contrary, the United States argues, Article 3.2 limits the Appellate Body to looking to 'customary rules of interpretation of public international law,' not prior decisions and by recognizing that 'Recommendations and rulings of the DSB cannot add to or diminish the rights and obligations provided in the covered agreements.' Moreover, it is the 'Ministerial Council and the General Council [that] shall have the exclusive authority to adopt interpretations of this Agreement and of the Multilateral Trade Agreements' under Article IX of the Marrakesh Agreement Establishing the World Trade Organization, not the Appellate Body. Panels are instructed by DSU Article 11 to 'make an objective assessment of the matter before it, including an objective assessment of the facts of the case and the applicability of and conformity with the relevant covered agreements.' Ignoring legal arguments in deference to the Appellate Body, the United States argues, would fail that standard. And structurally, the United States observes that the role of both the panels and Appellate Body are to assist the Dispute Settlement Body, representing the full membership of the WTO, in resolving disputes, not to develop WTO law.

II. Furthering Interests

But it is impossible to ignore the overlap between the United States' positive assessment and self-interest. The Appellate Body's doctrine of precedent has developed alongside its views on the permissibility and use of a series of trade measures known as remedies. The United States has interpreted the rules in ways that allow for more and larger anti-dumping and countervailing duties against other members. Over a series of decisions, the Appellate Body has rejected these interpretations, most notably a calculation method known as 'zeroing.' Rejecting the Appellate Bodies views, the United States has continued to apply versions of these interpretations, and in the disputes that have followed, the United States has at times convinced panels that its interpretation is correct. These remedies cases have thus served as the primary battlefield for determining the force of Appellate Body precedents. The United States' desire to use these tools (most notably against Chinese imports), U.S. complaints that the Appellate Body has overreached and gotten the law wrong, and U.S. complaints about

Appellate Body precedent are impossible to disentangle.[43] As noted above, for the United States to have its way on these rules, it needs to convince panels to depart from Appellate Body interpretations, eliminate or shrink Appellate Body review, and/or limit the effect of dispute settlement decisions that go against it. Precedent is part and parcel of that fight. Even if no appellate mechanism emerges with jurisdiction over the United States, it will still want to limit the effect of past Appellate Body decisions.

Other members though have disagreed with Appellate Body interpretations, some consistently and vociferously. Yet no other member has launched (or arguably even supported) a broadside attack against Appellate Body precedent. This might be surprising given the reasonableness of the United States' textual arguments. Perhaps it could be argued that the United States is uniquely positioned to and interested in promoting flexibility as opposed to stability. Competition with China simply looms larger for the United States than others, who, if also concerned, are more worried that a trade war (or wars) will end up hurting them. Maybe. But the singular nature of this critique, its timing, and the response seem to call out for something more. And it is here that a sociological account can be revealing, not only in describing the current conflict over precedent, but also in explaining some of its odder features.

III. Culture Clubs

A fuller explanation of the current fight might start by focusing on the relative peace between 2008, when the 'cogent reasons' standard was announced, and 2018, when the United States issued its anti-precedent broadside. Following some discussion at the meetings of the Dispute Settlement Body in 2007 and 2008, the Appellate Body's standards regarding the weight of its precedents disappear from the agenda until 2018. Even

43 Lester and Bacchus (n. 6) ('Of course, underlying this semantic debate is the true U.S. concern. The United States has long hoped that, in deciding new appeals, new members of the Appellate Body would overrule the judgments of previous members of the Appellate Body on an assortment of legal issues of political significance to the United States, particularly on antidumping, subsidies, and safeguards.').

in 2008, only Chile,[44] and perhaps Colombia,[45] seemed to join the United States in expressing concern over the standard. Japan, India, and the European Union actually expressed their approval.[46] On the few occasions that 'cogent reasons' did reappear at the DSB in the intervening decade, it was simply as the accepted Appellate Body standard.[47]

Nor did other members fight the standard in disputes before panels or the Appellate Body. Members sometimes tried to shape the standard,[48] but more often argued within it.[49] Members, of course, did not always want a prior Appellate Body precedent to apply to their dispute. But the main

---

44 Chile expressed some 'concern' that some of the Appellate body's language regarding the DSU and its precedents 'could lead to unfortunate conclusions regarding the nature of the dispute settlement system, and Chile hoped that this would not become a trend likely to constrain panels in future disputes, and above all, that this would not alter the nature of the rights and obligations negotiated by the Membership.' WTO, *Minutes of Meeting of Dispute Settlement Body – Statement by Chile* (20 May 2008) WT/DSB/M/250, para. 68.

45 'While recognizing the need to provide security and predictability to the multilateral trading system through the development of a consistent line of jurisprudence, Colombia wished to recall that the Ministerial Conference and the General Council alone were empowered to adopt authoritative interpretations.' Ibid para. 72.

46 Ibid paras. 57, 60, and 69; WTO, *United States: Continued Existence and Application of Zeroing Methodology – Report of the Appellate Body* (4 February 2009) WT/DS350/AB/R, para. 363 ('The European Communities underscores that it agrees with this reasoning of the Appellate Body in *US – Stainless Steel (Mexico)* "without reservation."'); WTO, *US Use of Zeroing in Anti-Dumping Measures Involving Products from Korea – EU Third Party Submission* (18 January 2011) WT/DS402/R, para. 8 ('In other words, WTO panels are obliged to correctly apply the law; in the context of this dispute this also means that the Panel should follow the rulings of the Appellate Body where the Appellate Body has previously interpreted the same legal questions. Otherwise, the security and predictability enshrined in Article 3.2 of the DSU would be put in serious danger.').

47 WTO, *Minutes of Meeting of Dispute Settlement Body – Statement by Japan* (19 January 2010) WT/DSB/M/278, para. 84 ('Even assuming that this change in the analytical approach did not amount to a departure from the legal interpretations previously made by the Appellate Body in similar situations, which, the Appellate Body had explained, must be made with "cogent reasons"...').

48 WTO, *United States: Continued Existence and Application of Zeroing Methodology – Report of the Appellate Body* (4 February 2009) WT/DS350/AB/R, para. 363–65 (showing the European Union argument that only Appellate Body, not panels, can invoke 'cogent reasons').

49 WTO, *United States: Use of Zeroing in Anti-Dumping Measures Involving Products from Korea – Report of the Panel* (18 January 2011) WT/DS402/R, para. VII.32 ('However, we agree with Korea that adopted reports create legitimate expectations among WTO Members and that "following the Appellate Body's conclu-

argument raised by members other than the United States was not that precedent was of no weight or merely persuasive, but instead that there were 'cogent reasons' to depart from it.

With the exception of the United States, members seemed to basically accept the Appellate Body's description of the horizontal and vertical effects of its prior interpretations.[50] And the best explanation for why lies not in their analysis of the text or a careful cost-benefit analysis of varying rules, but the fact that the Appellate Body's pronouncement largely captured members' practice and expectations. As the Appellate Body had earlier noted, members already argued as if GATT decisions had at least some precedential authority, and those practices largely carried over to the WTO era. As Mariana Clara Andrade observes, the development by the Secretariat of tools like the WTO Analytical Index, replete with references to prior decisions, only made that practice easier.[51] And those practices echoed those surrounding other international courts, which seemed to adopt de facto doctrines of precedent even when the treaties creating them seemed to explicitly deny such authority.[52] In fact, WTO Appellate Body Member Giorgio Sacerdoti observed that the 'cogent reasons' standard was borrowed from the International Court for the Former Yugoslavia, because it had a similar system of appellate review.[53] Arguing from precedent and about precedent seemed normal; WTO practitioners had long been acculturated to some version of that practice.[54]

---

sions in earlier disputes is not only appropriate, but is what would be expected from panels, especially where the issues are the same."').

50 Andrade, 'Precedent in the WTO: Retrospective Reflections for a Prospective Dispute Settlement Mechanism' (2020) *JIDS*, 1 (13).

51 Andrade (n. 50) 14. For more on the role of the Secretariat in panel and Appellate Body decisionmaking, Pauwelyn and Pelc, 'Who Writes the Rulings of the World Trade Organization? A Critical Assessment of the Role of the Secretariat in WTO Dispute Settlement' (2019), <https://papers.ssrn.com/sol3/papers.cfm?abstract_id=3458872>.

52 Robert McDougall suggests that '[t]he European Union (i.e., the European Commission) may be more comfortable with activist adjudicators, given the contribution the CJEU has made to constructing the internal EU legal order.' McDougall, 'Crisis in the WTO: Restoring the WTO Dispute Settlement Function' (October 2018) 194 *CIGI Papers*, 11 <https://www.cigionline.org/sites/default/files/documents/Paper%20no.194.pdf> accessed 18 October 2020.

53 Andrade (n. 50) 14.

54 Ibid 5 fn. 20 (observing that the Appellate Body was likely responding to submissions from the parties themselves suggesting that prior precedents deserved some presumptive weight).

Except in the United States. This might seem paradoxical. Strong doctrines of precedent are often associated with the Anglo-American common law system and training in Anglo-American schools and firms. American lawyers are often blamed for importing stronger arguments about precedent into transnational practice.[55] In this case, though, U.S. opposition to a doctrine of WTO precedent started even before *US – Stainless Steel (Mexico)*. In the DSB meeting following *US – Oil Country Tubular Goods Sunset Reviews*, the U.S. representative questioned the Appellate Body's 'expectation' that panels would follow prior Appellate Body interpretation, observing that nothing in the DSU authorized a doctrine of 'stare decisis.'[56] And following the Appellate Body's pronouncements in *US – Stainless Steel (Mexico)*, the United States continued to push back against the rule at the next DSB meeting[57] and in its subsequent submissions in disputes.[58] Opposition to the 'cogent reasons' standard was becoming part of the practice and culture of the U.S. Trade Representative's Office (USTR). And within that culture, it found fertile ground to grow. Appellate Body overreach, judicial activism, and obiter dicta were, and continue to be, common USTR complaints. Amongst those complaints, the Appellate Body's claims to precedential authority fit a common narrative—a story of

55 Alford, 'The American Influence on International Arbitration' (2013) 19 *Ohio St. J. on Disp. Resol.*, 69 (82–87).

56 WTO, *Minutes of Meeting of Dispute Settlement Body – Statement by the US* (17 December 2004) WT/DSB/M/180, para. 43 ('The United States was also confused as to whether the Appellate Body was now suggesting for the first time that stare decisis existed in WTO dispute settlement.').

57 WTO, *Minutes of Meeting of Dispute Settlement – Statement by the US* (20 May 2008) WT/DSB/M/250, para. 47–55.

58 WTO, *United States: Use of Zeroing in Anti-Dumping Measures Involving Products from Korea – Report of the Panel* (18 January 2011) WT/DS402/R, para. A.11 ('To the extent that Korea suggests that the Panel should simply base its findings upon a "consistent line of Appellate Body Reports," however, it should be noted that prior panel and Appellate Body reports are not binding on panels considering other disputes.'); USTR, *Appellee Submission of the US in US: Continued Existence and Application of Zeroing Methodology* (1 December 2008), paras. 46–49 <https://ustr.gov/sites/default/files/uploads/agreements/morocco/pdfs/dispute_settlement/ds350/asset_upload_file233_13332.pdf > accessed 18 October 2020 ('As the Appellate Body has explained, adopted dispute settlement reports are not binding, except with respect to resolving the particular dispute between the parties to that dispute. Only the Ministerial Conference and the General Council have the exclusive authority to adopt binding interpretations of the covered agreements. And treating prior reports as binding outside the scope of the original dispute would add to the obligations of the United States and other Members, inconsistent with Articles 3.2 and 19.1 of the DSU.').

a self-aggrandizing body of experts, claiming the mantle not just of a court, but of a self-appointed 'high court' of trade law,[59] neglecting its dispute settlement role in favor of filling interpretive gaps and developing rules well beyond the disputes before it or its treaty-defined mandate. And it is a story that found an eager dramatist in current U.S. Trade Representative Robert Lighthizer, a well-known skeptic of judicialization[60] shaped by pre-WTO fights and diplomacy.[61] The United States' regular reminder to other members that the Appellate Body was not designated a court and its members specifically not labelled judges might sound to some trifling and technical, but within this narrative, it is a key principled point. And ironically, it is here that U.S. experience with courts casts a dark shadow.

American lawyers may be familiar with common-law-style arguments from precedent, but an education steeped in legal realism and a highly politicized Supreme Court has also attuned them to see judges as political actors and sensitized them to claims of judicial activism.[62] Casting the

---

59 Lighthizer, 'How to Set World Trade Straight' (20 August 2020) *Wall St. J.* ('But over time it came to see itself as something else—a high court empowered to create a new common law of free trade.').

60 Vidigal, 'Living Without the Appellate Body: Multilateral, Bilateral and Plurilateral Solutions to the WTO Dispute Settlement Crisis' (2019) 20 *J. World Investment & Trade*, 862 (865); DePillis, 'Robert Lighthizer Blew Up 60 Years of Trade Policy. Nobody Knows What Happens Next' (13 October 2020) *ProPublica*, <https://www.propublica.org/article/robert-lighthizer-blew-up-60-years-of-trade-policy-nobody-knows-what-happens-next> accessed 18 October 2020 ('"The fact that the Appellate Body had ruled against the U.S. repeatedly was the primary reason Lighthizer was determined to bring down the WTO," said a former USTR official.'); Lighthizer, 'U.S. Trade Policy Priorities – Speech at the Center for Strategic and International Studies' (18 September 2017), <https://www.csis.org/analysis/us-trade-policy-priorities-robert-lighthizer-united-states-trade-representative> accessed 18 October 2020; Ikenson and Lighthizer, 'Is the WTO Dispute Settlement System Fair?' (26 February 2007) *Council on Foreign Relations*, <https://www.cfr.org/article/wto-dispute-settlement-system-fair> accessed 18 October 2020 (worrying about 'judicial activism' and observing that 'The WTO dispute settlement system is veering off course, and is increasingly a threat to the legitimacy of the entire body.').

61 Vela, 'Charge of the Lighthizer Brigade' (2 October 2018) *Politico* <https://www.politico.eu/article/the-charge-of-the-robert-lighthizer-brigade-trade-war-us-donald-trump/> accessed 18 October 2020 ('The goal here is to revive the strong-arm tactics he used as deputy USTR against Japan in the 1980s.').

62 USTR, *Report on the Appellate Body of the World Trade Organization* (February 2020), 50 <https://ustr.gov/sites/default/files/Report_on_the_Appellate_Body_of_the_World_Trade_Organization.pdf> accessed 18 October 2020 ('Thus, any "clarification" resulting from the system cannot take the form of judicial activism by panels or the Appellate Body.').

Appellate Body as a would-be common-law court[63] is both a familiar reference and one weighed down with baggage. This tendency to see judging as inherently political likely played a role in USTR's willingness to break community norms, 'politicize' the dispute settlement process, and refuse to reappoint U.S. panel members and block the appointment or reappointment of others who USTR suspected were voting against its positions.

But the importance of the sociological story is most obvious in the United States' own stated position. As the appointment crisis built and the deadline to keep the Appellate Body operational loomed, other members sought to work with the United States to find a solution. An informal process facilitated by Ambassador David Walker of New Zealand recommended various reforms. But the United States explained that a commitment to paper reforms would not be enough. As Ambassador Dennis Shea, U.S. Permanent Representative to the World Trade Organization, explained, 'To find a solution to the concerns raised, WTO Members will need to reach a shared understanding that the Appellate Body has failed to follow the rules agreed by Members and the role assigned to it by the Members.'[64] Some members, Shea observed, 'appear willing to tolerate – or even encourage' the positions taken by the Appellate Body, and '[i]f we WTO Members cannot agree that we should be concerned that the Appellate Body has broken the plain rules that Members agreed to in the DSU, then it is difficult to see how we can find solutions to a "problem" we do not agree exists.'[65] The question that members must answer before any progress might be made is 'why did the Appellate Body feel free to disregard the clear text of the agreements?'

The United States thus frames the problem as cultural or sociological: Many other states—wrongly, in the United States' view—see no problem with what the Appellate Body has done, including with regard to the precedential weight of its decisions. Other members may simply view the Appellate Body and authority differently than the United States. As

63 U.S. Mission to International Organizations in Geneva, 'Statements by the United States at the Meeting of the WTO Dispute Settlement Body Geneva' (18 December 2018), para. 15 <https://geneva.usmission.gov/wp-content/uploads/sites/290/Dec18.DSB_.Stmt_.as-deliv.fin_.public.pdf> accessed 18 October 2020 ('WTO Members did not establish a common law system or a system of precedent').

64 U.S. Mission to International Organizations in Geneva, 'Statements Delivered to the General Council by Ambassador Dennis Shea, U.S. Permanent Representative to the World Trade Organization' (15 October 2019) <https://geneva.usmission.gov/2019/10/15/statements-by-the-united-states-at-the-wto-general-council-meeting/> accessed 18 October 2020.

65 Ibid.

Ambassador Shea explains, 'some WTO Members believe that the Appellate Body is an "international court" and its members are "judges" who inherently have more expansive authority than is provided in the DSU, for example, to create "jurisprudence" and fill gaps in the WTO agreements. This view may be shared by some who have served on the Appellate Body.'[66] What the United States seeks is a 'shared understanding'[67] of both the problem and the 'proper' role of the Appellate Body.

On precedent specifically, that 'shared understanding' requires more than an agreement 'that "precedent" is not created through WTO dispute settlement,' but an actual shift in practice. '[W]hy' asks Shea, 'did some WTO Members advocate for the Appellate Body to assert that its interpretations must be followed by panels absent unidentified cogent reasons? And why then does the Appellate Body assert a precedential value for its reports like an authoritative interpretation that only WTO Members in the Ministerial Conference or General Council can give?'[68]

Given its view that the differences with other members regarding the Appellate Body are the result of deep cultural fissures, it is perhaps unsurprising that the United States seems satisfied to let the Appellate Body wither away, replaced, if at all, by a body with very different powers and cultural cues. Commercial arbitration has been the model suggested by both Lighthizer[69] and Shea for WTO dispute settlement—a model suggesting ad hoc arbitrators and self-contained decisions, where '[t]he rulings of these one-off panels should only apply to the parties in the dispute and not become part of an ever-evolving body of trade jurisprudence.'[70] Rather than providing for appeals, the United States would support 'a mechanism that would allow WTO members to set aside panel opinions in exceptional cases.'[71]

But even if the Appellate Body is no more, the United States' complaints have had some desired effects. Precedent is back on the table at

66 Ibid.
67 Ibid.
68 Ibid.
69 Lighthizer (n. 59).
70 Dreyer, 'WTO: The definitive end of optimism on the Appellate Body' (29 September 2020) *Borderlex* <https://borderlex.eu/2020/09/29/wto-the-definitive-end-of-optimism-on-the-appellate-body/> accessed 18 October 2020.
71 Lighthizer (n. 59). This suggestion echoes Mariana Clara de Andrade's suggestion that removing the hierarchy implied by the Appellate Body might in-and-of-itself lighten the burden imposed by prior precedents. Andrade (n. 50) 15.

the WTO[72] in a way it had not been from 2008 and 2018. Members are discussing it again at the DSB, and even where supporting the current Appellate Body practice, members are apt to recall that there is no binding rule of stare decisis in the DSU.[73] Some have defended the Appellate Body by rejecting the idea that Appellate Body has even claimed precedential authority.[74] The overall effect is a subtle shift in the relative weight of precedent, as some of the Appellate Body's presumed authority is allowed to evaporate. And most notably, panelists may have felt the burden lighten as well.[75] Just before the Appellate Body was sent into hibernation, a panel hearing a dispute between Canada and the United States adopted the Appellate Body's 'cogent reasons' standard but, nonetheless, found reason to depart from prior interpretations, suggesting a potential way forward.[76] The United States actually 'commend[ed] the panel for doing its own

72 WTO, *Minutes of Meetings of the Dispute Settlement Body – Statement by Japan* (18 December 2018) WT/DSB/M/423, para. 4.31 (critiquing 'cogent reasons' standard); WTO, *Fostering a Discussion on the Functioning of the Appellate Body, Addressing the Issue of Precedent – Communication from Honduras* (4 February 2019) WT/GC/W/761 (laying out options including banning reliance in precedent); WTO, *Informal Process on Matters Related to the Functioning of the Appellate Body – Communication from Japan and Australia* (18 April 2019) WT/GC/W/768, p. 2:
'Issue of precedential value of interpretation by the Appellate Body
7. Members confirm that an interpretation by the Appellate Body of any WTO provision does not constitute a precedent for posterior interpretations.
8. Members confirm that panels may adopt an interpretation of a WTO provision that is different from the one developed by the Appellate Body.
9. Members reaffirm the important role of the dispute settlement system in providing security and predictability, as stated in paragraph 2 of Article 3 of the DSU.'

73 WTO, *Minutes of Meetings of the Dispute Settlement Body – Statement by Singapore* (18 December 2018) WT/DSB/M/423, para. 4.32; Ibid, *Statement by Australia*, para. 4.30.

74 Ibid, *Statement by Brazil*, para. 4.29.

75 Some suggest that other members shared many of the United States' concerns, even if they were quieter about it. If true, this narrative only reinforces the cultural component of the story. Those practicing around the WTO and AB may have had mixed views regarding precedent, but practice flowed towards the perceived community norm, each actor (aside from the U.S.) converging around what they thought others, including the AB itself, expected to hear. As the U.S. complaints got louder (amplified by a credible threat of action), the cultural norms shifted, pleasing the United States became as important as pleasing the AB or each other, and simmering discontent was allowed to bubble over into a chorus of resentment.

76 WTO, *United States: Anti-Dumping Measures Applying Differential Pricing Methodology to Softwood Lumber from Canada – Report of the Panel* (9 April 2019) WT/

interpretive analysis, and for having the courage to stand up to the undue pressure that the Appellate Body has been putting on panels for many years.'[77] Canada has appealed the decision into the void, but the panel's softer reading of standard might still have some influence as the multilateral interim appeal arrangement (MPIA) or other future mechanisms.

E. Towards a Sociology of International Precedent

The picture that emerges from this richer story of WTO precedent is one of overlapping communities of practice, drawn together through practice before the WTO panels, the Appellate Body, and the meetings of the DSB, but pulled apart by differences in views over precedent and the Appellate Body's role. Like soap bubbles or cells, some slowly merge together to form a larger whole, while others emerge, separate, and pull away. All of the practitioners in this story are members simultaneously of a series of communities—the community created by everyday life in their respective ministries and in their broader governments, the community created by inter-governmental practice in Geneva, the community of practitioners around the Appellate Body and WTO secretariat.[78] The convergence first, around citations to GATT and WTO precedent, and then around the 'cogent reasons' standard reflects the consolidation of a dominant community at the WTO with its own identity. As practice within that community thickens, the center of gravity shifts, the gravitational pull of these other communities weaken, and all are pulled closer together. But the continued opposition of the United States shows how practice within USTR has defied these forces; differences between USTR and the WTO Appellate Body fuel an intensifying sense of identity within USTR around its own practices and interpretations, slowly pushing these communities apart. Once largely overlapping with the others, the USTR community is drifting

---

DS534/R; Ridi, 'United States—Anti-Dumping Measures Applying Differential Pricing Methodology to Softwood Lumber from Canada' (2020) 114 *AJIL*, 735.

77 USTR, 'United States Prevails on "Zeroing" Again: WTO Panel Rejects Flawed Appellate Body Findings' (9 April 2019) <https://ustr.gov/about-us/policy-offices/press-office/press-releases/2019/april/united-states-prevails-"zeroing"> accessed 18 October 2020.

78 Andrade (n. 50) 13, 15 (on the role of the Secretariat in fostering a culture of precedent). Soave, 'Who Controls WTO Dispute Settlement? Socio-Professional Practices and the Crisis of the Appellate Body' (2020) *Italian Y.B. Int'l L.*, 13.

away, bonded with the others now by only the narrowest of overlaps through which views are shared and hashed out.

The clash over precedent at the WTO suggests the importance of a sociological account that is attendant to the individuals who might invoke or respond to arguments from precedent, their training, their history, their politics, and their identities. Only by looking at the culture developing around the WTO can we explain the relatively smooth emergence of a consensus practice of precedent among non-U.S. members. Only by paying attention to the culture of USTR, the historical baggage carried by its leadership, the training of its lawyers, and the reigning politics and policies of trade which frame its work, can we understand the depth of U.S. opposition to the 'cogent reasons' standard announced by the Appellate Body.

But the sociological account does more than simply explain patterns of precedent. It turns precedents into a type of dye test. Following the paths of particular precedents through international law as they pass from advocates to judges, from one decision to the next, and from one tribunal's practice to another, can reveal the shifting shapes of international law's communities of practice. The strange journey of the *Tadic* decision, tracked through citations from its origins in the International Criminal Tribunal for Yugoslavia to the International Court of Justice and investment arbitration tribunals into U.S. federal courts and, perhaps most surprisingly, into a U.S. Department of Justice White Paper on the legality of targeted killings,[79] describes a vast and connected community of international and domestic lawyers. But precedents dropped or blocked can also provide a map of clogs and disconnects—signs that a community of practice has not formed or is fraying. Precedents become a bellwether of change, of convergence and disjuncture, a leading indicator of how the international system is developing, whether centrifugal or centripetal forces seem to dominate.

Studying these patterns of precedent thus requires new tools. Rich case studies of international lawyers and practices, built on ethnography, interviews, and surveys need to be developed. Sources beyond tribunal decisions—textbooks and syllabi, briefs and submissions, internal memoranda and speeches—need to be unearthed and studied for their role in amplifying and transmitting precedents across legal communities, in imbuing particular precedents and those who can wield them with professional capital. And these studies need to be complemented by network analyses,

---

79 Cohen, 'Lawyers and Precedent' (2013) 46 *Vanderbilt J. Int'l L.*, 1025 (1030).

studies that can track and trace precedents as they make their journeys from decision to decision within and across fora.[80]

F. Conclusion

Once treated as something of an oddity, the emergence of practices of precedent in international law has moved both to the center of research agendas, and in the case of U.S. complaints about the WTO, diplomatic agendas as well. But what a sociological account of international precedent promises is not just an account of precedent, but of international law, its practitioners, and its construction as a whole. Precedent became a gateway to exploring how international law works and, perhaps more importantly, how it changes.

Bibliography

Emanuel Adler, *Communitarian International Relations: The Epistemic Foundations of International Relations* (Routledge, London 2005)

Roger P. Alford, 'The American Influence on International Arbitration' (2003) 19 *Ohio St. J. on Disp. Resol.*, 69

Kenneth Anderson, 'The Rise of International Criminal Law: Intended and Unintended Consequences' (2009) 20 *Eur. J. Int'l L.*, 331

Mariana Clara de Andrade, 'Precedent in the WTO: Retrospective Reflections for a Prospective Dispute Settlement Mechanism' (2020) 11 *J. Int'l Disp. Settlement*, 1

Pierre Bourdieu, 'The Force of Law: Toward a Sociology of the Juridical Field' (1987) 38 *Hastings LJ*, 805

Jutta Brunnée and Stephen J. Toope, *Legitimacy and Legality in International Law: An Interactional Account* (Cambridge University Press, Cambridge 2010)

Harlan Grant Cohen, 'Lawyers and Precedent' (2013) 46 *Vanderbilt J. Int'l L.*, 1025

Harlan Grant Cohen, 'Theorizing International Precedent' in Andrea Bianchi, Daniel Peat, and Matthew Windsor (eds), *Interpretation in International Law* (Oxford University Press, Oxford 2015)

80 Jeffrey Kucik and Sergio Puig, 'Extending Trade Law Precedent' (forthcoming 2021), *Vanderbilt J. Int'l L.* (finding that the WTO Appellate Body has in fact followed and extended its own precedent since developing the 'cogent reasons' standard).

Harlan Grant Cohen, 'Undead Wartime Cases' (2009) 15 *Tulane L. Rev.*, 957

Lydia DePillis, 'Robert Lighthizer Blew Up 60 Years of Trade Policy. Nobody Knows What Happens Next' (13 October 2020) *ProPublica* <https://www.propublica.org/article/robert-lighthizer-blew-up-60-years-of-trade-policy-nobody-knows-what-happens-next> accessed 18 October 2020

Yves Dezalay and Bryant G. Garth, *Dealing in Virtue: International Commercial Arbitration and the Construction of a Transnational Legal Order* (University of Chicago Press, Chicago 1998)

Iana Dreyer, 'WTO: The Definitive End of Optimism on the Appellate Body' (29 September 2020) *Borderlex* <https://borderlex.eu/2020/09/29/wto-the-definitive-end-of-optimism-on-the-appellate-body/> accessed 18 October 2020

Laurence R. Helfer and Anne-Marie Slaughter, 'Toward a Theory of Effective Transnational Adjudication' (1997) 107 *Yale LJ*, 273

Hirabayashi v. United States, 320 U.S. 81 (1943)

Daniel J. Ikenson and Robert E. Lighthizer, 'Is the WTO Dispute Settlement System Fair?' (26 February 2007) *Council on Foreign Relations* <https://www.cfr.org/article/wto-dispute-settlement-system-fair> accessed 18 October 2020

Marc Jacob, 'Precedents: Lawmaking Through International Adjudication' (2011) 12 *German LJ*, 1005

Korematsu v. United States, 323 U.S. 214 (1944)

Jeffrey Kucik and Sergio Puig, 'Extending Trade Law Precedent' (forthcoming 2021) *Vanderbilt J. Int'l L*

Jens Lehne, *Crisis at the WTO: Is the Blocking of Appointments to the WTO Appellate Body by the United States Legally Justified?* (Carl Grossman Publishers, Berlin 2019)

Simon Lester and James Bacchus, 'Of Precedent and Persuasion: The Crucial Role of an Appeals Court in WTO Disputes' (2019) 74 *Free Trade Bulletin*

Robert E. Lighthizer, 'How to Set World Trade Straight' (20 August 2020) *Wall St. J.*

Robert E. Lighthizer, 'U.S. Trade Policy Priorities – Speech at the Center for Strategic and International Studies' (18 September 2017) <https://www.csis.org/analysis/us-trade-policy-priorities-robert-lighthizer-united-states-trade-representative> accessed 18 October 2020

Katerina Linos, *The Democratic Foundations of Policy Diffusion* (Oxford University Press, Oxford 2013)

David Luban, 'Military Necessity and the Cultures of Military Law' (2013) 26 *Leiden J. Int'l L.*, 315

David MacArthur, 'NAFTA Chapter 11: On an Environmental Collision Course with the World Bank' [2003] *Utah L. Rev.*, 913

Robert McDougall, 'Crisis in the WTO: Restoring the WTO Dispute Settlement Function' (October 2018) *194 CIGI Papers* <https://www.cigionline.org/sites/default/files/documents/Paper%20no.194.pdf> accessed 18 October 2020

Joost Pauwelyn and Krzysztof Pelc, 'Who Writes the Rulings of the World Trade Organization? A Critical Assessment of the Role of the Secretariat in WTO Dispute Settlement' (2019) <https://papers.ssrn.com/sol3/papers.cfm?abstract_id=3458872> accessed 18 October 2020

Ex parte Quirin, 317 U.S. 1 (1942).

Niccolò Ridi, 'The Shape and Structure of the "Usable Past": An Empirical Analysis of the Use of Precedent in International Adjudication' (2019) 10 *J. Int'l Disp. Settlement*, 200

Niccolò Ridi, 'United States—Anti-Dumping Measures Applying Differential Pricing Methodology to Softwood Lumber from Canada' (2020) 114 *Am. J. Int'l. L.*, 735

Anthea Roberts, 'Clash of Paradigms: Actors and Analogies Shaping the Investment Treaty System' (2013) 107 *Am. J. Int'l L.*, 45

Tommaso Soave, 'Who Controls WTO Dispute Settlement? Socio-Professional Practices and the Crisis of the Appellate Body' (2020) *Italian Y.B. Int'l L.*, 13

William M. Snyder, 'Communities of Practice: Combining Organizational Learning and Strategy Insights to Create a Bridge to the 21st Century' (August 1997) *Community Intelligence Labs* <http://www.co-i-l.com/coil/knowledge-garden/cop/cols.shtml> accessed 18 October 2020

Trump v. Hawaii, 138 S. Ct. 2392 (2018).

U.S Mission to International Organizations in Geneva, 'Statements by the United States at the Meeting of the WTO Dispute Settlement Body Geneva' (18 December 2018) <https://geneva.usmission.gov/wp-content/uploads/sites/290/Dec18.DSB_.Stmt_.as-deliv.fin_.public.pdf> accessed 18 October 2020

U.S. Mission to International Organizations in Geneva, 'Statements Delivered to the General Council by Ambassador Dennis Shea, U.S. Permanent Representative to the World Trade Organization' (15 October 15 2019) <https://geneva.usmission.gov/2019/10/15/statements-by-the-united-states-at-the-wto-general-council-meeting/> accessed 18 October 2020

USTR, 'Appellee Submission of the US in US: Continued Existence and Application of Zeroing Methodology' (1 December 2008) <https://ustr.gov/sites/default/files/uploads/agreements/morocco/pdfs/dispute_settlement/ds350/asset_upload_file233_13332.pdf> accessed 18 October 2020

USTR, 'Report on the Appellate Body of the World Trade Organization' (February 2020) <https://ustr.gov/sites/default/files/Report_on_the_Appellate_Body_of_the_World_Trade_Organization.pdf> accessed 18 October 2020.

USTR, 'Report on the Appellate Body of the World Trade Organization' (February 2020) <https://ustr.gov/sites/default/files/Report_on_the_Appellate_Body_of_the_World_Trade_Organization.pdf> accessed 18 October 2020, 50

USTR, 'United States Prevails on "Zeroing" Again: WTO Panel Rejects Flawed Appellate Body Findings' (9 April 2019) <https://ustr.gov/about-us/policy-offices/press-office/press-releases/2019/april/united-states-prevails-"zeroing"> accessed 18 October 2020

Jakob Hanke Vela, 'Charge of the Lighthizer Brigade' (2 October 2018) *Politico* <https://www.politico.eu/article/the-charge-of-the-robert-lighthizer-brigade-trade-war-us-donald-trump/> accessed 18 October 2020

Geraldo Vidigal, 'Living Without the Appellate Body: Multilateral, Bilateral and Plurilateral Solutions to the WTO Dispute Settlement Crisis' (2019) 20 *J. World Investment & Trade*, 862

Erik Voeten, 'Does a Professional Judiciary Induce More Compliance?: Evidence from the European Court of Human Rights' (27 March 2012) <http://papers.ssrn.com/sol3/papers.cfm?abstract_id=2029786> accessed 18 October 2020

WTO, *Fostering a Discussion on the Functioning of the Appellate Body, Addressing the Issue of Precedent – Communication from Honduras* (4 February 2019) WT/GC/W/761

WTO, *Informal Process on Matters Related to the Functioning of the Appellate Body – Communication from Japan and Australia* (18 April 2019) WT/GC/W/768

WTO, *Japan: Taxes on Alcoholic Beverages – Report of the Appellate Body* (4 October 1996) WT/DS8/AB/R, WT/DS10/AB/R and WT/DS11/AB/R14

WTO, *Minutes of Meeting of Dispute Settlement Body* (20 May 2008) WT/DSB/M/250

WTO, *Minutes of Meeting of Dispute Settlement Body – Statement by Japan* (19 January 2010) WT/DSB/M/278

WTO, *Minutes of Meeting of Dispute Settlement Body – Statement by the US* (17 December 2004) WT/DSB/M/180

WTO, *Minutes of Meetings of Dispute Settlement Body* (18 December 2018) WT/DSB/M/423

WTO, 'Panels Established to Review Claims Against Trade Measures of Costa Rica, Russia, Saudi Arabia' (18 December 2018) <https://www.wto.org/english/news_e/news18_e/dsb_18dec18_e.htm> accessed 18 October 2020

WTO, *United States: Anti-Dumping Measures Applying Differential Pricing Methodology to Softwood Lumber from Canada – Report of the Panel* (9 April 2019) WT/DS534/R

WTO, *United States: Continued Existence and Application of Zeroing Methodology – Report of the Appellate Body* (4 February 2009) WT/DS350/AB/R

WTO, *United States: Final Anti-Dumping Measures on Stainless Steel from Mexico – Report of the Appellate Body* (30 April 2008) WT/DS344/AB/R

WTO, *United States: Import Prohibition of Certain Shrimp and Shrimp Products (Article 21.5- Malaysia) – Report of the Appellate Body* (22 October 2001) WT/DS58/AB/RW

WTO, *United States: Sunset Reviews of Anti-Dumping Measures on Oil Country Tubular Goods from Argentina- Report of the Appellate Body* (29 November 2004) WT/DS268/AB/R

WTO, *United States: Use of Zeroing in Anti-Dumping Measures Involving Products from Korea* (18 January 2011) WT/DS402/R

Reasoning with past cases at the CJEU: linguistic, institutional and systemic constraints

Elina Paunio[1]

I. Introduction

This chapter looks at three groups of factors, linguistic, institutional and systemic, that have an impact on judicial decision-making at the Court of Justice of the European Union ('the Court' or the 'CJEU') with the aim of shedding light on some of the reasons that inform the Court's judicial style, in particular with regard to how it uses past cases in its reasoning.

EU law is multilingual and this has an effect on both the law that the Court interprets and its own judgments. Multilingualism also has an effect on the way the Court reasons to reach a particular outcome in a case.

On the one hand, EU law is equally authentic in all official languages of the European Union, languages that correspond to the official languages of the Member States. EU law comes about in a complex legislative procedure that combines drafting and translation at different stages of the process. The final product lacks an obvious linguistic foundation given that all versions are equally authentic. On the other hand, the Court is itself a multilingual *and* a monolingual institution. Internally, the Court is monolingual: the internal working language is French and the Court deliberates the cases brought before it in that language. Externally, however, the Court is multilingual. As a corollary to equal authenticity of official languages, judgments must be translated and published in all those languages. Translation is therefore omnipresent in proceedings before the Court.

In addition to those factors, this chapter will explore a number of other *internal* linguistic, institutional and systemic factors that have an effect on how the Court works. Those include linguistic diversity within judges' chambers and the use of French as the working language. Other factors examined include the Court's structure, the collegiality of decision-making as well as the Court's case load. Uncovering those factors is important for

---

1 Legal secretary at the Court of Justice of the European Union. All views expressed in this paper are those of the author.

the overall understanding of how the Court's case law develops and how past cases are used as justification in legal reasoning. Indeed, the process by which the case law of the Court comes about may have an important effect on the output of that institution.

II. The Linguistic Context

1. The Law

The Court operates in a multilingual systemic setting. Its main task is to interpret multilingual EU law, equally authentic in all official languages of the European Union.

The EU legislative procedure combines in a unique way drafting and translation at different stages of the legislative process. As this author has explained in more detail elsewhere,[2] drafting and translating EU legislation do not form a linear process. A legislative text is not first drafted in a specific language and then translated into the other official languages. Instead, drafting and translation are intertwined and often overlapping. The final product is a result of work in committees, working groups, teams. Several translators may work on the same document, even with the same target language text. Translation gets lost in the institutional arrangements: there is no way of clearly separating drafting legislation from translating legislation.

EU law-making forms a process where texts rotate and develop in a circular manner. Linguistic versions are redrafted and retranslated several times. In this sense, problems related to legal translation are multiplied by difficulties stemming from the overall process in which EU law evolves. Even the preparatory stages of law-making are the result of complex translation processes. For example, a draft regulation, directive and a generally applicable decision initiated in an English or French draft can receive feedback from Member State delegations. This feedback may require additional translation in different directions.[3] More stages of translation and

2 Paunio, *Legal Certainty in Multilingual EU law: Language, Discourse and Reasoning* (2013) 10.

3 Bengoetxea, 'Multilingual and multicultural legal reasoning: The European Court of Justice, in Kjær & Adamo (eds), Linguistic Diversity and European Democracy (2011) 101.

both linguistic and political revision take place at the Council and the Parliament.

The final version in each of the official languages therefore carries traces of earlier phases of the process. All the elements of translation and text production are multiplied. As explained, official language versions are usually collective products: the source text does not remain stable throughout the process, but gets rewritten by new authors, then retranslated by the same translator or possibly someone else. Moreover, it is not uncommon that the source language changes during this process.[4] Due to these particularities, no 'original' text exists that could function as the reference text for judicial interpretation by the Court. As the Court has explained, 'the wording used in one language version of a provision of EU law cannot serve as the sole basis for the interpretation of that provision, or be made to override the other language versions. Provisions of EU law must be interpreted and applied uniformly in the light of the versions existing in all languages of the European Union. Where there is divergence between the various language versions of an EU legislative text, the provision in question must be interpreted by reference to the general scheme and purpose of the rules of which it forms part'.[5]

EU law therefore exists only through a process of translation.[6] On the one hand, from a purely linguistic perspective, EU law does not have its own language so that it must be expressed through all the official languages. As was mentioned, legislation is not drafted in any particular language: it comes about in a process that constitutes a mix of language and politics. Translators input in drafting law is considerable.[7] This inevitably results in translation problems that the Court needs to clarify through its case law. On the other hand, from a more systemic perspective, EU law must be transposed into national law. As the Court reminded national courts already in *CILFIT*, 'even where the different language versions are entirely in accord with one another, [EU] law uses terminology which is

---

4 Koskinen, *Beyond Ambivalence. Postmodernity and the Ethics of Translation* (2000) 88.

5 CJEU, C-81/19, judgment of 9 July 2020, Banca Transilvania, EU:C:2020:532, paragraph 33.

6 Azoulai, 'La jurisprudence de la Cour de justice des Communautés européennes et le paradigme de la traduction', in Bailleux et al (eds), *Traduction et droits européens: enjeux d'une rencontre* (2009) 118, 121.

7 Paunio, *Legal Certainty in Multilingual EU law: Language, Discourse and Reasoning* (2013) 19.

peculiar to it. Furthermore, ... legal concepts do not necessarily have the same meaning in [EU] law and in the law of the various Member States.'[8]

This is also the reason why the Court often recalls that a particular concept, which appears in a provision of an EU law instrument that does not contain any reference to national laws, 'must be regarded as an autonomous concept of EU law and interpreted uniformly throughout the European Union'.[9] Such concepts can include anything from 'parody'[10] in the context of EU copyright law to that of an 'undertaking'[11] as a matter of EU competition law.

Even though EU law exists in many linguistic versions, those versions are assumed to denote one normative notion of EU law, that those versions express the same concepts (i.e. each linguistic version of EU law draws from the same EU law meaning).[12] In this sense, it could be argued that where official language versions differ, they may offer multifaceted, sometimes contradictory and ambiguous raw material, which functions as the starting point of the Court's interpretation.[13]

2. *The Institution*

Like the law it interprets, the Court is multilingual too. As a corollary to the equal authenticity of all official languages, any one of the official languages of the EU Member States may be the language of the case at the Court.

This is arguably particularly important for the proper functioning of the preliminary ruling procedure laid down in Article 267 TFEU. That proce-

---

8 CJEU, 283/81, judgment of 6 October 1982, Cilfit and Others, EU:C:1982:335, paragraph 19.

9 See, among many, CJEU, C-288/19, judgment of 20 January 2021, Finanzamt Saarbrücken, EU:C:2021:32, paragraph 38.

10 CJEU, C-201/13, judgment of 3 September 2014, Deckmyn and Vrijheidsfonds, EU:C:2014:2132, paragraph 15.

11 C-152/19 P, judgment of 25 March 2021, Deutsche Telekom v Commission, EU:C:2021:238 paragraph 72 and case law cited.

12 McAuliffe, 'Precedent at the ECJ: The Linguistic Aspect' (2013) 15 *Current Legal Issues*, 483, 492.

13 Kjær, 'Nonsense: The CILFIT Criteria Revisited: from the Perspective of Legal Linguistics' in Weiler et al (eds), *The New Legal Realism: Essays in Honour of Hjalte Rasmussen* (2010) 297. Kjær offers an interesting account about how, from a linguistic perspective, EU legislation in fact lacks a stable meaning before the CJEU pins that meaning down through its case law.

dure is commonly described in the literature as an instrument for a certain type of judicial dialogue. That dialogue is crucial for the development and enforcement of EU law and for ensuring that EU law is applied uniformly across the EU. This is because the procedure constitutes an interface allowing a conversation to take place between the Court and national courts on how to interpret EU law. Indeed, judicial dialogue between the Court and national courts that have the authority to apply EU law is a constitutional feature of the EU legal order and it constitutes an inherent part of EU law.[14] In that procedure, whereas the Court has jurisdiction to *interpret* EU law, it is for the national courts to *apply* that law in the specific context of the case pending before them. From this division of labour also follows that the Court has no competence in interpreting the meaning of national law, examine whether national law is in conformity with EU law or to apply the rule in the specific context of the case at hand.

The importance of that procedure becomes readily apparent when the following is considered. The EU has over 500 million citizens and a great many companies, but there are only 27 judges and 11 Advocates General at the CJEU. Consequently, national judges must apply EU law in practice in all official languages. These judges turn EU law into enforceable law of the land within each Member State. Without guidance on how to do so, judges from different legal backgrounds might easily arrive at different interpretations of the same EU law concepts, even though these concepts have an autonomous EU law meaning and ought not to be applied differently in light of national law. To protect the unity and effectiveness of EU law, therefore, the Court provides guidance on the correct interpretation of EU law where a national court has doubts as to the correct meaning of EU law.[15]

In references for preliminary rulings, the language of procedure is the language of the national court that has made the request for a preliminary ruling. In direct actions, the applicant can, in principle, choose the language of procedure.[16] In that case, the language of procedure is the official language of that state. Member States are entitled to use their

---

14 Lenaerts & Gutierrez-Fons 'To say what the law of the EU is: methods of interpretation and the European Court of Justice' (2014) 20 *The Columbia Journal of European Law*, 3, 48.

15 Cuyvers, 'Preliminary References under EU Law', in Ugirashebuja et al (eds), *East African Community Law* (2017), 275, 275 who makes the observation in an interesting comparative study on East African and European integration.

16 This is so unless the defendant is a Member State or a natural or legal person holding the nationality of a Member State.

own language in their written statements and observations and their oral submissions when they intervene in a direct action or participate in a preliminary reference procedure. Although, as a rule, the Court publishes its judgments in all official languages, only the version in the language of procedure is the authentic version of a judgment.[17]

For both practical and traditional reasons,[18] however, the Court operates in a single working language. That language is French. Irrespective of the language of procedure or the nationality and language skills of the judges involved in a particular case, judgments are drafted in French. They are also deliberated in French. Therefore, when a case (other than a French language case) is brought to the Court, the very first step in the procedure involves translation: the application, appeal or, in the preliminary ruling procedure under Article 267 TFEU, the request for a preliminary ruling must first be translated into French so that the Court can start working on the case.

Because of the linguistic setup of the Court, that is to say that the Court has a single working language but communicates towards the outside world in all official languages, translation is omnipresent in proceedings before the Court. In practical terms, the translation department of the Court, which constitutes approximatively half of the entire workforce of the Court and which is divided into language sections, or translation units, plays an important role in the communicative process that takes place between the Court and its interlocutors, most notably national courts. In this communicative process, so-called lawyer-linguists, who must hold a law degree but also be able to translate into their mother tongue from at least two other official languages, are responsible for translating documents into the working language of the Court and subsequently into all of the official EU languages.

The preliminary ruling procedure constitutes the most important type of procedure in the Court's docket.[19] In that procedure, lawyer-linguists translate all written documents drafted externally into all official languages. They also translate all documents drafted internally, which include the notice of the questions referred for a preliminary ruling in the Official

---

17 Interestingly, the first request for a preliminary ruling was made in Irish only in 2020. See, CJEU, C-64/20, UH v An tAire Talmhaíochta Bia agus Mara, Éire and An tArd-Aighne, EU:C:2021:207.

18 Arnull 'The working language of the CJEU: time for a change?' (2018), *European Law Review*, 904 (905–906) on the reasons why the language chosen as the working language was French at the time when the Court was established.

19 Annual report, Court of Justice of the European Union, 2019, p. 54.

Journal of the EU, the Opinion of the Advocate General, the judgment and the press release with the summary of the judgment. Therefore, the work of lawyer-linguists is both essential for the proper functioning of the Court and for the reception of the Court's case law in the Member States.

More specifically, as regards *input*, the French translation unit ensures that incoming procedural documents, such as decisions for a preliminary ruling and parties' observations are translated into French. With regard to *output*, the other translation units ensure that the Court's judgments are translated from French into the other official languages of the European Union.[20] With the current number of official languages and current workload, this means that (where *pivot* translation[21] is not used) there are 552 potential language combinations and over 1.2 million pages to translate every year.[22]

III. The Court's Judicial Style

1. From a French model to a sui generis style

Before the 1980's, the Court's drafting style was inspired by French drafting. Judgments consistently followed syllogistic structure. Reasoning was succinct, the tone was distant and the style abstract.[23] This style reflected the idea that courts, through a deductive and syllogistic approach, merely discovered the correct interpretation of the law and then applied it to the case in question. Such a system, of which the French *Cour de Cassation* offers a paradigmatic example, relies on expertise, authority and hierarchy, rather than on argumentation to achieve legitimacy.[24]

---

20 The Advocates General's Opinions are also translated, although the language combinations vary. This is because of the leeway that Advocates General enjoy in choosing the language in which they wish to draw up their Opinions.

21 Documents in certain languages (this concerns in particular post-2004 enlargement languages) are translated into a particular 'pivot language'. The text is only then translated from that pivot language into the other EU official languages, and vice versa.

22 Annual report, Court of Justice of the European Union, 2019, p. 27.

23 Bobek, 'The Court of Justice of the European Union' (2014) 2 *Research Papers in Law*, 15.

24 Hinarejos, 'Social Legitimacy and the Court of Justice of the EU: Some Reflections on the Role of the Advocate General' (2011 – 2012) 14 *Cambridge YB EurLegal Stud*, 615 (626).

Although the French model remains visible in the Court's institutional format and the style of reasoning, the drafting style has nevertheless gradually changed and moved further away from those roots. That said and despite the Court still being closely connected to the civilian legal tradition, the CJEU is today a unique transnational court that encompasses 27 Member States and multiple legal traditions.[25] This has an impact on the style of the Court's judgments, which is distinct from any other court. That style is difficult to tie to a particular cultural context. Indeed, with successive enlargements, Member States from different legal traditions have brought with it judges and practitioners with different views on the Court's judicial style. Still, even though French-inspired single sentence structure of judgments has been abandoned, the Court's judicial style is characterized by abstract and deductive reasoning, fixed structure and the absence of any dissenting or concurring opinions.[26]

The overall structure of a judgment is fixed. Because templates are used, each judgment has the same structure based on numbered paragraphs. A judgment systematically begins with a short summary of the case, followed by a description of the legal framework, the relevant facts, procedure and the questions referred. The CJEU's appraisal follows those introductory sections. Sometimes (especially in direct actions) also a separate section on the parties arguments and claims is included in the judgment.

In addition to those formal elements, also the reasoning follows a stable pattern. The Court's style of reasoning has been described as 'self-referential'.[27] This refers to the Court's frequent use of its own past statements as justification in its reasoning. While referring to its own case law is by no means unusual for a supreme court,[28] it is the way it uses past cases

25 Ibid.

26 Ibid.

27 Jacob, *Precedents and Case-based Reasoning in the European Court of Justice — Unfinished Business* (2014) 117. See, for example, CJEU, C-330/16, judgment of 1 June 2017 Zarski, EU:C:2017:418, paragraphs 25 and 26; C-438/05, judgment of 11 December 2007, International Transport Workers' Federation and Finnish Seamen's Union, EU:C:2007:772 and C-341/05, judgment of 18 December 2007, Laval un Partneri, EU:C:2007:809. On formulaic jurisprudence, Azoulai 'La fabrication de la jurisprudence communautaire', in Mbongo et al (eds), *Dans la fabrique du droit européen: scènes, acteurs et publics de la Cour de justice des Communautés européennes* (2009) 153, 165–166.

28 As Jääskinen points out, however, most – if not all – supreme courts in the world refer to their own case law as justification and, in this sense, the CJEU is no different. See Jääskinen, 'Oma ja muiden oikeuskäytäntö oikeuslähteenä ylimpien

in reasoning that arguably sets the CJEU apart from other courts that set precedent.

2. *Abstract reasoning with past cases*

In EU law, there are no clear rules regarding the precedential value of past decisions. Unlike *stare decisis* in the United States, for example, EU law lacks an official doctrine of precedent. It has nevertheless been argued that EU law operates with its own system of de facto binding precedent.[29] As the supreme court of the EU, however, the CJEU cannot – quite obviously – be bound by its own previous case law. It is clear though that the Court places particular emphasis on the coherence of its own case law. This is understandable given that the preliminary ruling procedure is based on the need to ensure the uniform application of EU law in the Member States.[30]

The Court's style of reasoning is generally perceived as formalistic and abstract. One of the features of the Court's judicial style that may help explain this impression is repetition: the Court's reasoning is characterised by abstract statements from past cases, or the use of 'cluster citations'.[31]

---

suomalaisten ja eurooppalaisten tuomioistuimien ratkaisutoiminnassa' (2020) 7–8 *Lakimies*, 1205, 1207.

29 Tridimas, 'Precedent and the Court of Justice: A Jurisprudence of Doubt?', in Dickson et al (eds), Philosophical Foundations of European Union Law (2012), 307, 308 making a comparison to stare decisis. See also McAuliffe, 'The Limitations of a Multilingual Legal System' (2013), *International Journal for the Semiotics of Law*, 861, 882 explaining how it is possible to speak of 'linguistic precedent' in the context of the production of CJEU case law. Because of the frequent use of 'copy-and-paste' from previous decisions, the linguistic form of a statement, rather than the legal holding, becomes binding on future decisions of the Court.

30 Jääskinen, 'Oma ja muiden oikeuskäytäntö oikeuslähteenä ylimpien suomalaisten ja eurooppalaisten tuomioistuimien ratkaisutoiminnassa' (2020) 7–8 *Lakimies* 1205, 1209. On the role of national courts in the process of applying the Court's statements at the national level from the perspective of multilingualism, see Derlén, *Multilingual Interpretation of European Union Law* (2009).

31 Bobek, 'The Court of Justice of the European Union' (2014) 2 *Research Papers in Law*, 16. See also Jääskinen, 'Oma ja muiden oikeuskäytäntö oikeuslähteenä ylimpien suomalaisten ja eurooppalaisten tuomioistuimien ratkaisutoiminnassa' (2020) 7–8 *Lakimies* 1205, 1209 and Jacob, *Precedents and Case-based Reasoning in the European Court of Justice — Unfinished Business* (2014) 101, who notes that over 95 % of all case law references made in Grand chamber judgments are string citations.

Those statements could be described as building blocks for other cases. The CJEU only rarely substantially engages with the reasons of a previous decision in order to distinguish or overrule.

The following extract from the Court's judgment in *Brey*[32] concerning the interpretation of Directives 2004/38[33] and Regulation No 883/2004[34] offers an illustration of how the Court may use past statements as justification in its reasoning:

> '51... it should be borne in mind that Regulation No 883/2004 seeks to achieve the objective set out in Article 48 TFEU by preventing the possible negative effects that the exercise of the freedom of movement for workers could have on the enjoyment, by workers and their families, of social security benefits (see, to that effect, Chuck, paragraph 32).
> 52 It is in order to achieve that objective that, through the waiver of residence clauses under Article 7 thereof, Regulation No 883/2004 provides, subject to the exceptions set out therein, for the cash benefits falling within its scope to be exportable in the host Member State (see, to that effect, Case C-20/96 Snares [1997] ECR I-6057, paragraphs 39 and 40).
> 53 By contrast, although the aim of Directive 2004/38 is to facilitate and strengthen the exercise of the primary and individual right – conferred directly on all Union citizens by the Treaty – to move and reside freely within the territory of the Member States (see Case C-127/08 Metock and Others [2008] ECR I-6241, paragraphs 82 and 59; Case C-162/09 Lassal [2010] ECR I-9217, paragraph 30; and Case C-434/09 McCarthy [2011] ECR I-3375, paragraph 28), it is also intended, as is apparent from Article 1(a) thereof, to set out the conditions governing the exercise of that right (see, to that effect, McCarthy, paragraph 33, and Joined Cases C-424/10 and C-425/10 Ziolkowski and Szeja [2011] ECR I-14035, paragraphs 36 and 40), which include, where residence

32 CJEU, C-140/12, judgment of 19 September 2013, Brey, EU:C:2013:565, paragraphs 51 to 56.

33 Directive 2004/38/EC of the European Parliament and of the Council of 29 April 2004 on the right of citizens of the Union and their family members to move and reside freely within the territory of the Member States amending Regulation (EEC) No 1612/68 and repealing Directives 64/221/EEC, 68/360/EEC, 72/194/EEC, 73/148/EEC, 75/34/EEC, 75/35/EEC, 90/364/EEC, 90/365/EEC and 93/96/EEC (OJ L 158, 30.4.2004, p. 77).

34 Regulation (EC) No 883/2004 of the European Parliament and of the Council of 29 April 2004 on the coordination of social security systems (OJ L 166, 30.4.2004, p. 1).

is desired for a period of longer than three months, the condition laid down in Article 7(1)(b) of the directive that Union citizens who do not or no longer have worker status must have sufficient resources.

54 It is apparent from recital 10 in the preamble to Directive 2004/38, in particular, that that condition is intended, inter alia, to prevent such persons becoming an unreasonable burden on the social assistance system of the host Member State (Ziolkowski and Szeja, paragraph 40).

55 That condition is based on the idea that the exercise of the right of residence for citizens of the Union can be subordinated to the legitimate interests of the Member States – in the present case, the protection of their public finances (see, by analogy, Case C-413/99 Baumbast and R [2002] ECR I-7091, paragraph 90; Zhu and Chen, paragraph 32; and Case C-408/03 Commission v Belgium [2006] ECR I-2647, paragraphs 37 and 41).

56 In a similar vein, Article 24(2) of Directive 2004/38 allows a derogation from the principle of equal treatment enjoyed by Union citizens other than workers, self-employed persons, persons who retain such status and members of their families who reside within the territory of the host Member State, by permitting that State not to confer entitlement to social assistance, in particular for the first three months of residence (see Joined Cases C-22/08 and C-23/08 Vatsouras and Koupatantze [2009] ECR I-4585, paragraphs 34 and 35).'

The extract offers an example of how the Court may employ its own case law as justification for rule-like postulates or major legal premises.[35] It may refer to its case law also in the context of descriptive statements.[36] Those statements are not case specific and contain general statements. They can therefore be detached flexibly from a particular context and used again as justification in other cases and contexts.

The Court does not operate with any strict hierarchy between different sources of precedent. The Court refers rather freely to statements from previous cases as justification. In principle, the source of precedent is

---

35 Jacob, *Precedents and Case-based Reasoning in the European Court of Justice — Unfinished Business* (2014) 113 on how the Court uses precedent. See, among many, CJEU, C-648/15, judgment of 12 September, Austria v Germany, EU:C:2017:664, paragraph 39.

36 See CJEU, C-365/16, AFEP and Others, EU:C:2017:378, paragraph 22 and CJEU, C-325/08, judgment of 16 March 2010, Olympique Lyonnais, EU:C:2010:143, paragraphs 41 and 42 regarding previously made factual assertions.

therefore potentially ever growing and in a state of flux. This aspect is highlighted by *how* past cases are used in reasoning.

Ad verbatim string citations, or close to verbatim rendition of past statements in judgments do not engage with the facts of previous cases. This textualist attitude to case law contrasts with the way the Court deals with multilingual legislation it interprets. A typical feature of the Court's use of past cases is that it does distinguish or explain the ratio for holding a particular statement applicable. Indeed, the Court lacks established doctrines of *ratio decidendi* or *obiter dictum*. Moreover, a single decision can become 'established case law'. Statements may be de-contextualised and transposed to new cases and contexts.[37] As a corollary to that practise, the Court rarely openly departs from its previous case law, even though development and new orientations in the case law take place constantly.[38]

Growing case numbers and a bigger court have created a risk of inconsistencies across different chambers. In that context, the concern for preserving the internal unity and coherence of the case law has been suggested as an explanation for the CJEU's judicial style and its reliance on past statements from the case law. Indeed, using past statements as justification may be seen as a way to signal coherence and stability across the different chambers of the Court.[39]

Beyond those considerations, however, the case law the CJEU produces – and the choices made regarding the use of case law in reasoning – is, however, not a simple matter of a chamber of judges drawing up a judgment. The case law and the Court's reasoning are products of a unique multi-layered and multilingual process in which many actors are

---

37 From an empirical perspective, see Derlén and Lindholm, 'Goodbye van Gend en Loos, Hello Bosman? Using Network Analysis to Measure the Importance of Individual CJEU Judgments' (2014) 20 *European Law Journal*, 667 and Šadl, 'Precedent in the Sui Generis Legal Order: A Mine Run Approach' (2014) 20 *European Law Journal*, 544.

38 For an example of express overturning, see CJEU, C-127/08, judgment of 25 July 2008, Metock and Others, EU:C:2008:449. It is more common to use other techniques. For a more modest way to distinguish, see CJEU, C-365/16, judgment of 17 May 2017, AFEP and Others, EU:C:2017:378, paragraph 34. The Court can also depart from previous case law through a technique that could be called 'avoidance'. See C-413/14, judgment of 6 September 2017, Intel Corporation, EU:C:2017:632, paragraphs 133 et seq. omitting to refer to CJEU, C-23/14, judgment of 6 October 2015, Post Danmark, EU:C:2015:651.

39 Bobek, 'The Court of Justice of the European Union' (2014) 2 *Research Papers in Law*, 6.

involved.[40] The following section sheds light on three closely interrelated groups of factors that may have an impact on the Court's judicial style.

IV. Constraints Related to Language, the Court's Set-Up and Its Role in the EU Legal System

1. Language

The decision-making at the Court is constrained by language(s). Linguistic diversity affects the decision-making process of the Court at every step of the procedure.

The members of the Court (judges and advocates general), legal secretaries (référendaires), lawyer-linguists and other lawyers working in the research and documentation service come from diverse cultural, linguistic and legal backgrounds. European legal traditions vary considerably as concerns the role and importance of case law as a source of law, but also as concerns more generally the style of legal reasoning expected from courts.

The Court works and deliberates in French. The possibility of relying on past statements made by the Court, but also the need to strictly follow a considerable number of drafting conventions and house-style, arguably facilitates the work of legal secretaries who assist judges in drafting documents such as preliminary reports and judgments. With regard to the role of legal secretaries, it is important to keep in mind that while officially it is the reporting judge who is responsible for drafting the judgment according to what is agreed on by the chamber in secret deliberations, in reality it is often his/her legal secretary who drafts the text.[41] Seen from that perspective, it has been argued that the repetition of past statements from the case law may be of particular assistance to those not working in their own mother tongue and who have not been educated in the French legal tradition. Indeed, it should not be forgotten that the majority of legal secretaries are working in a language other than their native tongue.[42]

---

40 McAuliffe, 'Behind the Scenes at the Court Of Justice: Drafting EU Law Stories' in Nicola and Davies (eds), *EU Law Stories: Contextual and Critical Histories of European Jurisprudence* (2017) 35, 36.

41 McAuliffe, 'Behind the Scenes at the Court Of Justice: Drafting EU Law Stories' in Nicola and Davies (eds), *EU Law Stories: Contextual and Critical Histories of European Jurisprudence* (2017) 35, 46.

42 See, in more detail, on how that factor affects the drafting of judgments, McAuliffe 'La traduction dans l'office des juges européens', in Bailleux et al (eds),

In fact, McAuliffe has suggested on the basis of interviews conducted at the Court that legal secretaries tend to consider, on the one hand, that the use of French in drafting judgments constrains their freedom in reasoning and that there is pressure to cite previous case law word-to-word. On the other hand, however, the practice of word-to-word citation of past statements has been described by some as a 'safety-net': it is assumed that material mistakes can be avoided in fields requiring particular technical expertise.[43]

The Court also employs francophone lawyers known as lecteurs d'arrêt and francophone proof readers. Their task is to verify citations and the conformity of the judgments with house-style, but also more generally, to harmonise texts produced at the Court.[44] The intervention of the lecteurs d'arrêt in the drafting process certainly enhances stylistic coherence across the chambers of the Court, but may also contribute to the impression of impersonal and repetitive style.

Beyond those micro-level factors, the macro-level institutional element of multilingualism and the fact that judgments must be translated into other official languages is arguably the most obvious explanation for the fixed structure of judgments, but also more specifically for the way the Court reasons with past cases. The importance of verbatim re-production and repetition in reasoning can be understood properly only in the light of the role that translation plays at the Court. Because all the judgments of the Court must be translated into over 20 languages, there is an obvious need to streamline the language and structure of judgments and to rely on already translated sentences as much as possible.

The Recommendations issued by the Court to national courts concerning the submission of preliminary ruling requests epitomise the concerns of efficiency and ease of translation, which inform judicial work at the Court. Those recommendations highlight the constraints of translation in the procedure before the Court stating that 'owing to the consequential need to translate it into all the official languages of the European Union,

---

Traduction et droits européens: enjeux d'une rencontre (2009) 24, 39. However, it has been calculated that 42% of legal secretaries are citizens of Belgium, France and Luxembourg. See Huyne Zhang, 'The Faceless Court' (2015) *King's College London Law School Research Paper No 45*, 27.

43 McAuliffe, 'Behind the Scenes at the Court Of Justice: Drafting EU Law Stories' in Nicola and Davies (eds), *EU Law Stories: Contextual and Critical Histories of European Jurisprudence* (2017) 35, 47.

44 Susan Wright 'The Language of the Law in Multilingual Contexts: Unpicking the English of the EU Courts' Judgments' (2016) 37 *Statute Law Review*, 156, 158.

the request for a preliminary ruling should... be drafted simply, clearly and precisely by the referring court or tribunal, avoiding superfluous detail.'[45]

The standardised language used by the Court and the fixed form of its judgments are therefore not merely tools seeking to ensure stylistic coherence, but arguably constitute from a more practical perspective a tool designed to facilitate translation. Indeed, a curiosity in the procedure before the Court is that the final version of a judgment, as deliberated on by the members of the relevant Chamber, is not usually the authentic version of the judgment.

An interesting point of comparison here is the European Court of Human Rights in Strasbourg (the ECtHR). The ECtHR system of precedent is explored in more detail by Frese and Palmer Olsen & Christensen in other chapters of this edited volume.

Unlike the CJEU that has one working language, the ECtHR has two, English and French. However, no equivalent to the CJEU translation system exists, whereby all published judgments are translated to 23 other official languages. At the ECtHR, judgments are published in one (or sometimes both) of the two working languages. It has been shown that unlike legal secretaries drafting judgments at the CJEU, their counterparts working at the Strasbourg court are less constrained by internal drafting guidelines and house-style. The latter group of legal secretaries possesses in other words more freedom in drafting.[46] That might however not only be explained by linguistic, but also systemic differences between EU law and the ECHR. Secondary EU legislation is certainly more voluminous, but also far more technical than the relatively limited number of human rights texts that the ECtHR is called upon to interpret. The ECtHR is also less constrained by translation and there is no similar concern related to primacy or direct effect as is in the context of the interpretation and application of EU law. In that regard, an important contribution to further study would be to analyse how those differences impact on the reception of the respective courts judgments in the Member States.

---

45 Recommendations to the attention of national courts concerning the submission of preliminary ruling proceedings (OJ, C 439, 2016, p. 1).

46 McAuliffe 'La traduction dans l'office des juges européens', in Bailleux et al (eds), *Traduction et droits européens: enjeux d'une rencontre* (2009) 24, 30–32.

2. *Collegiality and secret deliberations*

As mentioned earlier, the authentic version of a judgment is the version in the language of procedure. Therefore, the authentic version of a CJEU judgment is in fact a translation of the version agreed upon by the judges in their secret deliberations.

The Court adjudicates in chambers of three or five judges, the Grand Chamber or the Full Court. There are no dissenting or concurring opinions. In accordance with Article 32 of the Rules of Procedure of the Court, deliberations are secret and the conclusions reached by the majority of the judges after final discussion shall determine the decision of the Court. Unlike in some other jurisdictions therefore, legal secretaries are not allowed to sit in on the oral deliberations.[47] It is also worth pointing out that unlike for instance at the ECtHR, the CJEU deliberates a case allocated to a particular chamber on the basis of a written draft judgment prepared by the referring judge.[48]

The linguistic and legal diversity of the Court is also reflected in deliberations. Because the Court does not work with dissenting opinions, a unanimous judgment delivered by the Court and in particular the reasoning contained therein may or may not constitute a compromise: a judgment is a collective document.[49] Moreover, just as the legal secretaries, the majority of judges that deliberate cases (usually orally) in French, on the basis of a draft judgment drawn up in French, without the legal secretaries being present in those deliberations, are not French native speakers.

The problems stemming from cultural, linguistic and legal differences, which judges encounter in secret deliberations and which must be overcome to reach a compromise are summarised by Sir Konrad Schiemann, a former judge at the Court: 'a self-evident truth to a French lawyer is frequently not a self-evident truth to an English lawyer'.[50] However, the 'fact of having to speak French, which has been the Court's working lan-

---

47 Ibid, 31.

48 McAuliffe, 'Behind the Scenes at the Court Of Justice: Drafting EU Law Stories' in Nicola and Davies (eds), *EU Law Stories: Contextual and Critical Histories of European Jurisprudence* (2017) 35, 38.

49 See, for example, CJEU, C-34/09, judgment of 8 March 2011, Ruiz Zambrano, EU:C:2011:124 as an often cited example of a case where collegiality might lead to extremely succinct reasoning.

50 Schiemann 'The application of general principles of Community law by English courts', in Jacobs et al (eds), *European Community Law in the English Courts* (1998) 137, 139.

guage since 1952, in the deliberation room and having to draft judgments in French, puts the non-francophones at a definite disadvantage vis-à-vis their brethren from France, Belgium and Luxembourg. Being of course accomplished gentlemen, they would never consciously take advantage of their colleagues' handicap; but the full mastery of a language — is an irresistible weapon; and the owner of that weapon will not be likely to refrain from using it.'[51]

3. *Caseload*

Together with the EU itself, the Court has transformed from a community of six Member States with a broadly shared understanding of the role of courts to a Union of 27 Member States encompassing different legal traditions and expectations regarding the role of its highest court. In the words of Judge Prechal, the Court has transformed over the years from a family to a factory.[52]

In addition to successive enlargements of the EU, the transformation is at least partly due to the fact that, unlike many other supreme courts, the Court does not control its docket as regards, in particular, requests for a preliminary ruling.[53] The Court has been successful in bringing national

---

51 Mancini and David Keeling, 'Language, culture and politics in the life of the European Court of Justice' (1995) 1 *Columbia Journal of European Law*, 397, 398.

52 Interview with the judge Sacha Prechal of 18 December 2013, available at https://europeanlawblog.eu/2013/12/18/interview-with-judge-sacha-prechal-of-the-european-court-of-justice-part-i-working-at-the-cjeu/ accessed 8 June 2021.

53 In the context of direct actions Article 58a of the Statute of the Court of Justice provides that an appeal brought against a decision of the General Court concerning a decision of (a) the European Union Intellectual Property Office; (b) the Community Plant Variety Office; (c) the European Chemicals Agency; or (d) the European Union Aviation Safety Agency an shall not proceed unless the Court of Justice first decides that it should be allowed to do so on the basis of a separate request to that effect annexed to the appeal (see Article 170a of the Rules of Procedure). On docket control and the success of constitutional courts in ensuring legitimacy, see Fontana, 'Docket control and the Success of Constitutional Courts', in Ginsburg et al (eds), *Handbook of Comparative Constitutional Law* (2011), 624 (636). According to Fontana, allowing constitutional courts 'to decide what to decide proves crucial to the success of these courts. A court empowered to set its agenda is a court that can avoid excessive political conflict and ensure maximum compliance. ... there is no issue more important than an issue that appears to be the most simple: the content and structure of the docket of the court.'

courts on board and in encouraging them to pose questions on the proper interpretation of EU law in the context of the preliminary ruling procedure under Article 267 TFEU. To encourage a judicial dialogue, the Court for example systematically reminds national courts that they are free to make further requests, even where a specific request is deemed manifestly inadmissible pursuant to Article 53(2), of the Rules of Procedure. According to the Court, 'the referring court retains the right to submit a new request for a preliminary ruling when it is in a position to provide the Court with all the information enabling the Court to give a ruling on the question referred'.[54]

The importance and success of the preliminary ruling procedure has resulted in a paradox. The more the preliminary ruling procedure is used, the more burdensome dealing with those requests becomes for the CJEU. As a result, there is a clear risk that the quality of reasoning deteriorates and that the Court's ability to provide authoritative guidance to national courts weakens, with the paradoxical result of weakening the system of preliminary references itself.[55] Indeed, in that procedure, lower instance courts may choose to put questions of interpretation to the Court where they deem appropriate. Instead, courts of last instance are under an obligation to do so, unless the exception laid down by the CJEU in *CILFIT* applies.[56]

For example, whereas from 2007 to 2011, references for a preliminary ruling constituted more than half of the proceedings before the CJEU, cases decided in this procedure constitute now more or less two thirds of all cases decided. In absolute numbers, the judicial activity of the Court has also steadily increased over time. In the early period, when the Court was founded in the 1950s, the Court had less than 50 new cases each year. In the 1970s, the CJEU dealt with around 100 to 200 new cases each year. In the 1990s, the CJEU (excluding cases dealt by the Court of First Instance) dealt with between 300 and 500 cases. Since 2001 there have

---

54 See, for example, CJEU, order of 1 October 2020, GR and Others, EU:C:2020:771, paragraph 34 and case law cited.

55 Lenaerts, 'The Unity of European Law and the Overload of the ECJ – The System of Preliminary Rulings Revisited' (2005) *The Global Community: Y.B. Int'l L. Jurisprudence*, 211, 212.

56 CJEU, 283/81, judgment of 6 October 1982, Cilfit and Others, EU:C:1982:335, paragraph 21.

been between 400 and 850 new cases each year.[57] In 2019, 966 new cases were introduced of which 641 under the preliminary ruling procedure.[58]

Despite the increase in the number of cases, the Court has been able to accelerate the handling of cases by adapting its Rules of Procedure and using reasoned orders on the basis of Articles 53, 99 and 181 of the Rules of Procedure to deal with cases more swiftly. Those provisions allow the Court to dispose of cases speedily and efficiently. Internally, the Court has also taken a number of organisational measures to enhance its efficiency, such as monitoring the progress of individual cases against indicative internal deadlines for the main stages of the judicial procedure, digitising procedural documentary flows, and enhancing accountability.[59]

From the perspective of efficiency and timeliness, the use of reasoned orders presents obvious advantages. Importantly, most orders are not published, meaning that they are only translated into the language of the procedure.

However, it seems possible to presume that repetition of statements from previous case law is more frequent in orders than in judgments. This would appear to be the case in particular with regard to orders based on Article 99 of the Rules of Procedure. This provision gives the Court the possibility to rule by way of a reasoned order where a question referred to it for a preliminary ruling is identical to a question on which the Court has already ruled; where the reply to such a question may be clearly deduced from existing case law; or where the answer to the question referred for a preliminary ruling admits of no reasonable doubt. Indeed, recourse to a reasoned order typically presupposes that the answer to the question referred can be deduced from existing case law.

From the perspective of efficiency, brief reasoning based on statements made in past cases may be useful in order to ensure speedy resolution of (easy) cases. However, as mentioned above, the Court plays an important role in the EU legal system in pinning down the meaning of EU law and ensuring that it is interpreted uniformly across the European Union by providing national courts with authoritative guidance. Bearing that in mind, there are obvious challenges involved in allocating resources (both those related to translation and to drafting of judgments and orders) wisely

---

57 See in more detail on the evolution of the Court's docket over the decades Pierdominici, *The Mimetic Evolution of the Court of Justice of the EU: A Comparative Law Perspective* (2020) 234.

58 Annual report, Court of Justice of the European Union, 2019, p. 54.

59 Special report of the Court of Auditors 2017, p. 19.

and in ensuring sufficient quality of reasoning, especially in cases that cannot be dealt with by way of order.[60]

4. *Discussion: Legitimacy Through Reasoning*

A judgment issued by the Court is a collegiate document. This is easily overlooked in legal literature, which tends to focus on the Court as a rational actor and to analyse the soundness of the Court's legal reasoning in a particular case from a substantive perspective or its coherence with regard to previous body of case law in the same field. As Michal Bobek, currently an Advocate General at the Court, has pointed out, 'even though we tend to refer to a court as "it", a court is always "they"'.[61] The 'they' in this instance are not only judges though. The 'they' are also Advocates General, legal secretaries, lecteurs d'arrêt, proofreaders, and lawyer-linguists.

Drawing up the final version of a CJEU judgment is not simply a matter of a chamber of judges deciding on a case in secret deliberations. The process involves multiple authors working in a language that is not necessarily their mother tongue. That process, which begins with translation and ends with translation, includes multiple layers of translation between 24 official EU languages.[62]

For the emergence of uniform EU law, the way the Court reasons is not without consequence. The application of EU law, as interpreted by the Court, remains in the hands of national courts. This highlights the importance of judicial dialogue in the construction and development of EU law. Indeed, to be able to speak with authority, the Court's reasoning must be clear and persuasive.

In a multilingual and multi-layered legal system the continuous conversation that takes place between the Court and national courts in the preliminary ruling procedure is a way to deliberate a common understanding about norms and concepts in the multilingual EU legal system. The Court's legitimacy and its ability to convince its audience, especially the

---

60 On how quality standards could be applied in adjudication, Bengoetxea, 'Quality Standards in Judicial Adjudication: The European Court of Justice', in Müller et al (eds.), *Festschrift für Heike Jung* (2007), 47 *et seq*.

61 Bobek, 'The Court of Justice of the European Union' (2014) 2 *Research Papers in Law*, 10.

62 McAuliffe, 'Behind the Scenes at the Court Of Justice: Drafting EU Law Stories' in Nicola & Davies (eds), *EU Law Stories: Contextual and Critical Histories of European Jurisprudence* (2017) 35, 39.

highest courts of the Member States, regarding the correct interpretation of EU law, and by extension, its ability to achieve its goal that EU law is uniformly interpreted and applied across the EU, is closely connected to the quality of its reasoning. In multi-layered systems of governance, like that of the EU, the need to guarantee a constructive judicial dialogue among different courts is of particular importance for determining whether the CJEU enjoys legitimacy.[63] Indeed, where the participants in that dialogue do not share the same cultural and linguistic background and expectations, it may be argued that 'discursive legitimacy' that comes from making reasoning explicit, transparent and convincing becomes central to achieving legitimacy. Such a view on legitimacy accepts that there are several possible interpretations of the law, and that in choosing one, judges in fact make law, rather than just apply it. In doing so, they are expected to assess the merits and consequences of all possible interpretations. This makes the decision look more like a carefully weighed discussion than a syllogism.[64]

Whether the Court's reasoning achieves such legitimacy has become a particularly pressing issue. In recent years, not only the constitutional importance but also the political and societal sensitivity of some cases brought before the Court have certainly contributed to its visibility beyond its traditional audience of national courts.[65] Weiler predicted this development already over twenty years ago: the 'Court will… be called upon to adjudicate disputes which will, inevitably, subject it to public debate of a breadth and depth it is unaccustomed to… Its overall visibility is bound to grow and it will be judged by a media and public opinion far more informed than before.'[66]

The fixed structure of judgments and citing verbatim paragraphs from previous cases arguably carries certain institutionalized, status-bound authority. However, such reasoning may lack in persuasive power needed

---

63 Lenaerts, 'How the ECJ thinks: a study in judicial legitimacy' (2013) 36 *Fordham Int'l L.J.*, 1302, 1306.

64 Hinarejos, 'Social Legitimacy and the Court of Justice of the EU: Some Reflections on the Role of the Advocate General' (2011 – 2012) 14 *Cambridge YB EurLegal Stud*, 615, 627.

65 See, for example, CJEU, C-188/15, judgment of 14 March 2017, Bougnaoui and ADDH, EU:C:2017:204; CJEU, C-157/15, judgment of 14 March 2017, G4S Secure Solutions, EU:C:2017:203; CJEU, C-511/18, C-512/18 and C-520/18, judgment of 6 October 2020, La Quadrature du Net and Others, EU:C:2020:791 and CJEU, C-619/18, judgment of 24 June 2019, Commission v Poland (Independence of the Supreme Court), EU:C:2019:531.

66 Weiler, *The Constitution of Europe* (1999) 207.

to convince a pluralist audience of the interpretation of the law it puts forward and in the final analysis, for ensuring the Court's legitimacy. Because of multilingualism and the role translation plays in the proceedings before the Court though, it is not straightforward to remedy many of the linguistic and institutional constraints discussed previously and thus to substantially change the way the Court reasons, and in particular the way it uses past cases in its reasoning.

Some authors have suggested dissenting or concurring opinions as a way for the Court to engage in more discursive reasoning.[67] Indeed, the rationale of a separate opinion is that the majority cannot readily ignore a separate opinion without engaging with the reasons put forward in it. Introducing dissenting opinions would also probably involve a change of style for the majority judgment since explaining their position vis-à-vis the dissenter would require a different approach to reasoning.[68]

Separate opinions and the corresponding lengthening of majority opinions, in any of the Court's possible configurations would pose many challenges of its own. This would arguably be the case even if the number of such opinions per judge were limited and recourse to such opinions were limited to certain types of cases, for example to those dealt with by the Grand Chamber. The most obvious problems are practical ones and relate to issues discussed above. A change of style would undoubtedly put added pressure on the already overburdened translation service. Moreover, a change of style imposed by separate opinions might have significant spill over effects, most notably on the resources needed to translate such opinions, but also more broadly on the Court's working methods. Another concern is whether separate opinions might reduce the legitimacy and persuasiveness of the Court's judgments, given that it would no longer speaks with one voice.

While it may seem unsatisfactory to object to reform for practical (and financial) reasons, it is an objection that also has merit from a systemic perspective. The equality of all official languages is an important constitutional principle, which makes any proposal to change the current linguistic setup of the Court difficult. Moreover, the doctrines of primacy and direct effect that have contributed to the special character of EU law should

---

67 See for an extensive analysis, Perju, 'Reason and Authority in the European Court of Justice' (2009) 49 *Virginia Journal of International Law*, 307. See also, from a comparative standpoint, Keleman, 'Dissenting Opinions in Constitutional Courts' (2013) 14 *German Law Journal*, 1345.

68 Edward, 'How the Court of Justice Works' (1995) 20 *European Law Review*, 539, 557.

not be overlooked here. Because of those principles, it is important that the Court's judgments are translated into all official languages. This is paramount for ensuring that a open dialogue with national courts can take place.

The Opinions drafted by the Court's Advocates General may enhance the discursive legitimacy of the Court without substantially changing the style or the structure of the judgments themselves. This is because Opinions may function as a channel that sheds some insight into the Court's reasoning through transparency and discursiveness and a form of input into that reasoning that might otherwise be lacking.[69] Indeed, an Opinion may increase the impression of less abstract and formalist reasoning of the Court in two ways: in a single case if a judgment and the Opinion published in that same case are considered as a whole and more generally, as a critical voice within the Court.

In the past, the Advocates General provided an Opinion (though sometimes a very short one) in every case. However, their role today is different: Advocates General are typically called upon to conclude only in the more complex cases, without exception in Grand Chamber cases, but also in many of the five judges' chamber cases. Within these generally either legally or technically complex or politically sensitive cases, the Advocates General not only provide a description of the state of the law and a proposal on how to solve the case in question, but also a broader and oftentimes critical analysis of the CJEU's case law in the field of law in question.[70]

That said, even though the role of Advocates General Opinions is certainly valuable in prompting debate within and beyond the Court and providing a counterbalance to the Court's succinct and formulaic judicial style, the value of Opinions as a way to ensure discursive legitimacy arguably remains limited. An Opinion constitutes a separate legal analysis published before the final judgment of the CJEU is deliberated. This means that a judgment can at least theoretically position itself vis-à-vis the Opinion, but not the other way around. Indeed, while Advocates General contribute to the decision-making of the Court with critical and discursive elements by providing, for example, in-depth analysis of the state of the case law, an Advocate General can only critically analyse the Court's case law generally, but not the judgment in the case in which the Opinion is

69 Hinarejos, 'Social Legitimacy and the Court of Justice of the EU: Some Reflections on the Role of the Advocate General' (2011 – 2012) 14 *Cambridge YB EurLegal Stud*, 615, 625–632.

70 Bobek, 'The Court of Justice of the European Union' (2014) 2 *Research Papers in Law*, 14.

delivered. Moreover, an Advocate General's Opinion does not force the judges to explain their position in a way that a dissenting opinion probably would, and the Court does not generally engage with the position of the Advocate General in its judgements.

V. Concluding Remarks

This chapter explored factors that inform the emergence of the CJEU case law and in particular the use of past cases as source of justification in reasoning. The way the Court reasons cannot be detached from the process and the actors involved in drawing up that case law: in the case of the Court, the process of judicial decision-making constitutes a multi-layered process of collective decision-making, drafting and translation and the input of staff from different legal and linguistic backgrounds form an integral part of that process.

Although qualitative and quantitative concerns are common to every judicial body, they are particularly important for supreme courts like the CJEU as the highest court of the EU. Indeed, the Court's judgments, and the reactions to them by national courts, are a way to deliberate, through a dialogue, common understanding about norms and concepts in the multi-layered and multilingual EU legal system. The Court's authority in convincing its audience, especially the highest courts of the Member States, is linked to the quality of its legal reasoning. How to ensure that the CJEU is able successfully to guide national courts in the day-to-day application of EU law also in the future?

The Court's set-up and, in that context, the need to translate all published judgments, to accommodate different approaches to legal reasoning in a collective decision, and the increasing caseload arguably contribute to the Court's 'self-referential' style of reasoning and in particular the formulaic use of past statements from the case law. The challenge would therefore seem to be to find a way to reconcile, on the one hand, the need for transparent and discursive reasoning that would engage more openly with previous cases and, on the other hand, the constraints of the linguistic and institutional setting in which the Court operates.

Bibliography

Anthony Arnull, 'The working language of the CJEU: time for a change?' (2018) 43 *European Law Review*, 904

Louic Azoulai, 'La jurisprudence de la Cour de justice des Communautés européennes et le paradigme de la traduction', in Alain Bailleux et al (eds), *Traduction et droits européens: enjeux d'une rencontre* (Facultés universitaires Saint Louis, Bruxelles 2009), 119

Louic Azoulai, 'La fabrication de la jurisprudence communautaire', in Pascal Mbongo et al (eds), *Dans la fabrique du droit européen: scènes, acteurs et publics de la Cour de justice des Communautés européennes* (Bruylant, Brussels 2009), 153

Joxerramon Bengoetxea, 'Quality Standards in Judicial Adjudication: The European Court of Justice', in Egon Müller et al (eds.), *Festschrift für Heike Jung* (Nomos Verlag, Baden-Baden 2007), 47

Joxerramon Bengoetxea, 'Multilingual and multicultural legal reasoning: The European Court of Justice, in Anne Lise Kjær and Silvia Adamo (eds), *Linguistic Diversity and European Democracy* (Ashgate Publishing, Farnham 2011), 97

Michal Bobek, 'The Court of Justice of the European Union' (2014) 2 *Research Papers in Law* 2/2014

Armin Cuyvers, 'Preliminary References under EU Law', in Emmanuel Ugirashebuja et al (eds), *East African Community Law* (Brill, Leiden 2017), 275

Matthias Derlén, *Multilingual Interpretation of European Union Law* (Kluwer Law International, Alphen aan den Rijn 2009)

Matthias Derlén and John Lindholm, 'Goodbye van Gend en Loos, Hello Bosman? Using Network Analysis to Measure the Importance of Individual CJEU Judgments' (2014) 20 *European Law Journal*, 667

David Edward, 'How the Court of Justice Works' (1995) 20 *European Law Review*, 539

David Fontana, 'Docket control and the Success of Constitutional Courts', in Tom Ginsburg & Rosalind Dixon (eds), *Handbook of Comparative Constitutional Law* (Edward Elgar, Cheltenham 2011), 624

Alicia Hinarejos, 'Social Legitimacy and the Court of Justice of the EU: Some Reflections on the Role of the Advocate General' (2011–2012) 14 *Cambridge YB EurLegal Stud*, 615

Angela Huyne Zhang, 'The Faceless Court' (2015) *King's College London Law School Research Paper No 45*

Marc Jacob, *Precedents and Case-based Reasoning in the European Court of Justice — Unfinished Business* (Cambridge University Press, Cambridge 2014)

Niilo Jääskinen, 'Oma ja muiden oikeuskäytäntö oikeuslähteenä ylimpien suomalaisten ja eurooppalaisten tuomioistuimien ratkaisutoiminnassa' (2020) 7–8 *Lakimies*, 1205

Katalin Kelemen, 'Dissenting Opinions in Constitutional Courts' (2013) 14 *German Law Journal*, 1345

Anne Lise Kjær, 'Nonsense: The CILFIT Criteria Revisited: from the Perspective of Legal Linguistics' in Joseph Weiler et al (eds), *The New Legal Realism: Essays in Honour of Hjalte Rasmussen* (Djøf Forlag, København 2010), 297

Kaisa Koskinen, *Beyond Ambivalence. Postmodernity and the Ethics of Translation* (Tampereen yliopistopaino, Tampere 2000)

Koen Lenaerts, 'The Unity of European Law and the Overload of the ECJ—The System of Preliminary Rulings Revisited' (2005) 1 *The Global Community: Y.B. Int'l L. Jurisprudence*, 211

Koen Lenaerts, 'How the ECJ thinks: a study in judicial legitimacy' (2013) 36 *Fordham Int'l L.J.*, 1302

Koen Lenaerts, & José Antonio Gutiérrez-Fons, 'To say what the law of the EU is: methods of interpretation and the European Court of Justice' (2014) 20 *The Columbia Journal of European Law*, 3

Giuseppe Mancini and David Keeling, 'Language, culture and politics in the life of the European Court of Justice' (1995) 1 *Columbia Journal of European Law*, 397

Karen McAuliffe 'La traduction dans l'office des juges européens', in Alain Bailleux et al, (eds), *Traduction et droits européens: enjeux d'une rencontre* (Facultés universitaires Saint Louis, Bruxelles 2009), 24

Karen McAuliffe, 'Precedent at the ECJ: The Linguistic Aspect' (2013) 15 *Current Legal Issues*, 483

Karen McAuliffe, 'The Limitations of a Multilingual Legal System' (2013) 26 *International Journal for the Semiotics of Law*, 861

Karen McAuliffe, 'Behind the Scenes at the Court Of Justice: Drafting EU Law Stories' in Fernanda Nicola & Bill Davies (eds), *EU Law Stories: Contextual and Critical Histories of European Jurisprudence* (Cambridge University Press, Cambridge 2017), 35

Elina Paunio, *Legal Certainty in Multilingual EU Law: Language, Discourse and Reasoning at the European Court of Justice* (Ashgate Publishing, Farnham 2013)

Vlad Perju, 'Reason and Authority in the European Court of Justice' (2009) 49 *Virginia Journal of International Law*, 307

Sacha Prechal, Interview with judge Sacha Prechal of the Court of Justice: 'Part I: Working at the CJEU' of 18 December 2013. Available at <https://europeanlawblog.eu/2013/12/18/interview-with-judge-sacha-prechal-of-the-european-court-of-justice-part-i-working-at-the-cjeu/> accessed on 10 April 2021

Leonardo Pierdominici, *The Mimetic Evolution of the Court of Justice of the EU: A Comparative Law Perspective* (Palgrave MacMillan, Cham, 2020)

Urska Šadl, 'Precedent in the Sui Generis Legal Order: A Mine Run Approach' (2014) 20 *European Law Journal*, 544

Konrad Schiemann 'The application of general principles of Community law by English courts', in Francis Jacobs et al (eds), *European Community Law in the English Courts* (Clarendon, Oxford 1998), 137

Takis Tridimas, 'Precedent and the Court of Justice: A Jurisprudence of Doubt?', in Julie Dickson et al (eds), *Philosophical Foundations of European Union Law* (Oxford University Press, Oxford 2012), 307

Joseph Weiler, *The Constitution of Europe* (Cambridge University Press, Cambridge 1999)

Susan Wright 'The Language of the Law in Multilingual Contexts: Unpicking the English of the EU Courts' Judgments' (2016) 37 *Statute Law Review*, 156

Special report of the Court of Auditors no 14/2017: Performance review of case management at the Court of Justice of the European Union, p. 19. Available at: <https://www.eca.europa.eu/Lists/ECADocuments/SR17_14/SR_CJEU_EN.pdf> accessed 9 April 2021

The Year in Review, Annual Report, Court of Justice of the European Union, 2019. Available at: <https://curia.europa.eu/jcms/upload/docs/application/pdf/2020-05/ra_pan_2019_interieur_en_final.pdf> accessed 9 April 2021

Precedents – A Question of Memory*

Julius Schumann

I. Introduction

Whether one is looking at the common law or the civil law, courts both here and there use prior decisions to create subsequent decisions. Some do so by citing them in the judgement; others consider them without referencing to these prior decisions in the text of the judgement.[1] Reference to previous decisions indicates a knowledge of them, regardless of whether they are accorded a binding effect or are merely used as supporting arguments. For the aim of this text, the notion of "precedent" should therefore be defined broadly as a "past event [...] which serves as a guide for present action".[2] The fact that this knowledge of precedents can lessen the costs of decision-making has inspired *Posner* and *Landes* from a law & economics perspective to consider a body of precedents in a given area of law as a

* I would like to thank Ulrike Frauenberger-Pfeiler, Caterina Grasl, Mario Hössl-Neumann, Stephanie Nitsch, Julian Pehm and the participants of a seminar hosted by Ars Iuris Vienna for helpful comments on my text to make my arguments on some points clearer. As always, the responsibility for any imperfections in the text rests with the author alone.

1 Cf for example the discussion at the Conseil d'Etat in the report of the groupe de travail sur la rédaction des décisions de la juridiction administrative présidé par le président Philippe Martin, 'Rapport' 30–32 <https://www.conseil-etat.fr/Media/actualites/documents/2012/rapport_redaction_decisions_juradm_2012> accessed 12 July 2021; see Weber, *Der Begründungsstil von Conseil constitutionnel und Bundesverfassungsgericht: Eine vergleichende Analyse der Spruchpraxis* (2019) 206–208 and regarding the development at the French Cour de cassation see 188–192 as well as the 'Rapport de la Commission de réflexion sur la réforme de la Cour de cassation' 129-178 <https://www.courdecassation.fr/IMG///Rapport%20-sur%20la%20r%C3%A9forme%20de%20la%20Cour%20de%20cassation.pdf> accessed 12 July 2021; see also Taruffo, 'Institutional Factors Influencing Precedents' in MacCormick and Summers (eds), *Interpreting Precedents: A Comparative Study* (1997) 454–455.

2 Duxbury, *The Nature and Authority of Precedent* (2008) 1; on the question of a binding effect of previous decisions on future decisions in civil law jurisdictions, see Kodek, 'Precedents in Private Law – A Civil Law Perspective', in this volume.

capital stock that diminishes in value by time and overruling.[3] It is as *Baker* phrased it, neither in the common law nor in the civil law world a "court can afford to ignore the way the court has acted in the past".[4] If we go along with *Posner*'s metaphor, we can pose the question how this capital stock is preserved and how it is accessed when needed. At the time *Posner* and *Landes*' study was published, lawyers still had to rely on printed law reports. Nowadays, databases give access to a high number of decisions and make keyword search an everyday tool. This is a development that has not stopped at the courts. The change in the media in which precedents are preserved has given rise to publications on the influence of media on legal research and the use of precedents stemming, somewhat unsurprisingly, primarily from Anglo-American legal scholars.[5] Yet, the German literature on legal methodology also offers some reflections on how to deal with this change in the way court decisions are processed.[6]

---

3 Posner, *Economic analysis of law* (2014) 759–760 et 769; Landes and Posner, 'Legal Precedent: A Theoretical and Empirical Analysis' (1976) 19 *The Journal of Law & Economics*, 249.

4 Baker, 'Preface' in Baker (ed), *Judicial Records, Law Reports, and the Growth of Case Law* (2013) 5.

5 E.g.: Berring, 'Collapse of the Structure of the Legal Research Universe: The Imperative of Digital Information' (1994) 69 *Washington Law Review*, 9; Berring, 'Legal Research and the World of Thinkable Thoughts' (2000) 2 *The Journal of Appelate Practice and Process*, 305; Ezra Dodd Church, 'Technological Conservatism: How Information Technology Prevents the Law from Changing' (2004) 83 *Texas Law Review*, 561; Devins and Klein, 'The Vanishing Common Law Judge?' (2017) 165 *University of Pennsylvania Law Review*, 595; Hanson, 'From Key Numbers to Keywords: How Automation Has Transformed the Law' (2002) 94 *Law Library Journal*, 563; Harvey, *Collisions in the Digital Paradigm: Law and Rule-Making in the Internet Age* (2017) 152–171; Katsh, *The Electronic Media and the Transformation of Law* (1989) 17–48; Kuh, 'Electronically Manufactured Law' (2008) 22 *Harvard Journal of Law & Technology*, 223; Outler, 'Mapping the Achieved Values of Legal Reference Books onto the Digital Future' (2015) 34 *Legal Reference Services Quarterly*, 177; Tiersma, *Parchment, Paper, Pixels: Law and the Technologies of Communication* (2010); a Canadian view: Vries, 'Legal Research, Legal Reasoning and Precedent in Canada in the Digital Age' (2018) 487 *Advocates' Quarterly*, 1.

6 E.g.: Schuhr, 'Rechtsprechungsdatenbanken als Format rechtlicher Information – Hilfsmittel oder Ersatz für Kommentare?' in Funke and Lachmayer (eds), *Formate der Rechtswissenschaft* (2017); Raselli, 'Gedanken über den Einfluss computergestützter Informationsverarbeitung auf die Rechtsprechung' (2002) *SJZ*, 605; Strauch, 'Wandel des Rechts durch juristische Datenbanken' (2007) *DVBl*, 1000; Lepsius, 'Kontextualisierung als Aufgabe der Rechtswissenschaft' (2019) 74 *Juristenzeitung*, 793; Reimer, *Juristische Methodenlehre* (2020) Rz 405; Strauch, *Methodenlehre des gerichtlichen Erkenntnisverfahrens: Prozesse richterlicher Kognition* (2017) 601–613; Wolf, 'Richterliche Entscheidungsroutinen als Gegenstand und Leitfaden der

This text aims to steer the debate on the media of precedents back to the fundamental question of how precedents are made available and accessible to the court itself. For this purpose, the text starts by examining supreme courts from an organizational perspective not only as major actors in creating precedents[7] but also in preserving the memory of them.[8] In this regard, the reasoning of decisions will be considered not only as a justification to the parties, but rather as a way of shaping the court's recollections. Therefore, the text pays special attention to archives and their technical development. Finally, a significant actor outside the court will be touched upon, namely legal scholarship. Thereby, the specific relationship between legal scholarship and the courts in the preservation of memory will be addressed.

II Storing and Retrieving Decisions at the Court

Duxbury starts the first chapter of his well-known book "The Nature and Authority of Precedent" by speaking of precedents as the "usable past".[9] But what is it that makes the past usable? It takes particular efforts in courts to make the past available and accessible and to thereby create their own "institutional memory". Introducing the term of "institutional memory", this section will show that by taking a look at different Central European Supreme Courts, it becomes clear that storing and retrieving the memory of previous decisions plays a significant role in their structure and administration.

---

juristischen Methodenlehre: zivilrechtliche Perspektiven' in Reimer (ed), *Juristische Methodenlehre aus dem Geist der Praxis?* (2016) 86.

7 Their role is often simply a result of the hierarchical court organization, cf Taruffo (n 1) 437–440.

8 See their role in maintaining databases in several jurisdictions at II.A.c.

9 See the heading of the Introduction to Duxbury (n 2) 1; he is not, of course, the first person to use this term in connection with precedents: Ridi, 'The Shape and Structure of the 'Usable Past': An Empirical Analysis of the Use of Precedent in International Adjudication' (2019) 10 *Journal of International Dispute Settlement*, 200, 202 (fn 8).

A. Storing: Institutional Measures for an Institutional Memory

a. What Makes a Memory Institutional?

In the early common law, before the rise of printed law reports in the 16th century,[10] judges and barristers discussed the law in court, recalling legal arguments and decisions[11] mainly from memory during the proceedings.[12] *Tiersma* describes this interplay between barristers and judges as a form of "institutional memory".[13] However, given the growing number of decisions, lawyers and judges no longer made the common law common knowledge.[14] Yet, this did not make the need for an institutional memory vanish. In addition to the memories stored in the minds of judges and lawyers, additional measures had to be taken. They all shape the institutional memory of courts today.

The term institutional memory, also commonly referred to as "organizational memory",[15] is understood from a functional perspective[16] as „stored information from an organization's history that can be brought to bear on present decisions"[17] and its definition is unsurprisingly close to a basic notion of precedent.[18] The principal idea is that an organization is able

10 Ibbetson, 'Case-Law and Doctrine' in Schulze and Seif (eds), *Richterrecht und Rechtsfortbildung in der Europäischen Rechtsgemeinschaft* (2003) 33; Ross, 'The Memorial Culture of Early Modern English Lawyers: Memory as Keyword, Shelter, and Identity, 1560–1640' (1998) 10 *Yale JL & Human*, 229, 313; Tiersma (n 5) 181.

11 See the historical connection between the rise in the importance of decisions as sources and the first records of decisions: Tiersma (n 5) 179–180. However, the principle of binding precedent was not established before the 19th century, see e.g. Plucknett, *A Concise History of the Common Law* (2010) 349–350.

12 Tiersma (n 5) 178–179.

13 Ibid.

14 Tiersma (n 5) 215–216.

15 The term used is often linked to a specific underlying concept, for an overview of trends in research of organizational memory see e.g. Casey, *Organizational identity and memory: A multidisciplinary approach* (2019) 17–60.

16 Cf the categorization of four different perspectives: Foroughi and others, 'Organizational Memory Studies' (2020) 41 *Organization Studies*, 1725, 1730–1738.

17 Walsh and Ungson, 'Organizational Memory' (1991) 16 *The Academy of Management Review*, 57, 61; cf also Jain, 'Is Organizational Memory a Useful Capability?: An Analysis of Its Effects on Productivity, Absorptive Capacity, and Adaption' in Argote and Levine (eds), *The Oxford Handbook of Group and Organizational Learning* (2020) 295.

18 Duxbury (n 2) 1; Jacob, *Precedents and case-based reasoning in the European Court of Justice: Unfinished business* (2014) 10.

to store and retrieve acquired knowledge[19] – an approach that can also be applied to courts as organizations.[20]

The loci, which *Walsh* and *Ungson* in their foundational work call "storage bins",[21] in which this knowledge is stored range from individuals, culture, and transformation to the structure and ecology of an organization.[22] Additionally, organizational knowledge can be stored outside the organization, in so called external archives, such as former members of the organization or others in the environment of the organization that keep records.[23] Thus, one can identify organizational memory as "a structure of repositories in which different forms of knowledge are stored, and from which knowledge can be retrieved".[24] Looking at a court from this organizational perspective, various loci or knowledge repositories can be identified. Previous decisions, which are of interest here, are usually communicated verbally or in writing. Without dwelling on the controversial explicit vs tacit knowledge dichotomy[25], we can therefore consider them explicit knowledge. These decisions as documents produced in the organization of courts constitute a distinct formalized way of memory. Courts use these documents when recollecting a specific case. This reliance on documents in remembering past events also shows a weakness, not only in relation to courts, of the identified retention bins of *Walsh and*

19 See already Walsh and Ungson (n 17), 62–70.

20 Reflections on an institutional memory in courts can be found, for example, in: Creamer and Godzimirska, 'Trust in the Court: The Role of the Registry of the European Court of Human Rights' (2019) 30 *European Journal of International Law*, 665, 681–682; Jacob (n 18) 84–86; Lundmark, *Charting the Divide Between Common and Civil Law* (2012) 352 Reiter, *Gerichtsinterne Organisation: Best Practices* (2015) 252–257; Schweighofer, 'Knowledge management and administration of justice' (2004) 18 *International Review of Law, Computers & Technology*, 47; cf also the observations of Haberler, *Die höchstgerichtliche Entscheidung: Eine empirische Studie zur Entscheidungsfindung in Zivilrechtssachen am OGH* (2014) 74–82.

21 Walsh and Ungson (n 17), 63.

22 Ibid 63–66; see also Jain (n 17) 298–301.

23 Walsh and Ungson (n 17), 66–67.

24 Fiedler and Welpe, 'How do organizations remember? The influence of organizational structure on organizational memory' (2010) 31 *Organization Studies*, 381, 382.

25 See Hedesstrom and Whitley, 'What is Meant by Tacit Knowledge? Towards a Better Understanding of the Shape of Actions' (2000) *ECIS 2000 Proceedings* <https://aisel.aisnet.org/ecis2000/29> accessed 12 July 2021 and their differentiation into two schools the "difficulty school" and the "de facto school"; Taal, *Working separately together* (2016) 27–29.

Ungson. They mention "records and files" only in passing as "a memory aid" to individuals. Although judges themselves are the other major repository of previous decisions, this does not, however, reflect the present-day significance of such records in courts, which are kept in databases for decades independently of individuals. Similar criticism is voiced in the literature on organizational knowledge theory particularly with regard to the extensive use of computer-based information technologies in organizations today.[26] Yet, even before this technological development, significant knowledge repositories in the form of structured decision collections can be found in courts. This part of organizational memory will be referred to here as the (internal) archive in order to conceptually include non-digital document-storage in addition to databases.[27] Yet, the aim of this chapter is not to define all sorts of loci possible at courts, but rather to exemplify in the next section which institutional measures are taken to support the development of an organizational memory regarding decisions a court has rendered.

b. Lawyers at the Court

Today, lawyers are widely actors external to the court who depend on the published memory of the court as a source for their submissions and can only encourage recollection from the published memory in a specific case.[28] They can be considered external archives in *Walsh* and *Ungson*'s sense.[29] The close institutionalized connection that *Tiersma* describes with regard to the early common law no longer exists.[30] Nevertheless, also in the 20th century a court-affiliated advocacy can be observed as making a contribution to an institutional memory. One example for this is the Ger-

---

26 Olivera, 'Memory Systems In Organizations: An Empirical Investigation Of Mechanisms For Knowledge Collection, Storage And Access' (2000) 37 *Journal of Management Studies*, 811, 813; Stein and Zwass, 'Actualizing Organizational Memory with Information Systems' (1995) 6 *Information Systems Research*, 85, 90.

27 Jain (n 17) 301 classifies databases as "external archives", but since they are different from other external archives as defined by Walsh and Ungson and are also not external, this terminology has been avoided here.

28 See also the observations of Tiersma (n 5) 215–216; lawyers involved in the proceedings who publish in this role can be regarded as an exception here.

29 See above II.A.a.

30 Tiersma (n 5) 215–216 mentions the increasing size of the legal community as a reason for that.

man Supreme Court.[31] Even today, only those lawyers who are admitted to proceedings before the German Supreme Court may represent clients before the latter in civil matters ("Rechtsanwälte am Bundesgerichtshof"). There are currently thirty-eight of them.[32] Already during the time of the "Reichsgericht", the predecessor of today's Supreme Court, the lawyers were part of the small group that was able to consult on the internal collection of decisions.[33] Their contribution to an institutional memory becomes even more evident by looking at the participation of *Philipp Möhring*, a lawyer at the Supreme Court, in the publication of the internal collection of decisions ("Nachschlagewerk") in the 1950s, which contained annotations of the judgements by judges and lawyers.[34] It should also be mentioned that the initiative for such an internal collection did not come from the judges but from the Chief Public Prosecutor at the Reichsgericht.[35]

c. *Facilities of the Court*

A substantial contribution to an institutional memory can be seen in the case of such "advocates" who are not entrusted with party representation but who take on a special role at the court itself. Such are for example the "Parquet général" at the Cour de cassation[36] or the Advocate General at the CJEU,[37] who both contribute to the observance of the Court's previous

---

31 Throughout the text, the term "German Supreme Court" refers to the Bundesgerichtshof.

32 Rechtsanwaltskammer am BGH, 'Verzeichnis' <https://www.rak-bgh.de/verzeichnis> accessed 12 July 2021.

33 Schubert and Glöckner, *Nachschlagewerk des Reichsgerichts Bürgerliches Gesetzbuch: §§ 1 – 133* (1994) XII.

34 Schneider, 'Einfluß und Aufgaben der Anwaltschaft am Bundesgerichtshof' in Krüger-Nieland (ed), *25 Jahre Bundesgerichtshof* (1975) 84–85; Walker, 'Die richterliche Veröffentlichungspraxis in der Kritik' (1998) 34 *JurPC*, Abs. 1 – 163, Abs. 117 <https://www.jurpc.de/jurpc/show?id=19980034> accessed 12 July 2021.

35 Schubert and Glöckner (n 33) XX, who, however, note that judges may only have been hiding behind his request.

36 Ferrand, 'Der Avocat général bei der Cour de cassation und die richterliche Rechtsfortbildung in Frankreich' (2016) 80 *Rabels Zeitschrift für ausländisches und internationales Privatrecht*, 288, 294.

37 Jacob (n 18) 199–200; Mortelmans, 'The Court Under the Influence of its Advocates General: An Analysis of the Case Law on the Functioning of the Internal Market' (2005) 24 *Yearbook of European Law*, 127.

case law.[38] The "Generalprokuratur" (Procurator General's Office) at the Austrian Supreme Court[39] can also be regarded as such a body, even though its field of activity was limited at an early stage and it is now active in criminal matters only.[40]

Nevertheless, the Austrian Supreme Court took on a pioneering role in fostering the creation of an institutional memory for the courts of the 19th and 20th centuries by the court administration. The reason for the call for a common memory at the court at that time lay in the increase in the number of judges resulting from an enlargement of the court's jurisdiction, with the simultaneous demand for a uniform application of the law also in the new territories.[41] In addition to the creation of comprehensive decision archives in the middle of the 19th century, the Court established the so-called "Evidenzbüro" at the beginning of the 19th century. This special office, which still exists today, was and is responsible for keeping records of decisions and making judges aware of them. Its most significant contribution is the creation of headnotes extracted from decisions, called "Rechtssätze".[42] To a growing extent, it is also responsible for providing legal research to today's judges.[43]

A quite similar function is fulfilled by the Italian Ufficio del Massimario at the Corte di Cassazione, whose origins date back to the year 1924.[44] This office does not only extract headnotes, the so-called "massima",[45]

---

38 However, the closeness between the court and the *Parquet général* at the Cour de cassation resulted in convictions on Article 6 ECHR by the ECtHR: Ferrand (n 36), 299–304.

39 Throughout the text, the term "Austrian Supreme Court" refers to the Oberster Gerichtshof.

40 Aicher, 'Geschichte der Generalprokuratur' in Kohl and Reiter-Zatloukal (eds), *"... das Interesse des Staates zu wahren": Staatsanwaltschaften und andere Einrichtungen zur Vertretung öffentlicher Interessen. Geschichte, Gegenwart, Perspektiven* (2018) 119–122.

41 Wahle, 'Vorwort' in Redaktionsausschuss des Obersten Gerichtshofes (ed), *Die Judikate und Sprüche des Obersten Gerichtshofes seit seinem Bestande* (1950) VIII.

42 Cf § 14 OGHG and § 76 Z 3 'Geschäftsordnung des Obersten Gerichtshofes 2019' <https://www.ogh.gv.at/media/ogh-geo-2019.pdf> accessed 12 July 2021. However, the creation of headnotes is usually made in consultation with the panel of the Supreme Court that has rendered the decision.

43 Danzl and Hopf, *Oberster Gerichtshof* (2017) 113–114.

44 Giovanni Amoroso, 'Nomofilachia e Massimario' 3 <https://www.cortedicassazione.it/cassazione-resources/resources/cms/documents/Il_precedente_ed_il_ruolo_del_Massimario_s07.pdf> accessed 12 July 2021.

45 Diedrich, *Präjudizien im Zivilrecht* (2004) 510–519; Romito and Tracogna, 'Standardization of Judicial Practice in Italy' (2013) 3 *Union of Jurists of Romania Law*

from the decisions as the Evidenzbüro in Austria does but also supplies information on previous case law.[46] Such a facility can also be found at the ECtHR, where the Jurisconsult of the ECtHR Registry "is responsible for ensuring the consistency of case-law and supplying opinions and information, in particular to the trial benches and the members of the Court".[47] The Research and Documentation Directorate at the CJEU, besides doing research on legal systems of the member states, also provides an early review of all requests for a preliminary ruling. Moreover, it is under the supervision of the Judge-Rapporteur responsible for the summaries of the judgments and orders published in the European Court Reports and the processing of decisions for several research tools.[48] Another example of this kind is the Service de la documentation, des études et du rapport (SDER), which is the documentation, research, and reporting department at the Cour de cassation.[49] The work of these institutions goes beyond decision preparation. In most cases, they are also responsible for maintaining archives such as databases, some of which are open to the public.[50] Such offices are sometimes supplemented or surrogated by référendaires or law clerks which are assigned to individual judges or panels for support

---

Review, 1, 14–15; Siltala, *A Theory of Precedent: From Analytical Positivism to a Post-Analytical Philosophy of Law* (2000) 128–132; Taruffo and La Torre, 'Precedent in Italy' in MacCormick and Summers (eds), *Interpreting Precedents: A Comparative Study* (1997) 148–149.

46 David, *International Encyclopedia of Comparative Law. Vol 2: The Legal Systems of the World, Their Comparison and Unification: Chapter 3: Sources of Law* (1984) 195; Romito and Tracogna (n 45), 11; Schlagböhmer, 'Das automatisierte juristische Informationssystem des Kassationsgerichtshofes in Rom „Italgiure"' (1975) 4 *Datenverarbeitung im Recht*, 61, 61–65.

47 ECtHR, 'ECHR Registry' <https://www.echr.coe.int/Documents/Registry_ENG.pdf> accessed 12 July 2021; see also Creamer and Godzimirska (n 20), 681–682; for a more general discussion of the registries and legal secretariats in international judicial institutions as legal memory see: Cartier and Hosse, 'The Role of Registries and Legal Secretariats in International Judicial Institutions' in Romano, Alter and Shani (eds), *The Oxford Handbook of International Adjudication* (2013) 721–723.

48 CJEU, 'Research and Documentation Directorate' <https://curia.europa.eu/jcms/jcms/Jo2_11968/> accessed 12 July 2021.

49 Cour de cassation, 'About the Court' <https://www.courdecassation.fr/about_the_court_9256.html> accessed 12 July 2021.

50 See e.g. the "Rechtsinformation des Bundes – Justiz" that is inter alia filled by the Austrian Supreme Court: http://ris.bka.gv.at.

in the legal research.[51] Well-known examples of these are the CJEU[52], the German Supreme Court[53], and – outside Europe – the US Supreme Court.[54]

A mere post-processing of the decisions is undertaken by the "Dokumentationsstelle" at the German Supreme Court,[55] which primarily prepares decisions for the database of the provider "juris"[56], the Centro Elettronico di Documentazione (C.E.D.), which inter alia prepares the decision for Italgiure,[57] as well as the Library Directorate of the CJEU, which complements the Research and Documentation Directorate in the dissemination of decisions by publishing the decisions on the EUR-Lex and Curia sites.[58]

d. Panels and Specialization

The need for a shared memory of decisions at a court is particularly evident when the court is split into several panels[59] as is quite usual in Central Europe.[60] However, a division of the Court bears a certain risk that

51 Uzelac, 'Supreme Courts in the 21st Century: should organisation follow the function?' (2019) *Studia Iuridica*, 125, 127.

52 Jacob (n 18) 200–201; Kenney, 'Beyond Principals and Agents' (2000) 33 *Comparative Political Studies*, 593, 604–612; see also Paunio,'Reasoning at the CJEU: linguistic, institutional and systemic constraints', in this volume.

53 Stürner, 'Sharing Responsibility: The German Federal Court of Justice and the Civil Appellate System' in Bravo-Hurtado and van Rhee (eds), *Supreme Courts under Pressure: Controlling Caseload in the Administration of Civil Justice* (2021) XX; see also, for example, a study of the German Bundesverfassungsgericht: Kranenpohl, *Hinter dem Schleier des Beratungsgeheimnisses: Der Willensbildungs- und Entscheidungsprozess des Bundesverfassungsgerichts* (2010) 88–91.

54 Kenney (n 52), 601–604.

55 Schliebs, 'Dokumentationsstelle, Nachschlagewerk und Entscheidungsversand des Bundesgerichtshofs' in Geiß (ed), *Festschrift aus Anlaß des fünfzigjährigen Bestehens von Bundesgerichtshof, Bundesanwaltschaft und Rechtsanwaltschaft beim Bundesgerichtshof* (2000) 761–773.

56 See 'juris' <http://www.juris.de> accessed 12 July 2021.

57 Corte di Cassazione, 'CED' <https://www.cortedicassazione.it/corte-di-cassazione/it/ced.page> accessed 19 May 2021.

58 CJEU, 'Library Directorate' <https://curia.europa.eu/jcms/jcms/Jo2_11875/en/> accessed 12 July 2021.

59 Taruffo (n 1) 447.

60 Schönberger, 'Höchstrichterliche Rechtsfindung und Auslegung gerichtlicher Entscheidungen: 2. Referat' in Grzeszick, Calliess and Lienbacher (eds), *Grundsatzfragen der Rechtsetzung und Rechtsfindung. Referate und Diskussionen auf der*

the knowledge at the Court is divided as well. Supreme courts have tried to counterbalance this potential disparity of information insofar as judges are assigned to specialized panels. Such specialized panels, therefore, contribute to the development of an institutional memory as they enable in-depth study of court practice on a specific subject and encourage the exchange between similarly specialized judges.[61] Moreover, such panels provide not only an informal opportunity for exchange among judges at the court,[62] but also a formal one in the panel itself.[63] However, there is a certain risk that the knowledge of one formation is not shared among members of other formations.[64] Furthermore, a splitting of the judicial body according to subject matters cannot completely prevent that a panel is faced with a legal question that has already been decided by another panel. This is, of course, particularly evident when, as at the Austrian Supreme Court, there is a mixed system between special competences of panels (senates) and an additional distribution of cases on a single (more general) matter among all panels.[65] Also, the further subdivision

---

Tagung der Vereinigung der Deutschen Staatsrechtslehrer in Münster vom 5. bis 8. Oktober 2011 (2012) 308–309.

61 Ibid 313; cf also Maultzsch, *Streitentscheidung und Normbildung durch den Zivilprozess: Eine rechtsvergleichende Untersuchung zum deutschen, englischen und US-amerikanischen Recht* (2012) 398–399; this can also be viewed critically: Neumayr, 'Lauter Bäume, kein Wald' in Christandl et al. (eds), *Intra- und Interdisziplinarität im Zivilrecht: Jahrbuch junger Zivilrechtswissenschaftler* (2018) 14–15.

62 On the importance of the court cafeteria for informal exchanges between panels, see: Stegmaier, *Wissen, was Recht ist: Richterliche Rechtspraxis aus wissenssoziologischethnografischer Sicht* (2009) 306; for more general observations of such informal exchanges see a study at the Austrian Supreme Court: Haberler (n 20) 76–78; an interesting study also stems from Taal (n 25), which, however, does not differentiate according to the type of knowledge that is shared (see therefore the limitations of this study on pp 122–125).

63 See the findings of the study regarding knowledge sharing of Baas, *De meerwaarde van meervoud. Verschillen en overeenkomsten tussen meervoudige en enkelvoudige rechtspraak, in het bijzonder in civiele zaken* (2020) 329.

64 Cf Jain (n 17) 299.

65 This is also a significant difference to the BGH: Kodek, 'Funktion und Arbeitsweise des OGH – die Binnensicht' in Kodek (ed), *Zugang zum OGH: Vorträge des Symposiums "Zugang zum OGH in Zivil- und Strafsachen"* (2012) 102; Neumayr, 'Lauter Bäume, kein Wald' (n 61) 14; for an English overview on the structure of the Austrian Supreme Court see e.g. Scholz-Berger, 'Access to the Austrian Oberster Gerichtshof: Attempts to Strike a Balance Between Adequate Workload and Adequate Review' in Bravo-Hurtado and van Rhee (eds), *Supreme Courts under Pressure: Controlling Caseload in the Administration of Civil Justice* (2021) 108–109.

of specialized divisions into sections as present at the Cour de cassation[66] does not facilitate the transfer of knowledge. Due to the risk of divergent decisions, legislators, such as those in France,[67] Germany,[68] and Austria,[69] have made efforts to resolve such inconsistencies between the panels by procedural solutions, namely the enlargement of the formation.[70] In Germany and Austria these solutions were accompanied by the creation of archives as knowledge repositories. In the Austrian monarchy, the Court even went so far as to tie the enlargement of its panels expressly to the contents of archives.[71] Thus, senates could depart from legal questions already answered by the court and entered as headnotes in the collections called "Spruchrepertorium" resp "Judikatenbuch" only by enlarging the panel. This mechanism was finally abolished at the end of the 1960s due to constitutional concerns.[72]

e. *Archives*

Archives offer organizations the most comprehensive way to store knowledge.[73] In particular, they allow the intentional storage of knowledge.[74] Historically, courts have always sought to collect their decisions since they map the activity of the court and form a common basis for the memory of trials.[75] It is therefore not surprising that courts have also benefited from

---

66 Cour de cassation, 'About the Court' <https://www.courdecassation.fr/about_the_court_9256.html> accessed 12 July 2021.

67 Ibid.

68 Stürner (n 53) 78.

69 Feldner, *Verstärkte Senate beim Obersten Gerichtshof: Rechtsprechung im Spannungsfeld zwischen Unabhängigkeit, Richtigkeit und Einheitlichkeit* (2001); Scholz-Berger (n 65) 108; critical with regard to the effectiveness of the instrument, for example: Neumayr, 'Lauter Bäume, kein Wald' (n 61) 14.

70 See also for a more detailed overview of these procedural solutions: Kodek, 'Precedents in Private Law – A Civil Law Perspective', in this volume.

71 See reg the development of these two collections during the monarchy: Wahle (n 41).

72 Fasching, 'Zur verfassungsrechtlichen Rechtfertigung der Bindung des Obersten Gerichtshofes an seine Entscheidungen' in Fasching (ed), *Festschrift für Hans Schima zum 75. Geburtstag* (1969) 143; Feldner (n 69) 22–25.

73 Jain (n 17) 301; Olivera (n 26), 814; see also Schweighofer (n 20), 50–51 et 53.

74 Olivera (n 26), 817.

75 See e.g. Baker (n 4) 7–8; Ibbetson and Wijffels, 'Case Law in the Making: The Techniques and Methods of Judicial Records and Law Reports' in Wijffels (ed), *Case Law in the Making: Vol 1: Essays* (1997); Stölzel, *Die Entwicklung des*

developments in the archival field. In addition to the "Präjudizienbücher" ("precedent books"),[76] other methods of filing were added from the 19th century onwards. In the 20th century, for example, card indexes also made their way into courts. They were used inter alia at the Supreme Courts in France[77], Italy[78], Germany[79], and Austria[80]. The result of centuries of development,[81] index cards were seen as a new form of modern office organization in the 20th century. In the German literature such card indexes were described as the "memory of the company"[82] or "mobile memory"[83].[84] The construction of such card index systems also requires an integration of these archives into the organization and its procedures.[85] The move to digital forms at most courts which mirror these archives is therefore hardly

---

gelehrten Richterthums in deutschen Territorien: eine rechtsgeschichtliche Untersuchung mit vorzugsweiser Berücksichtigung der Verhältnisse im Gebiete des ehemaligen Kurfürstenthums Hessen: Erster Band (1872) 177–186.

76 See for example the "Präjudizienbücher" at the Reichsgericht for each senate and also the "Nachschlagewerk" Schubert and Glöckner (n 33) XIV–XVI, or the "Spruchrepertorium" and the "Judikatenbuch" at the Austrian Supreme Court, Wahle (n 41).

77 David (n 46) 195; Szladits, *Guide to Foreign Legal Materials: French German Swiss* (1959) 61.

78 David (n 46) 195; Nagelsmeier-Linke, *Automatisierte juristische Informationssysteme: Gegenwärtiger Stand ihrer Entwicklung und ihre Bedeutung für die Bibliothekarische Praxis* (1980) 96.

79 Schubert and Glöckner (n 33) XXI, however, only an overview of the literature was recorded in this way. The "Nachschlagewerk", on the other hand, was stored in ring binders of the Leitz company at this time (see Gerstenkorn, 'Einführung: Die Dokumentation im Bereich der Bundesgerichte', in Gerstenkorn and Kirchner (eds), *Die Dokumentation der Bundesgerichte der Bundesrepublik Deutschland, Österreichs und der Schweiz* (1964) 5.

80 David (n 46) 195; Danzl and Hopf (n 43) 110.

81 For a concise history starting with Gessner's Bibliotheca universalis and the first card catalogue in a library in Vienna: Krajewski, *Paper machines: About cards & catalogs, 1548–1929* (2011); see also on the history of records: Vismann, Akten (2011).

82 Translated from Westphal, 'Grundzüge der Karteinutzung' in Löser and Couvé (eds), *Reformen in den städtischen Verwaltungen* (1930) 93.

83 Menzel, *Bürokunde: Schulausgabe* (1926) 30 quoted from Krajewski (n 81) 128.

84 See also other examples in Krajewski (n 81) 125–131; for principal considerations on memory and card indexes see Cevolini, 'Die Organisation des Gedächtnisses und das Gedächtnis der Organisation' in Dimbath and Heinlein (eds), *Die Sozialität des Erinnerns: Beiträge zur Arbeit an einer Theorie des sozialen Gedächtnisses* (2014).

85 Cevolini (n 84) 178.

surprising.[86] Whether we are looking at the Italian Italgiure,[87] the German Juris,[88] the French Database of the Cour de cassation,[89] or the Austrian RIS,[90] supreme courts have today transferred their archives into databases, most of which are even open to public.[91] Hence, the supreme courts are in line with the general trend regarding the importance of computer-based information technologies for the storing of organizational knowledge.[92] Therefore, the following section is concerned with the storing and retrieving of decisions from such archives.

B. *Retrieving from Archives*

a. *What We Store is What We Retrieve*

Even though it is a somewhat simple assertion, only what has been stored can be retrieved. Therefore, the appeal to a previous decision in terms of its content cannot go beyond the stored memory of the process of decision-making. Thus, from an archival perspective, the documentation function of decisions becomes apparent.[93] In order to distinguish what is stored in archives of the process of decision-making, a distinction can be made along with *Luhmann* between the making of a decision ("Herstellung") and the communication or recording of the rendered decision ("Darstellung").[94]

86 See also, for example, the description of the change in the Swiss courts: Raselli (n 6), 606.

87 'Italgiure' <http://www.italgiure.giustizia.it/> accessed 12 July 2021.

88 'juris' <http://www.juris.de> accessed 12 July 2021.

89 Cour de cassation, 'Jurisprudence' <https://www.courdecassation.fr/jurisprudence_2/> accessed 12 July 2021.

90 'RIS' <https://www.ris.bka.gv.at/Jus/> accessed 12 July 2021.

91 For an overview of case law databases in Europe see Marc van Opijnen and others, 'On-line Publication of Court Decisions in the EU: Report of the Policy Group of the Project 'Building on the European Case Law Identifier'' (2017) <https://www.bo-ecli.eu/uploads/deliverables/Deliverable%20WS0-D1.pdf> accessed 12 July 2021.

92 Olivera (n 26), 814.

93 Cf Brink, *Über die richterliche Entscheidungsbegründung: Funktion – Position – Methodik* (1999) 29–30; Kischel, *Die Begründung: Zur Erläuterung staatlicher Entscheidungen gegenüber dem Bürger* (2003) 45–47.

94 Luhmann, *Recht und Automation in der öffentlichen Verwaltung: Eine verwaltungswissenschaftliche Untersuchung* (1966) 51; see also: Albers, 'Höchstrichterliche Rechtsfindung und Auslegung gerichtlicher Entscheidungen: 1. Referat' in Grzeszick, Calliess and Lienbacher (eds), *Grundsatzfragen der Rechtsetzung und*

Although the process of making a decision influences the way the decision is communicated,[95] it must be acknowledged that little of the process of making a decision is reflected in the communication or recording of the decision.[96] What is to be communicated of the context in which a decision was rendered is formalized by the long-established style of judicial reasoning.[97] The context of a decision is to be understood in a broad sense here. The notion of context ranges inter alia from the facts underlying the decision, over the line of decisions in which the decision is embedded, to extra-legal factors of decision-making including, for example, the time and effort invested in the decision.[98] Furthermore, the context can also include the parties' strategies of argumentation in their submissions. Especially the "legalistic, deductive and magisterial style" traditional in Europe tends to suppress contextualizing elements from the decision and thus stands in contrast to the "substantive, discursive and personalized judicial style" of the reasoning in common-law jurisdictions.[99] For instance, the disclosure

---

Rechtsfindung. Referate und Diskussionen auf der Tagung der Vereinigung der Deutschen Staatsrechtslehrer in Münster vom 5. bis 8. Oktober 2011 (2012) 264–265; Lautmann, *Justiz – die stille Gewalt: Teilnehmende Beobachtung und entscheidungssoziologische Analyse* (2011) 201–224; Morlok, Kolbel and Launhardt, 'Recht als Soziale Praxis: Eine Soziologische Perpektive in der Methodenlehre' (2000) 31 *Rechtstheorie*, 15, 27; Trute, 'Klugheit in juristischen Entscheidungen' in Scherzberg (ed), *Klugheit: Begriff – Konzepte – Anwendungen* (2008) 142–143; also recently: Masing and others (eds), *Entscheidungen und Entscheidungsprozesse der Rechtsprechung: Décisions juridictionnelles et processus décisionnels. Dokumentation des 9. Treffens des Deutsch-Französischen Gesprächskreises für Öffentliches Recht 2018* (2020).

95 With regard to internal procedural rules, e.g.: Kaiser, 'Herstellung und Darstellung von Entscheidungen des Bundesverfassungsgerichts' in Masing et al. (eds), *Entscheidungen und Entscheidungsprozesse der Rechtsprechung: Décisions juridictionnelles et processus décisionnels. Dokumentation des 9. Treffens des Deutsch-Französischen Gesprächskreises für Öffentliches Recht 2018* (2020) 1.

96 Morlok, Kolbel and Launhardt (n 94), 27.

97 See also Albers (n 94) 269 seeing decisions as special format of communication.

98 Cf for example Haberler (n 20) 84–87.

99 Taruffo (n 1) 448–450; see also: Kötz, *Über den Stil höchstrichterlicher Entscheidungen* (1973); Rebhahn, 'Der Urteilsstil des OGH im Vergleich mit den Höchstgerichten Deutschlands, Frankreichs und Englands' in Fischer-Czermak (ed), *Festschrift 200 Jahre ABGB* (2011); MacCormick and Summers, 'Further General Reflections and Conclusions' in MacCormick and Summers (eds), *Interpreting Precedents: A Comparative Study* (1997) 536; see also Kodek, 'Precedents in Private Law – A Civil Law Perspective', in this volume and regarding the CJEU Paunio, 'Reasoning at the CJEU: linguistic, institutional and systemic constraints', in this volume.

of facts in the reasoning of the Supreme Courts of France and England is entirely different. While in England, the facts form a central element of the judgment, there are hardly any facts to be found in the decisions of the Cour de cassation.[100] Moreover, civil law jurisdictions were traditionally more reluctant to introduce dissenting and concurring opinions.[101] In this case, such opinions are therefore not recorded in the published decisions. This hides organizational conflicts.[102] Nor is the consideration of prior decisions disclosed in the form of citations in the reasoning of every supreme court.[103]

Yet, the less or more inaccurately the context is preserved, the more likely is the court to change or even lose this kind of memory due to inadequacies in the way knowledge is stored. And although the actual process of decision-making is barely reflected in the decision itself, a judge of the supreme court not involved in the decision-making process is dependent on the repositories of the institutional memory of the court. Repositories which may offer additional insights into the context of previous decisions are on the one hand additional documents and on the other hand – a very important source besides the decision as a written document – judges who have personal knowledge of the context.

Although written decisions are the main source of written memory, preparatory documents for decisions (e.g. drafts, notes of the judges) are stored as well. These documents can provide additional information on the context of the decision. In Germany, for instance, the so-called "Senatsheft", a record that contains such preparatory documents, remains at the Supreme Court after the decision has been rendered.[104] Preparatory documents become all the more important in cases where the communicated reasoning of the decision is brief, either because of the general style of the judgment[105] or because of the possibility of an abbreviated

---

100 Taruffo (n 1) 451.

101 Ibid 450–451.

102 Luhmann, *Funktionen und Folgen formaler Organisation* (1964) 114–115 et 248–249; see also Lautmann (n 94) 207.

103 Rebhahn, 'Der Urteilsstil des OGH im Vergleich mit den Höchstgerichten Deutschlands, Frankreichs und Englands' (n 99) 1551–1554; Taruffo (n 1) 454–455; however, see the recent developments at the Cour de cassation: Weber (n 1) 191.

104 Huber, '§ 299' in Musielak and Voit (eds), *Zivilprozessordnung* (2021) Rz 7; Schmidt-Räntsch, 'Die Rechtsprechung der obersten Gerichtshöfe des Bundes (OGB)' in Riesenhuber (ed), *Europäische Methodenlehre: Handbuch für Ausbildung und Praxis* (2015) 533.

105 See above.

reasoning under the relevant statutory law.[106] However, in general there are certain limitations as to what a document can represent of the reality of an organization.[107] Document-based archives carry the particular risk of organizational memory being interpreted in a way that is not shared by all judges.[108] As texts, these documents are also subject to different interpretations. Hence, individuals, namely judges themselves, play an important role in remembering previous decisions and their context. Specifically, they can usually also recall the extra-legal context of the decision if it was important to the case. However, this presupposes that there exists at least one individual who has memories of the decision-making process, meaning that the decision may not have been made too long ago, and that at least one judge of the panel must be willing and able to share his or her knowledge. In the absence of this repository, the organizational memory must consequently change to a purely text-based one.

Therefore, the decision has to serve as a twofold means of communication to both internal and external audiences. Insofar as the court itself refers to previous decisions, these decisions serve as a repository of organizational memory internally; insofar as they are given to the parties or to the (professional) public, they serve to legitimize the decision externally. In addition, supreme courts also have a central function vis-à-vis lower courts, which as such are also external addressees.[109] While parties (and their representatives) and the judges involved have a special level of knowledge about the case, the other addressees are first and foremost dependent on the written and published decision. For these, alternative repositories of the organizational memory besides the decision usually remain unavailable. For instance, the "Senatsheft" can only be accessed after 30 years have passed.[110] Therefore, courts must also keep in mind in their reasoning that this form of external communication remains the only source on the basis

106 See, for example, Schuhr's comment that abbreviated decisions in databases have little informative value for third parties: Schuhr (n 6) 162–164.

107 Coffey, 'Analysing Documents' in Flick (ed), *The SAGE Handbook of Qualitative Data Analysis* (2014) 369–370; Morlok, Kolbel and Launhardt (n 94), 27.

108 Jain (n 17) 301.

109 Albers (n 94) 269; cf Taruffo (n 1) 451.

110 Also on the importance of the "Senatsheft" for research: Fleischer, 'Schlussbetrachtung: Gesellschaftsrechtliche Zeitgeschichte im Fallformat' in Fleischer and Thiessen (eds), *Gesellschaftsrechts-Geschichten* (2018) 772 who additionally notes that the German Bundesarchivgesetz (Federal Archives Act) aims for a period of 30 years, after which the files are handed over to the Federal Archives where they can be accessed.

of which a large audience – including legal scholars and lower courts and sometimes even the courts themselves – may interpret a decision.[111]

b. Retrieving in the Digital Age

The second half of the 20th century brought supreme courts the possibility of storing decisions electronically.[112] This allowed the previously existing physical archives of decisions to be transferred to databases. These databases often continue to be filled by the courts themselves, although in contrast to the previous resources in print form, they are now usually available to a wider public. However, this change in the way decisions are stored has also led to a change in their retrieval. Even before the use of databases, supreme courts were concerned with making relevant decisions retrievable as quickly and as precisely as possible when needed. This was made possible by standardizing the way decisions are recorded.[113] In the age of printing, the courts designed pre-coordinated indexing systems.[114] Therefore, courts needed to determine an organizing system serving all users or judges, as the physical storage could only be arranged once and in one way.[115] Examples are the already mentioned card indexes or decision registers in book form, which were sorted by subject matter. From a civil law perspective, it is not surprising that the sorting of decisions at the Austrian Supreme Court has been guided by paragraphs and codes; a similar method can also be found at courts in Germany.[116] In addition, there was also a keyword index which led to the relevant paragraphs. These collections often used headnotes as they facilitated inferring the content of the referred decision from the registers or index cards.[117] The headnotes, which were initially

---

111 Cf Payandeh, *Judikative Rechtserzeugung: Theorie, Dogmatik und Methodik der Wirkungen von Präjudizien* (2017) 458–459.

112 Bing, 'Let there be LITE: a brief history of legal information retrieval' (2010) 1 *European Journal of Law and Technology* <https://link.gale.com/apps/doc/A240098684/AONE?u=43wien&sid=AONE&xid=a9328aaa> accessed 12 July 2021.

113 Cf Berring, 'Collapse of the Structure of the Legal Research Universe' (n 5) 21; Ezra Dodd Church (n 5), 574.

114 Berring, 'Collapse of the Structure of the Legal Research Universe' (n 5) 18–25; Hanson (n 5), 574.

115 Berring, 'Collapse of the Structure of the Legal Research Universe' (n 5) 22

116 Cf the annex in Gerstenkorn and Kirchner (eds), *Die Dokumentation der Bundesgerichte der Bundesrepublik Deutschland, Österreichs und der Schweiz* (1964).

117 See for example the "Paragraphenkarteikarte" at the Austrian Supreme Court on page 121 in ibid.

intended for internal use only, were in some states made available to practitioners outside the court.[118] This accessibility turned them in to a separate legal format for communicating decisions.[119] Today, judges have at their disposal case law databases that no longer bind them to pre-coordinated indexes.[120] With full-text storage also came full-text search. Users can via the online search mask design their own search by means of the keywords that they identify as relevant.[121]

i. Availability and Forgetting

Databases have hardly any storage limitations. Full-texts of decisions that would otherwise have filled entire shelves now only consume the space of the hard drives on which they are stored.[122] From a technical point of view, this enables a relatively comprehensive record of decisions without any limitations at the courts.[123] This technical possibility was also the impetus for a book by *Spiros Simitis* entitled "Informationskrise des Rechts und Datenverarbeitung" (Information Crisis of Law and Data Processing) 1970,[124] which received widespread attention in the German-speaking world.[125] With reference to different projects carried out at the time at

118 This was done at a relatively early stage in the 19th century in Austria regarding the "Judikatenbuch" and "Spruchrepertorium", see Wahle (n 41) XXVIII–XXXVIII.

119 Fleischer, 'Höchstrichterliche Leitsätze und richterliche Normbildung im Gesellschaftsrecht' (2018) 39 *ZIP*, 605, 607.

120 Taruffo (n 1) 452.

121 Kuh (n 5), 246; Vries (n 5), 27.

122 Harvey (n 5) 163; Katsh (n 5) 21.

123 See Jacob (n 18) 85: „It is hard to image that any modern technological innovation other than word processing has had such an effect on the practice of law as the introduction of searchable databanks.".

124 Simitis, *Informationskrise des Rechts und Datenverarbeitung* (1970); for a contextualization of this book, see for instance: Kaiser, *Die Kommunikation der Verwaltung: Diskurse zu den Kommunikationsbeziehungen zwischen staatlicher Verwaltung und Privaten in der Verwaltungsrechtswissenschaft der Bundesrepublik Deutschland* (2009) 130–131.

125 Cf e.g.: Geist, *Rechtsdatenbanken und Relevanzsortierung* (2017) 49; Jahnel, 'Rechtsdatenbanken für Wissenschaft und Praxis' (1988) *ÖJZ*, 301, 301; Kilian, 'Idee und Wirklichkeit der Rechtsinformatik in Deutschland' (2017) 33 *Computer und Recht*, 202, 204; Kramer, 'Informationskrise des Rechts und Veröffentlichungspraxis' (1976) *ZRP*, 84; Kreppel, 'Informationskrise, Verlagskrise und „Besseres Recht"' (1975) *NJW*, 2325; Prestel, *Datenverarbeitung im Dienste ju-*

the Corte di Cassazione and the Cour de cassation, *Simitis* demanded the use of electronic data processing to expand the systematic record of court decisions.[126] According to *Simitis*, the existing collections at the German courts were insufficient as they did not cover all decisions. In particular, the already existing "Nachschlagewerk"[127] could not remedy the situation. He therefore argued against a selection of decisions by the courts and in favor of comprehensive full-text storage. One of his aims was to avoid inconsistencies in case law.[128] Even if it has been realized in different ways, this is an approach that is still endorsed today.[129] In the Austrian legal information system (RIS), into which decisions are entered by the Supreme Court itself and which is used by the judges in their research on previous cases, all the decisions rendered in civil matters from 1991 onwards are stored in the database in full-text. In addition, the full-text of all decisions that were indexed in the so-called "Rechtssatzkartei" are currently included back to 1984.[130] Storing the full-text of decisions also brought a major change for retrieval.[131] The searcher no longer had to rely on abbreviations or headnotes of decisions. Whereas previously two steps were necessary, namely singling out the relevant decision via an index, with the content being conveyed by headnotes or abbreviations, and then looking for the decision in full-text in a separate register, the search can now be combined with retrieval of the full-text by a single click.[132] Nevertheless, for example, the official headnotes, called "Rechtssätze", continue to be used in Austria due to their advantage of being based on manual indexing by the court itself. Their advantage for the user is that they are not created for a single decision only but index all decisions concerning

---

ristischer Dokumentation: Ein Arbeits- und Funktionsvergleich zweier Systeme (1971) 1; Rödig, 'Axiomatisierbarkeit juristischer Systeme' (1972) 1 *Datenverarbeitung im Recht*, 170, 181 (fn 32).

126 Simitis (n 124) 67–82.

127 See above at II.A.b.

128 Simitis (n 124) 68–69.

129 Cf van Opijnen and others, 'On-line Publication of Court Decisions in the EU: Report of the Policy Group of the Project 'Building on the European Case Law Identifier'' (2017) <https://www.bo-ecli.eu/uploads/deliverables/Deliverable%20WS0-D1.pdf> accessed 12 July 2021.

130 'RIS-Justiz Description' <https://www.ris.bka.gv.at/UI/Judikatur/Justiz/Kontakt.aspx> accessed 12 July 2021.

131 However until the 1980s, texts of decisions were still often stored electronically in abbreviated form only: Holzleithner and Mayer-Schönberger, 'Das Zitat als grundloser Grund rechtlicher Legitimität' in Feldner and Forgó (eds), *Norm und Entscheidung: Prolegomena zu einer Theorie des Falls* (2000) 322.

132 Cf Berring, 'Collapse of the Structure of the Legal Research Universe' (n 5) 19.

the same legal statement.[133] Therefore, it can be assumed that keywords as well as headnotes have not entirely lost their importance. Yet, they have become an additional format of communication.[134]

However, as already implied, this new form of availability of decisions entails the loss of selection at courts in a twofold way. On the one hand, the court could formerly decide what to include in an index. Inclusion in a specific index therefore simultaneously conveyed the significance of a decision for the court itself.[135] Moreover, decisions not included in an index were also difficult to retrieve for the court. On the other hand, adding a headnote or a keyword to a decision indicated which content would be of particular importance to the court in future case law.[136] Thus, since recourse to the full-text usually depended on reading a headnote or a keyword, this determined the context in which a decision would be remembered.[137] This may still be partially the case today with respect to headnotes;[138] however, it does no longer take much effort to search through the decisions on which the headnotes are based. Unless the search is limited to annotated document sections,[139] the entire text of the decision is searched and retrieved.

From the perspective of the organizational memory described, a selection of content can be considered an intentional act of forgetting.[140]

---

133 The idea of these "Rechtssätze" is that even those decisions are indexed under a given "Rechtssatz" that make a dissenting or modifying statement. They are therefore intended to provide an up-to-date overview of a line of decisions of the Supreme Court. The related criticism shall not be dealt with here (see e.g. Rebhahn, 'Auf der Suche nach der ratio decidendi' in Jabloner et al. (eds), *Festschrift Heinz Mayer: Vom praktischen Wert der Methode* (2011) 585–588). The author of this text will address this topic in more detail in his dissertation.

134 Cf Wiederin, 'Der Leitsatz als juristisches Kommunikationsformat' in Kert and Lehner (eds), *Vielfalt des Strafrechts im internationalen Kontext: Festschrift für Frank Höpfel zum 65. Geburtstag* (2018) 779–780.

135 Cf Kuh (n 5), 243

136 See the "Signalfunktion" described by Rethorn, *Kodifikationsgerechte Rechtsprechung: Eine Untersuchung zur Bildung und zur Funktion von Leitsätzen* (1979) 76–81 resp the "Filterfunktion" of headnotes by Wiederin (n 134) 778–779.

137 Cf Jones, 'The Role of Official Headnotes in Legal Research' (1966) 59 *Law Library Journal*, 277; Kuh (n 5), 246–247; see also Kuh (n 5), 251–260 with some reflections from a cognitive science perspective on the influence of labelling and categorization in legal research.

138 See Wiederin (n 134) 778–779.

139 In the Austrian RIS it is possible to search the legal reasoning separately from the whole document.

140 Cf about legal commentaries: Kästle-Lamparter, 'Rezeption und Vergessen in der Welt der Kommentare' in Marsch, Münkler and Wischmeyer (eds),

The court, by considering or not considering decisions in the indexes, influenced its own recall of them. Moreover, by adding keywords and/or headnotes, it was possible to determine the content to be remembered as it directly influenced the retrieval.[141] Full-text and unlimited publication of decisions limits the possibility of such forgetting. As *Simitis* stated,[142] to prevent forgetting is as much the goal of digitalization as it was the aim of written records in general.[143] Today, there can be no doubt that digitalization has considerably simplified our "access to the past".[144] Yet, from an organizational perspective, forgetting can be regarded as beneficial. Forgetting allows "disruptive innovation" as the organization has no need to reference old principles.[145] This consideration may also be fruitfully extended to courts. As courts in continental Europe are otherwise forced to refer to previous judgments at least for consistency reasons,[146] by simply forgetting "insignificant" decisions a court could avoid the necessity of making reference. Even if the court is not bound by its previous decision, it is by forgetting that it can most easily take a new path without having to respect an old one. Thus, a new decision line can be formed without further need for justification. Conversely, full and unrestricted access to the past may lead to an extensive adaptation to already existing court practice.[147]

The "selection" of decisions is left to the technology of the database today. Since a real selection, meaning the withholding of decisions from the public, is not accepted for good reasons,[148] in times of growing databases relevance sorting is becoming more and more important.[149] The

Apokryphe Schriften: Rezeption und Vergessen in der Wissenschaft vom Öffentlichen Recht (2019) 101–102.

141 Uhlig, 'Leitsatzbildung' (1974) *DRiZ*, 75, 76.

142 Simitis (n 124) 69.

143 Cf also Ezra Dodd Church (n 5), 577–581; Ross (n 10), 305.

144 Ezra Dodd Church (n 5), 581–585.

145 Easterby-Smith and Lyles, 'In Praise of Organizational Forgetting' (2011) 20 *Journal of Management Inquiry*, 311, 313–314.

146 Cf MacCormick and Summers (n 99) 532–533.

147 Ezra Dodd Church (n 5), 585–586; Neumayr, 'Lauter Bäume, kein Wald' (n 61) 17; Strauch, 'Wandel des Rechts durch juristische Datenbanken' (n 6) 1006; Raselli (n 6), 607; see also the study of Devins and Klein (n 5).

148 Geist (n 125) 133–134; see also in this regard Kodek, 'Precedents in Private Law – A Civil Law Perspective', in this volume.

149 Regarding the relevance sorting in legal information retrieval see e.g.: Ashley, *Artificial Intelligence and Legal Analytics: New Tools for Law Practice in the Digital Age* (2017) 214–226; Geist (n 125) 83–129; van Opijnen and Santos, 'On the concept of relevance in legal information retrieval' (2017) 25 *Artif Intell Law*, 65.

criteria for a search algorithm are therefore of particular importance for the user.[150] The problem, however, is that these are rarely disclosed by the provider of the database.[151] Users are therefore left with a list that is based on their search criteria, but not (exclusively) sorted by them. However, even with the limited disclosure that is sometimes accessible,[152] it remains questionable whether users are currently sufficiently aware of this problem.[153] This becomes increasingly problematic as we move in the direction of deeper content analysis through further technical development.[154] At the same time, however, the technology of databases could be used to close the gap in the organization of information that has arisen as a result of the provision of full-text and the suppression of organizational systems from the days of print.[155] Yet if courts outsource the programming and maintenance of databases to external providers, they must be aware that this means that the structuring of a central repository is outsourced. Mechanisms of content classification must therefore be implemented in particularly close coordination with the courts and the user must also be made aware of them.

ii. Lost in Results

Since the increased use of such archives in the form of databases, there has been discussion about the extent to which databases are misused.[156] On the one hand, criticism centers on what is retrieved and, on the other hand, on how what is retrieved is used. The outcome of a search query is usually a list of results.[157] The more sophisticated the search engine, the more likely is it that this list will be sorted by relevance to meet the needs of the user.

---

150 Geist (n 125) 131–132; Mart, 'The Algorithm as a Human Artifact: Implications for Legal [Re]Search' (2017) 109 *Law Library Journal*, 387, 420; Strauch, 'Wandel des Rechts durch juristische Datenbanken' (n 6) 1003.

151 Geist (n 125) 130.

152 See e.g.: 'juris Trefferliste' <https://www.juris.de/jportal/portal/page/fshelp.psml?cmsuri=/hilfe/de/ep/weitere_suchfunktionen/trefferliste.jsp> accessed 12 July 2021.

153 Geist (n 125) 58–59 et 130.

154 Cf Ashley (n 149) 223–233; Bues, 'Artifical Intelligence im Recht' in Hartung, Bues and Halbleib (eds), *Legal Tech: Die Digitalisierung des Rechtsmarkts* (2018) 279; Harvey (n 5) 169–171.

155 See already Ezra Dodd Church (n 5), 592.

156 Taruffo (n 1) 452.

157 Ashley (n 149) 214.

However, even a mere Boolean search[158] is not uncommon in decision databases.[159] For the appearance of a decision in the list, it is therefore mainly important that the search word or – to a limited extent, i.e. when using specific symbols[160] – a similar word is found in the document. This is not changed by text-statistical methods that use the position of the word in the text for determining relevance.[161] This situation has led to criticism, particularly in the area of the common law, that no distinction is made between obiter dicta and holding.[162] This is indeed a distinction that the methods of retrieval in legal databases are not yet able to provide. Due to the search method itself, the focus is very much on the relevant keywords.[163] Moreover, the display of the result often leads the searcher by highlighting the search term directly in the relevant section of the document.[164] It is therefore assumed that this focus on snippets of the text[165] is also reflected in the reasoning of decisions in the form of "'law-byte' reasoning"[166] meaning "the over-reliance on bits of information".[167] *Tiersma* observes that American judges provide their holding as a kind of "sound bite" that can then easily be used in subsequent decisions.[168] It hardly needs to be mentioned that the electronic availability of texts also

158 A Boolean Search ranks decisions simply according to how completely the criteria of the search, consisting of the keywords and Boolean operators (e.g. AND, OR), are met: ibid 216; Geist (n 125) 65–67.

159 Geist (n 125) 65; the Austrian RIS, for example, offers no further relevance sorting.

160 Such are, for example, the asterisk (*) or the exclamation mark (!).

161 Geist (n 125) 99–101.

162 Devins and Klein (n 5), 600; Stinson, 'Why Dicta Becomes Holding and Why it Matters' (2010) 76 *Brooklyn Law Review*, 219, 76.

163 Bintliff, 'From Creativity to Computerese: Thinking Like a Lawyer in the Computer Age' (1996) 88 *Law Libr J*, 338, 345–346; Devins and Klein (n 5), 621; see also Tiersma (n 5) 216, who states that case law has become "more textual than it was before"; and see the result of a study showing that electronic researchers base their searches more on facts and words: Kuh and Krieger, 'Accessing Law: An Empirical Study Exploring the Influence of Legal Research Medium' (2014) 16 *Vand J Ent & Tech L*, 757, 777.

164 Kuh (n 5), 246; Vries (n 5), 27.

165 Stinson (n 162), 253; Tiersma (n 5) 217.

166 Lien, 'Technocentrism and the Soul of the Common Law Lawyer' (1998) 48 *American University Law Review*, 85, 88; also Hanson (n 5), 577–578; Vries (n 5), 31.

167 Vries (n 5), 31; see also the idea of a "rapid rule extraction" by Lien (n 166), 88.

168 Tiersma, 'The Textualization of Precedent' (2007) 82 *Notre Dame Law Review*, 1187–1278, 1260.

facilitates copy and paste.[169] *Tiersma* relates this to a general development of a "textualization of precedents"[170] in the common law. For him "the traditional analysis of the holding or *ratio decidendi* of a case [...] is being replaced by close reading of snippets of critical text".[171] In civil law countries, practitioners have always been more used to such sound bites because "broad formulations [...] which expresses a rule or a principle" are not uncommon in a reasoning.[172] In addition, headnotes are formed based on the decision texts, which are also usually characterized by a very abstract wording.[173] These "snippets" also regularly find their way into subsequent decisions. While, therefore, the use of text modules in decisions is not a new development brought about by the advent of databases,[174] fears that this practice could be strengthened by the use of databases are also expressed in the German literature.[175]

From the perspective of an organizational memory, the use of "snippets" from previous decisions in follow-up decisions must not only be seen in a negative light. Repeating what has already been said once shows a recall of the organizational memory. The provision of sound bites or broad formulations can be seen as enhancing such recall.[176] However, the question arises as to how successful such a recall is. Therefore, it should be regarded as problematic – as is usually implied in criticism – if such an extraction results in a complete independence of the statement from the decision and thus in a loss of context[177] – something which *Vries* describes as the "'disaggregation' of results".[178] Such a "disaggregation" is nothing else than an unintended alteration and therefore an "imperfect recall" of a memory,[179] which causes inconsistency in the court practice. *Jain* sees

---

169 Stinson (n 162), 247.
170 Tiersma (n 168).
171 Tiersma (n 5) 217–218.
172 Szladits (n 77) 514.
173 E.g. Fleischer (n 119), 607.
174 Strauch, *Methodenlehre des gerichtlichen Erkenntnisverfahrens* (n 6) 607; see e.g. Bähr, *Gesammelte Aufsätze: Band 1: Juristische Abhandlungen* (1895) 430.
175 Bydlinski, 'Die Regresskriterien bei der Schadenersatz-Gesamtschuld: Zugleich ein neuerliches Plädoyer gegen die Rechtssatz-Judikatur' (2013) *Richterzeitung*, 57, 57; Neumayr, 'Die Judikaturdokumentation RIS-Justiz im österreichischen Rechtsinformationssystem' (2015) *ZZPint*, 73, 95; Raselli (n 6), 607.
176 Lepsius (n 6), 797.
177 Vries (n 5), 34; see reg headnotes Wiederin (n 134) 779.
178 Vries (n 5), 28 under reference to Outler (n 5), 187–188.
179 Jain (n 17) 307–308.

such imperfect recalls as a form of forgetting in an organization.[180] Thus, this form of forgetting at the same time enables the formation of a new memory. It is inter alia in such cases that an outside perspective can be of help.

III Curation of Memory

A significant actor outside the court that shapes the memory of decisions is legal scholarship. It is therefore not surprising from this perspective that German legal scholarship is increasingly emphasizing the task of contextualizing decisions.[181] *Lepsius* sees this task especially in the context of an information overload in which legal science is supposed to fulfil a systematizing function.[182] This approach is based on the consideration that a "decontextualization" often happens when courts use prior decisions.[183] The aim is obviously to call upon legal scholarship to restore this context in its own formats. In contrast to a (mere) critical appraisal of a decision on a point of law, the aim is to transmit or retain the context of decision making in other formats than the decision itself.

However, legal scholarship remains limited to the sources at its disposal for reconstructing the context. It can therefore supplement the context of a decision beyond the wording communicated, especially where it is a matter of locating the decision in the context of previous case law[184] or academic discourse.[185] Hence, legal scholarship can, for example, reveal

180 Ibid 307.

181 Albers (n 94) 262–263; Fleischer (n 119), 608; Fleischer, 'Gesellschaftsrechts-Geschichten – eine Forschungsagenda' in Fleischer and Thiessen (eds), *Gesellschaftsrechts-Geschichten* (2018) 1–26; Lege, 'Die Realität des Rechts ist der Fall. 56 ketzerische Thesen im Geist des Pragmatismus' (2019) 5 *RphZ Rechtsphilosophie*, 416, 427; Lepsius (n 6); Payandeh (n 111) 465–472; Reimer (n 6) 218–219; Schönberger (n 60) 324.

182 Lepsius (n 6), 796–797.

183 Fleischer (n 181) 17–18; Hoffmann-Riem, *Innovation und Recht, Recht und Innovation: Recht im Ensemble seiner Kontexte* (2016) 135–137; critical: Wahl, 'Entwicklungspfade im Recht' (2013) 68 *Juristenzeitung*, 369, 375–377.

184 Langenbucher, *Die Entwicklung und Auslegung von Richterrecht: Eine methodologische Untersuchung zur richterlichen Rechtsfortbildung im deutschen Zivilrecht* (1996) 81–83; Wank, *Juristische Methodenlehre: Eine Anleitung für Wissenschaft und Praxis* (2020) 126–127; both authors, however, do not participate in the debate on contextualization.

185 Fleischer (n 110) 779–782.

connections with (uncited) prior decisions or present in more detail the dialogue between legal scholarship and practice that the decision may only hint at. The procedural context of a decision can also be elaborated beyond what is communicated in the decision itself.[186] Moreover, legal scholarship may also contribute to limit the broad formulation of these "snippets" by embedding them in a temporal context. As *Lepsius* states in relation to the case law of the German Constitutional Court ("Bundesverfassungsgericht"), legal scholarship is able to limit such broad formulations by embedding them in their temporal context to offer the court room for new case law.[187] In contrast, the facts of the case can usually only be inferred from the decision itself. As already mentioned above, the accounts given of facts are quite short in many jurisdictions, including the German-speaking ones.[188] Hence, legal scholarship can seldom provide additional information on this aspect of the context, but rather clarification where the context is in danger of being lost. Usually, legal scholarship has little access to the material of the deliberations. It is primarily dependent on documents that, like the "Senatsheft" at the German Supreme Court, are released for academic editing after a period of time.[189] Moreover, extra-legal factors of the context of a decision usually remain unaddressed, probably also due to a lack of sources, which would only allow conjecture.

The increasing importance of contextualization can be seen as an acknowledgement of the need for a more comprehensive curation of case law by legal scholarship, which, inter alia, provides a counterbalance to the comprehensive accessibility of decisions in the digital age. Legal commentaries, for example, which are a mere compilation of sound bites or headnotes from decisions, have certainly lost their usefulness[190] that they had in the age of print.[191] This can be observed by the fact that commentaries are increasingly losing their significance as a filter for decisions,[192] because the user can hardly avoid a full-text search in practice. However, as *Kästle-Lamparter* notes, this also means that the relevance measurement is lost –

186 Lepsius (n 6), 797.
187 Ibid 801–802.
188 Fleischer (n 181) 3; see also Langenbucher (n 186) 78–81, who has a very narrow definition of context.
189 See above at II.B.a.
190 Fleischer (n 119), 613; Payandeh (n 111) 459.
191 Hanson (n 5), 580; Vries (n 5), 25–27.
192 Kästle-Lamparter, 'Rezeption und Vergessen in der Welt der Kommentare' (n 140) 102; regarding the function of a legal commentary see also Kästle-Lamparter, *Welt der Kommentare* (2016) 311–332.

a task that, as described, database providers are now increasingly offering through technical solutions.[193] Nevertheless, the functions of organizing knowledge and also of shaping knowledge cannot be underestimated, especially in an existing information overload. One way to do this is to open up to methods which are adapted to these circumstances, such as the ones *Olsen* and *Christensen* as well as *Frese* show in this book, or methods of corpus linguistics as *Vogel*, *Pötters* and *Christensen* have described;[194] methods that, in addition to the doctrinal method, make it easier to move the view beyond the individual case and put it in the context of the other case law of a court.[195]

Thus, legal scholarship can offer the courts additional "archives" that can function as a supplement to the memory of the organization itself. From the perspective of memory, the incentive here is a special service of systematization that courts are not able to provide simply because of a lack of time and resources. Nonetheless, at the same time, legal scholarship, as an external actor, can in any case only provide an interpretative contribution. It is therefore often a framer rather than a preserver of memory.

IV Conclusion: The Court and its Past

When we speak of "a court", there lies a fiction behind this expression.[196] One "court" does not exist. However, speaking of "a court" expresses consistency. Ideally, a court does not contradict itself but deviates from its case law. This requires a memory that not only consists of that of the individual judges but can maintain consistency inter alia over long stretches of time and factual contexts. Already early on, courts took measures that supported an organizational memory necessary for this purpose. The increasing accessibility of full-text decisions, however, poses the challenge to courts that inconsistencies are more easily brought to light.[197] The court

---

193 See above at II.B.b.i.

194 Vogel, Pötters and Christensen, *Richterrecht der Arbeit – empirisch untersucht: Möglichkeiten und Grenzen computergestützter Textanalyse am Beispiel des Arbeitnehmerbegriffs* (2015), cf especially page 228 seq where they highlight the use of such analysis in making the structure of discourses visible from a more global perspective.

195 See Olsen and Christensen, 'The Weight of Precedent: From Abstract Theorizing to Concrete Application: The case of the ECtHR', in this volume.

196 Taruffo (n 1) 447–448; cf also Paunio,'Reasoning at the CJEU: linguistic, institutional and systemic constraints', in this volume.

197 Hanson (n 5), 580.

is therefore increasingly forced to (at least) deal with its prior decisions. Nevertheless, it may be doubted whether this development, conversely, leads to greater consistency.[198] The loss of selection and the growth of the number of decisions that a court must consider[199] make this much more difficult. Reasonings of decisions, which are based on broad, even law-like, formulations, take away additional leeway for subsequent decisions. This burden of the court's own previous decisions does not necessarily require a binding effect, but only the responsibility, which is also common in civil law jurisdictions, to take the past into account. Creating leeway again is possible through a comprehensive memory that does not consist of abstract legal statements only but offers the context in which a decision was made.[200] However, the context must also be stored for this purpose. Although legal scholarship can edit decisions and their context, it remains largely dependent on the sources that are accessible to it.

Bibliography

Gabriele Aicher, 'Geschichte der Generalprokuratur' in Gerald Kohl and Ilse Reiter-Zatloukal (eds), *"… das Interesse des Staates zu wahren": Staatsanwaltschaften und andere Einrichtungen zur Vertretung öffentlicher Interessen. Geschichte, Gegenwart, Perspektiven* (Verlag Österreich, Wien 2018) 119

Marion Albers, 'Höchstrichterliche Rechtsfindung und Auslegung gerichtlicher Entscheidungen: 1. Referat' in Bernd Grzeszick, Christian Calliess and Georg Lienbacher (eds), *Grundsatzfragen der Rechtsetzung und Rechtsfindung. Referate und Diskussionen auf der Tagung der Vereinigung der Deutschen Staatsrechtslehrer in Münster vom 5. bis 8. Oktober 2011* (De Gruyter, Berlin 2012) 257

Amoroso G, 'Nomofilachia e Massimario' <https://www.cortedicassazione.it/cassazione-resources/resources/cms/documents/Il_precedente_ed_il_ruolo_del_Massimario_s07.pdf> accessed 12 July 2021

Kevin D Ashley, *Artificial Intelligence and Legal Analytics: New Tools for Law Practice in the Digital Age* (Cambridge University Press, Cambridge 2017)

Reyer Baas, *De meerwaarde van meervoud. Verschillen en overeenkomsten tussen meervoudige en enkelvoudige rechtspraak, in het bijzonder in civiele zaken* (Wolters Kluwer, Deventer 2020)

198 Both Raselli (n 6), 606 and Strauch, 'Wandel des Rechts durch juristische Datenbanken' (n 6), 1003–1004 see certain preconditions that are necessary to realize the potential of coherence. Based on the above, it may be questionable whether these have been achieved.

199 Lepsius (n 6), 802.

200 Cf ibid 801–802; Payandeh (n 111) 465–470.

Otto Bähr, *Gesammelte Aufsätze: Band 1: Juristische Abhandlungen* (F. W. Grunow, Leipzig 1895)

John H Baker, 'Preface' in John H Baker (ed), *Judicial Records, Law Reports, and the Growth of Case Law* (Duncker Humblot GmbH, Berlin 2013) 5

Robert C Berring, 'Collapse of the Structure of the Legal Research Universe: The Imperative of Digital Information' (1994) 69 *Washington Law Review*, 9

Robert C Berring, 'Legal Research and the World of Thinkable Thoughts' (2000) 2 *The Journal of Appelate Practice and Process*, 305

Jon Bing, 'Let there be LITE: a brief history of legal information retrieval' (2010) 1 *European Journal of Law and Technology* < https://link.gale.com/apps/doc/A240098684/AONE?u=43wien&sid=AONE&xid=a9328aaa > accessed 12 July 2021

Barbara Bintliff, 'From Creativity to Computerese: Thinking Like a Lawyer in the Computer Age' (1996) 88 *Law Libr J*, 338

Stefan Brink, *Über die richterliche Entscheidungsbegründung: Funktion – Position – Methodik* (Lang, Frankfurt am Main 1999)

Micha-Manuel Bues, 'Artifical Intelligence im Recht' in Markus Hartung, Micha-Manuel Bues and Gernot Halbleib (eds), *Legal Tech: Die Digitalisierung des Rechtsmarkts* (C.H. Beck, Vahlen, Manz, München 2018) 275

Peter Bydlinski, 'Die Regresskriterien bei der Schadenersatz-Gesamtschuld: Zugleich ein neuerliches Plädoyer gegen die Rechtssatz-Judikatur' (2013) *Richterzeitung*, 57

Stephanie Cartier and Cristina Hosse, 'The Role of Registries and Legal Secretariats in International Judicial Institutions' in Cesare Romano, Karen J Alter and Yuval Shani (eds), *The Oxford Handbook of International adjudication* (Oxford University Press, Oxford 2013) 711

Andrea Casey, *Organizational identity and memory: A multidisciplinary approach* (Routledge, Taylor and Francis Group, New York, London 2019)

Alberto Cevolini, 'Die Organisation des Gedächtnisses und das Gedächtnis der Organisation' in Oliver Dimbath and Michael Heinlein (eds), *Die Sozialität des Erinnerns: Beiträge zur Arbeit an einer Theorie des sozialen Gedächtnisses* (Springer, Wiesbaden 2014) 167

Amanda Coffey, 'Analysing Documents' in Uwe Flick (ed), *The SAGE Handbook of Qualitative Data Analysis* (SAGE, London 2014) 367

Cosette D Creamer and Zuzanna Godzimirska, 'Trust in the Court: The Role of the Registry of the European Court of Human Rights' (2019) 30 *European Journal of International Law*, 665

Ezra Dodd Church, 'Technological Conservatism: How Information Technology Prevents the Law from Changing' (2004) 83 *Texas Law Review*, 561

Karl-Heinz Danzl and Herbert Hopf, *Oberster Gerichtshof* (3rd edn, NWV, Wien, Graz 2017)

René David, *International Encyclopedia of Comparative Law. Vol 2: The Legal Systems of the World, their Comparison and Unification: Chapter 3: Sources of Law* (J.C.B. Mohr (Paul Siebeck), Tübingen 1984)

Neal Devins and David Klein, 'The Vanishing Common Law Judge?' (2017) 165 *University of Pennsylvania Law Review*, 595

Frank Diedrich, *Präjudizien im Zivilrecht* (Kovač, Hamburg 2004)

Neil Duxbury, *The Nature and Authority of Precedent* (Cambridge University Press, Cambridge 2008)

Mark Easterby-Smith and Marjorie A Lyles, 'In Praise of Organizational Forgetting' (2011) 20 *Journal of Management Inquiry*, 311

Hans W Fasching, 'Zur verfassungsrechtlichen Rechtfertigung der Bindung des Obersten Gerichtshofes an seine Entscheidungen' in Hans W Fasching (ed), *Festschrift für Hans Schima zum 75. Geburtstag* (Manz, Wien 1969) 133

Birgit Feldner, *Verstärkte Senate beim Obersten Gerichtshof: Rechtsprechung im Spannungsfeld zwischen Unabhängigkeit, Richtigkeit und Einheitlichkeit* (Springer, Wien [u.a.] 2001)

Frédérique Ferrand, 'Der Avocat général bei der Cour de cassation und die richterliche Rechtsfortbildung in Frankreich' (2016) 80 *Rabels Zeitschrift für ausländisches und internationales Privatrecht*, 288

Marina Fiedler and Isabell Welpe, 'How do organizations remember? The influence of organizational structure on organizational memory' (2010) 31 *Organization Studies*, 381

Holger Fleischer, 'Gesellschaftsrechts-Geschichten – eine Forschungsagenda' in Holger Fleischer and Jan Thiessen (eds), *Gesellschaftsrechts-Geschichten* (Mohr Siebeck, Tübingen 2018) 1

Holger Fleischer, 'Höchstrichterliche Leitsätze und richterliche Normbildung im Gesellschaftsrecht' (2018) 39 *ZIP*, 605

Holger Fleischer, 'Schlussbetrachtung: Gesellschaftsrechtliche Zeitgeschichte im Fallformat' in Holger Fleischer and Jan Thiessen (eds), *Gesellschaftsrechts-Geschichten* (Mohr Siebeck, Tübingen 2018) 736

Hamid Foroughi and others, 'Organizational Memory Studies' (2020) 41 *Organization Studies*, 1725

Anton Geist, *Rechtsdatenbanken und Relevanzsortierung* (Österreichische Computer Gesellschaft, Wien 2017)

Hans Gerstenkorn, 'Einführung: Die Dokumentation im Bereich der Bundesgerichte', in Hans Gerstenkorn and Hildebert Kirchner (eds), *Die Dokumentation der Bundesgerichte der Bundesrepublik Deutschland, Österreichs und der Schweiz* (Bibliothek des Deutschen Bundestages, Bonn 1964) 1

Hans Gerstenkorn and Hildebert Kirchner (eds), *Die Dokumentation der Bundesgerichte der Bundesrepublik Deutschland, Österreichs und der Schweiz* (Bibliothek des Deutschen Bundestages, Bonn 1964)

Groupe de travail sur la rédaction des décisions de la juridiction administrative présidé par le président Philippe Martin, 'Rapport' <https://www.conseil-etat.fr/Media/actualites/documents/2012/rapport_redaction_decisions_juradm_2012> accessed 12 July 2021

Veronika Haberler, *Die höchstgerichtliche Entscheidung: Eine empirische Studie zur Entscheidungsfindung in Zivilrechtssachen am OGH* (Wiener Advocatur Bureau, Wien 2014)

F. A Hanson, 'From Key Numbers to Keywords: How Automation Has Transformed the Law' (2002) 94 *Law Library Journal*, 563

David Harvey, *Collisions in the Digital Paradigm: Law and Rule Making in the Internet Age* (Hart Publishing, Oxford, Portand Oregon 2017)

Ted Hedesstrom and Edgar Whitley, 'What is Meant by Tacit Knowledge? Towards a Better Understanding of the Shape of Actions' (2000) *ECIS 2000 Proceedings* <https://aisel.aisnet.org/ecis2000/29> accessed 12 July 2021

Wolfgang Hoffmann-Riem, *Innovation und Recht, Recht und Innovation: Recht im Ensemble seiner Kontexte* (Mohr Siebeck, Tübingen 2016)

Elisabeth Holzleithner and Viktor Mayer-Schönberger, 'Das Zitat als grundloser Grund rechtlicher Legitimität' in Birgit Feldner and Nikolaus Forgó (eds), *Norm und Entscheidung: Prolegomena zu einer Theorie des Falls* (Springer, Wien, New York 2000) 318

Michael Huber, '§ 299' in Hans-Joachim Musielak and Wolfgang Voit (eds), *Zivilprozessordnung* (18th edn, Vahlen 2021)

David J Ibbetson, 'Case-Law and Doctrine' in Reiner Schulze and Ulrike Seif (eds), *Richterrecht und Rechtsfortbildung in der Europäischen Rechtsgemeinschaft* (Mohr Siebeck, Tübingen 2003)

David J Ibbetson and Alain Wijffels, 'Case Law in the Making: The Techniques and Methods of Judicial Records and Law Reports' in Alain Wijffels (ed), *Case Law in the Making: Vol 1: Essays* (Duncker & Humblot, Berlin 1997) 29

Marc A Jacob, *Precedents and Case-Based Reasoning in the European Court of Justice: Unfinished Business* (Cambridge University Press, Cambridge 2014)

Dietmar Jahnel, 'Rechtsdatenbanken für Wissenschaft und Praxis' (1988) *ÖJZ*, 301

Amit Jain, 'Is Organizational Memory a Useful Capability?: An Analysis of Its Effects on Productivity, Absorptive Capacity, and Adaption' in Linda Argote and John M Levine (eds), *The Oxford Handbook of Group and Organizational Learning* (Oxford University Press, New York, NY 2020) 295

Richard F Jones, 'The Role of Official Headnotes in Legal Research' (1966) 59 *Law Library Journal*, 277

Anna B Kaiser, 'Herstellung und Darstellung von Entscheidungen des Bundesverfassungsgerichts' in Johannes Masing et al. (eds), *Entscheidungen und Entscheidungsprozesse der Rechtsprechung: Décisions juridictionnelles et processus décisionnels. Dokumentation des 9. Treffens des Deutsch-Französischen Gesprächskreises für Öffentliches Recht 2018* (Mohr Siebeck, Tübingen 2020) 1

Anna-Bettina Kaiser, *Die Kommunikation der Verwaltung: Diskurse zu den Kommunikationsbeziehungen zwischen staatlicher Verwaltung und Privaten in der Verwaltungsrechtswissenschaft der Bundesrepublik Deutschland* (Nomos Verlag, Baden-Baden 2009)

David Kästle-Lamparter, *Welt der Kommentare* (Mohr Siebeck, Tübingen 2016)

David Kästle-Lamparter, 'Rezeption und Vergessen in der Welt der Kommentare' in Nikolaus Marsch, Laura Münkler and Thomas Wischmeyer (eds), *Apokryphe Schriften: Rezeption und Vergessen in der Wissenschaft vom Öffentlichen Recht* (Mohr Siebeck, Tübingen 2019) 93

M. E Katsh, *The Electronic Media and the Transformation of Law* (Oxford University Press, New York, NY 1989)

Sally J Kenney, 'Beyond Principals and Agents' (2000) 33 *Comparative Political Studies*, 593

Wolfgang Kilian, 'Idee und Wirklichkeit der Rechtsinformatik in Deutschland' (2017) 33 *Computer und Recht*, 202

Uwe Kischel, *Die Begründung: Zur Erläuterung staatlicher Entscheidungen gegenüber dem Bürger* (Mohr Siebeck, Tübingen 2003)

Georg Kodek, 'Funktion und Arbeitsweise des OGH – die Binnensicht' in Georg Kodek (ed), *Zugang zum OGH: Vorträge des Symposiums "Zugang zum OGH in Zivil- und Strafsachen"* (Manz, Wien 2012) 99

Hein Kötz, *Über den Stil höchstrichterlicher Entscheidungen* (Universitätsverlag GmbH, Konstanz 1973)

Markus Krajewski, *Paper Machines: About Cards & Catalogs, 1548–1929* (MIT Press, Cambridge, Massachusetts 2011)

Helmut Kramer, 'Informationskrise des Rechts und Veröffentlichungspraxis' (1976) *ZRP*, 84

Uwe Kranenpohl, *Hinter dem Schleier des Beratungsgeheimnisses: Der Willensbildungs- und Entscheidungsprozess des Bundesverfassungsgerichts* (VS Verl. für Sozialwiss, Wiesbaden 2010)

Thomas Kreppel, 'Informationskrise, Verlagskrise und „Besseres Recht"' (1975) *NJW*, 2325

Katrina F Kuh, 'Electronically Manufactured Law' (2008) 22 *Harvard Journal of Law & Technology*, 223

Katrina F Kuh and H. S Krieger, 'Accessing Law: An Empirical Study Exploring the Influence of Legal Research Medium' (2014) 16 *Vand J Ent & Tech L*, 757–808

William M Landes and Richard A Posner, 'Legal Precedent: A Theoretical and Empirical Analysis' (1976) 19 *The Journal of Law & Economics*, 249

Katja Langenbucher, *Die Entwicklung und Auslegung von Richterrecht: Eine methodologische Untersuchung zur richterlichen Rechtsfortbildung im deutschen Zivilrecht* (Beck, München 1996)

Rüdiger Lautmann, *Justiz – die stille Gewalt: Teilnehmende Beobachtung und entscheidungssoziologische Analyse* (Springer VS, Wiesbaden 2011)

Joachim Lege, 'Die Realität des Rechts ist der Fall. 56 ketzerische Thesen im Geist des Pragmatismus' (2019) 5 *RphZ Rechtsphilosophie*, 416

Oliver Lepsius, 'Kontextualisierung als Aufgabe der Rechtswissenschaft' (2019) 74 *Juristenzeitung*, 793

Molly W Lien, 'Technocentrism and the Soul of the Common Law Lawyer' (1998) 48 *American University Law Review*, 85

Niklas Luhmann, *Funktionen und Folgen formaler Organisation* (Duncker & Humblot, Berlin 1964)

Niklas Luhmann, *Recht und Automation in der öffentlichen Verwaltung: Eine verwaltungswissenschaftliche Untersuchung* (Duncker & Humblot, Berlin 1966)

Thomas Lundmark, *Charting the Divide Between Common and Civil Law* (Oxford University Press, Oxford 2012)

D. Neil MacCormick and Robert S Summers, 'Further General Reflections and Conclusions' in D. Neil MacCormick and Robert S Summers (eds), *Interpreting Precedents: A Comparative Study* (Taylor and Francis, Florence 1997) 531

Susan N Mart, 'The Algorithm as a Human Artifact: Implications for Legal [Re]Search' (2017) 109 *Law Library Journal*, 387

Johannes Masing and others (eds), *Entscheidungen und Entscheidungsprozesse der Rechtsprechung: Décisions juridictionnelles et processus décisionnels. Dokumentation des 9. Treffens des Deutsch-Französischen Gesprächskreises für Öffentliches Recht 2018* (Mohr Siebeck, Tübingen 2020)

Felix Maultzsch, *Streitentscheidung und Normbildung durch den Zivilprozess: Eine rechtsvergleichende Untersuchung zum deutschen, englischen und US-amerikanischen Recht* (Mohr Siebeck, Tübingen 2012)

Martin Morlok, Ralf Kolbel and Agnes Launhardt, 'Recht als Soziale Praxis: Eine Soziologische Perpektive in der Methodenlehre' (2000) 31 *Rechtstheorie*, 15

K. Mortelmans, 'The Court Under the Influence of its Advocates General: An Analysis of the Case Law on the Functioning of the Internal Market' (2005) 24 *Yearbook of European Law*, 127

Marlene Nagelsmeier-Linke, *Automatisierte juristische Informationssysteme: Gegenwärtiger Stand ihrer Entwicklung und ihre Bedeutung für die Bibliothekarische Praxis* (K. G. Saur, München, New York, London 1980)

Matthias Neumayr, 'Die Judikaturdokumentation RIS-Justiz im österreichischen Rechtsinformationssystem' (2015) *ZZPint*, 73

Matthias Neumayr, 'Lauter Bäume, kein Wald' in Gregor Christandl et al. (eds), *Intra- und Interdisziplinarität im Zivilrecht: Jahrbuch junger Zivilrechtswissenschaftler* (Nomos, Baden-Baden 2018) 9

Fernando Olivera, 'Memory Systems In Organizations: An Empirical Investigation Of Mechanisms For Knowledge Collection, Storage And Access' (2000) 37 *Journal of Management Studies*, 811

Elizabeth Outler, 'Mapping the Achieved Values of Legal Reference Books onto the Digital Future' (2015) 34 *Legal Reference Services Quarterly*, 177

Mehrdad Payandeh, *Judikative Rechtserzeugung: Theorie, Dogmatik und Methodik der Wirkungen von Präjudizien* (Mohr Siebeck, Tübingen 2017)

Theodore Plucknett, *A Concise History of the Common Law* (5th edn, Liberty Fund Inc, Indianapolis 2010)

Richard A Posner, *Economic Analysis of Law* (9th edn, Wolters Kluwer Law & Business, New York, NY 2014)

Bernhard M Prestel, *Datenverarbeitung im Dienste juristischer Dokumentation: Ein Arbeits- und Funktionsvergleich zweier Systeme* (De Gruyter, Berlin/Boston 1971)

'Rapport de la Commission de réflexion sur la réforme de la Cour de cassation' <https://www.courdecassation.fr/IMG///Rapport%20-sur%20la%20r%C3%A9forme%20de%20la%20Cour%20de%20cassation.pdf> accessed 12 July 2021

Niccolò Raselli, 'Gedanken über den Einfluss computergestützter Informationsverarbeitung auf die Rechtsprechung' (2002) *SJZ*, 605

Robert Rebhahn, 'Auf der Suche nach der ratio decidendi' in Clemens Jabloner et al. (eds), *Festschrift Heinz Mayer: Vom praktischen Wert der Methode* (Manz, Wien 2011) 575

Robert Rebhahn, 'Der Urteilsstil des OGH im Vergleich mit den Höchstgerichten Deutschlands, Frankreichs und Englands' in Constanze Fischer-Czermak et al. (eds), *Festschrift 200 Jahre ABGB* (Manz, Wien 2011) 1539

Franz Reimer, *Juristische Methodenlehre* (2nd edn, Nomos, Baden-Baden 2020)

Catherine Reiter, *Gerichtsinterne Organisation: Best Practices* (Schulthess, Zürich 2015)

Dietrich Rethorn, *Kodifikationsgerechte Rechtsprechung: Eine Untersuchung zur Bildung und zur Funktion von Leitsätzen* (Duncker & Humblot, Berlin 1979)

Niccolò Ridi, 'The Shape and Structure of the 'Usable Past': An Empirical Analysis of the Use of Precedent in International Adjudication' (2019) 10 *Journal of International Dispute Settlement*, 200

Jürgen Rödig, 'Axiomatisierbarkeit juristischer Systeme' (1972) 1 *Datenverarbeitung im Recht*, 170

Andrea S Romito and Clara Tracogna, 'Standardization of Judicial Practice in Italy' (2013) 3 *Union of Jurists of Romania Law Review*, 1

Richard J Ross, 'The Memorial Culture of Early Modern English Lawyers: Memory as Keyword, Shelter, and Identity, 1560–1640' (1998) 10 *Yale JL & Human*, 229

Maria Schlagböhmer, 'Das automatisierte juristische Informationssystem des Kassationsgerichtshofes in Rom „Italgiure"' (1975) 4 *Datenverarbeitung im Recht*, 61

Rainer Schliebs, 'Dokumentationsstelle, Nachschlagewerk und Entscheidungsversand des Bundesgerichtshofs' in Karlmann Geiß (ed), *Festschrift aus Anlaß des fünfzigjährigen Bestehens von Bundesgerichtshof, Bundesanwaltschaft und Rechtsanwaltschaft beim Bundesgerichtshof* (Heymanns, Köln 2000) 761

Johanna Schmidt-Räntsch, 'Die Rechtsprechung der obersten Gerichtshöfe des Bundes (OGB)' in Karl Riesenhuber (ed), *Europäische Methodenlehre: Handbuch für Ausbildung und Praxis* (3rd edn, De Gruyter, Berlin 2015) 519

Herbert Schneider, 'Einfluß und Aufgaben der Anwaltschaft am Bundesgerichtshof' in Gerda Krüger-Nieland (ed), *25 Jahre Bundesgerichtshof* (Beck, München 1975) 71

Florian Scholz-Berger, 'Access to the Austrian Oberster Gerichtshof: Attempts to Strike a Balance Between Adequate Workload and Adequate Review' in Pablo Bravo-Hurtado and Cornelis H van Rhee (eds), *Supreme Courts under Pressure: Controlling Caseload in the Administration of Civil Justice* (Springer, Cham 2021) 105

Christoph Schönberger, 'Höchstrichterliche Rechtsfindung und Auslegung gerichtlicher Entscheidungen: 2. Referat' in Bernd Grzeszick, Christian Calliess and Georg Lienbacher (eds), *Grundsatzfragen der Rechtsetzung und Rechtsfindung. Referate und Diskussionen auf der Tagung der Vereinigung der Deutschen Staatsrechtslehrer in Münster vom 5. bis 8. Oktober 2011* (De Gruyter, Berlin 2012) 296

Werner Schubert and Hans P Glöckner, *Nachschlagewerk des Reichsgerichts Bürgerliches Gesetzbuch: §§ 1 – 133* (Keip, Goldbach 1994)

Jan C Schuhr, 'Rechtsprechungsdatenbanken als Format rechtlicher Information – Hilfsmittel oder Ersatz für Kommentare?' in Andreas Funke and Konrad Lachmayer (eds), *Formate der Rechtswissenschaft* (Velbrück Wissenschaft, Weilerswist 2017) 161

Erich Schweighofer, 'Knowledge management and administration of justice' (2004) 18 *International Review of Law, Computers & Technology*, 47

Raimo Siltala, *A Theory of Precedent: From Analytical Positivism to a Post-Analytical Philosophy of Law* (Hart, Oxford 2000)

Spiros Simitis, *Informationskrise des Rechts und Datenverarbeitung* (C.F. Müller, Karlsruhe 1970)

Peter Stegmaier, *Wissen, was Recht ist: Richterliche Rechtspraxis aus wissenssoziologischethnografischer Sicht* (VS Verlag für Sozialwissenschaften/GWV Fachverlage GmbH Wiesbaden, Wiesbaden 2009)

Eric W Stein and Vladimir Zwass, 'Actualizing Organizational Memory with Information Systems' (1995) 6 *Information Systems Research*, 85

Judith Stinson, 'Why Dicta Becomes Holding and Why it Matters' (2010) 76 *Brooklyn Law Review*, 219

Adolf Stölzel, *Die Entwicklung des gelehrten Richterthums in deutschen Territorien: eine rechtsgeschichtliche Untersuchung mit vorzugsweiser Berücksichtigung der Verhältnisse im Gebiete des ehemaligen Kurfürstenthums Hessen: Erster Band* (J. G. Cotta'schen Buchhandlung, Stuttgart 1872)

Hans-Joachim Strauch, 'Wandel des Rechts durch juristische Datenbanken' (2007) *DVBl*, 1000

Hans-Joachim Strauch, *Methodenlehre des gerichtlichen Erkenntnisverfahrens: Prozesse richterlicher Kognition* (Verlag Karl Alber, Freiburg, München 2017)

Michael Stürner, 'Sharing Responsibility: The German Federal Court of Justice and the Civil Appellate System' in Pablo Bravo-Hurtado and Cornelis H van Rhee (eds), *Supreme Courts under Pressure: Controlling Caseload in the Administration of Civil Justice* (Springer, Cham 2021) 75

Charles Szladits, *Guide to Foreign Legal Materials: French German Swiss* (Parker School of Foreign and Comparative Law, New York 1959)

Sandra Taal, *Working separately together* (Nomos/Stämpfli/Jan Sramek, Baden-Baden, Bern, Zürich 2016)

Michele Taruffo, 'Institutional Factors Influencing Precedents' in D. Neil MacCormick and Robert S Summers (eds), *Interpreting Precedents: A Comparative Study* (Taylor and Francis, Florence 1997) 437

Michele Taruffo and Massimo La Torre, 'Precedent in Italy' in D. Neil MacCormick and Robert S Summers (eds), *Interpreting Precedents: A Comparative Study* (Taylor and Francis, Florence 1997) 141

Peter M Tiersma, 'The Textualization of Precedent' (2007) 82 *Notre Dame Law Review*, 1187

Peter M Tiersma, *Parchment, Paper, Pixels: Law and the Technologies of Communication* (The University of Chicago Press, Chicago, London 2010)

Hans-Heinrich Trute, 'Klugheit in juristischen Entscheidungen' in Arno Scherzberg (ed), *Klugheit: Begriff – Konzepte – Anwendungen* (Mohr Siebeck, Tübingen 2008) 129

Sigmar Uhlig, 'Leitsatzbildung' (1974) *DRiZ*, 75

Alan Uzelac, 'Supreme Courts in the 21st Century: should organisation follow the function?' (2019) *Studia Iuridica*, 125

Marc van Opijnen M and others, 'On-line Publication of Court Decisions in the EU: Report of the Policy Group of the Project 'Building on the European Case Law Identifier'' (2017) <https://www.bo-ecli.eu/uploads/deliverables/Deliverable%20WS0-D1.pdf> accessed 12 July 2021

Marc van Opijnen and Cristiana Santos, 'On the concept of relevance in legal information retrieval' (2017) 25 *Artif Intell Law*, 65

Cornelia Vismann, Akten. Medientechnik und Recht (3rd edn, Fischer Taschenbuch Verlag, Frankfurt am Main 2011)

Friedemann Vogel, Stephan Pötters and Ralph Christensen, *Richterrecht der Arbeit – empirisch untersucht: Möglichkeiten und Grenzen computergestützter Textanalyse am Beispiel des Arbeitnehmerbegriffs* (Duncker & Humblot, Berlin 2015)

Jonathan de Vries, 'Legal Research, Legal Reasoning and Precedent in Canada in the Digital Age' (2018) 487 *Advocates' Quarterly*, 1

Rainer Wahl, 'Entwicklungspfade im Recht' (2013) 68 *Juristenzeitung*, 369

Karl Wahle, 'Vorwort' in Redaktionsausschuss des Obersten Gerichtshofes (ed), *Die Judikate und Sprüche des Obersten Gerichtshofes seit seinem Bestande* (1950) III

Reinhard Walker, 'Die richterliche Veröffentlichungspraxis in der Kritik' (1998) 34 *JurPC*, Abs. 1 – 163 <https://www.jurpc.de/jurpc/show?id=19980034> accessed 12 July 2021

James P Walsh and Gerardo R Ungson, 'Organizational Memory' (1991) 16 *The Academy of Management Review*, 57

Rolf Wank, *Juristische Methodenlehre: Eine Anleitung für Wissenschaft und Praxis* (Verlag Franz Vahlen, München 2020)

Ruth K Weber, *Der Begründungsstil von Conseil constitutionnel und Bundesverfassungsgericht: Eine vergleichende Analyse der Spruchpraxis* (Mohr Siebeck, Tübingen 2019)

Westphal, 'Grundzüge der Karteinutzung' in Ewald Löser and Richard Couvé (eds), *Reformen in den städtischen Verwaltungen* (C. Heymann, Berlin 1930)

Ewald Wiederin, 'Der Leitsatz als juristisches Kommunikationsformat' in Robert Kert and Andrea Lehner (eds), *Vielfalt des Strafrechts im internationalen Kontext: Festschrift für Frank Höpfel zum 65. Geburtstag* (NWV, Wien, Graz 2018) 765

Wilhelm Wolf, 'Richterliche Entscheidungsroutinen als Gegenstand und Leitfaden der juristischen Methodenlehre: zivilrechtliche Perspektiven' in Franz Reimer (ed), *Juristische Methodenlehre aus dem Geist der Praxis?* (Nomos, Baden-Baden 2016) 75

Precedents in Private Law – A Civil Law Perspective

Georg Kodek

A. *Introduction*

The purpose of this chapter is to look at "precedents" from a perspective of Civil Law. I'll try to do so not just for my own legal system, but will also look at France and Germany. A broader scope of analysis is necessary in order to avoid oversimplifications and misunderstandings which may arise if one attempts to extrapolate from just one legal system and in this way tries to gain insights into the Civil Law in general. Often even knowledgeable comparatists base their conclusions on the observations from only one legal system, thus failing to adequately take into account important differences among the various Civil Law countries.[1] Such an approach, while maybe sometimes necessitated by difficulties in accessing sufficient sources (and these difficulties may well include language problems), fails to perceive the differences that exist among the various members of the Civil Law family in terms of history, degrees of specificity of their respective civil codes and other laws, styles of (legal) writings in general and judgments in particular and, in general, legal culture.

The selection of the countries discussed in this paper is not accidental. Rather, France was one of the first countries to enact a civil code. Specifically, it was the first country to enact a civil code which, in large measure, is still in force today. Also, the French code has also been, in whole or in part, the model for civil codes in other countries from (parts of) Germany, Romania, Egypt, to Louisiana and Quebec, to name just a few. Therefore, it is not surprising that the distinction between the tasks of the legislature on the one hand and the courts on the other hand was very early developed (and succinctly expressed) there. On the other hand, Germany is the country which tremendously contributed to the "intellectualization" of civil law by the Legal History Movement (*Historische Rechtsschule*) of

1 An example for the wrong conclusions drawn from such a one-sided method is the comparative discussion of "case law" by Gutteridge, *Comparative Law* (1946) 88 ff, which apparently (without him telling so) is only based on observations gained from French law.

the 19th century. Even today one cannot but be impressed by the level of learning evidenced by German academic writings and court decisions. Also, Germany with its some 21,000 professional judges probably, in relation to its population, has the largest number of judges worldwide. Indeed, it is sometimes criticized as becoming a "Judges' State" (*Richterstaat*) – a development which by some authors has been described as a secret "revolution".[2] Therefore, it is particularly apt to look at Germany if we want to discuss the effect of judicial decisions. Finally, Austria is my home country where I have spent most of my professional life. While generally perceived, from a view of comparative law, as being a member of the German "family" of legal systems, Austria has a civil code which is almost 100 years older than the German code. Consequently, legal doctrine and practice, in spite of many contacts and influences between these two countries, developed quite differently.

I'll limit my discussion to private law (as opposed to public law which in Civil Law would include constitutional and administrative law, and criminal law). There are two reasons for this limitation of my short paper. The first one is trivial: Private law is the field of law I have practiced in, and written about, for some 35 years, whereas my experience in criminal law is limited to a short stint with the Kings County District Attorney in New York more than 30 years ago and a few criminal cases I heard many years ago at the beginning of my judicial career in Austria.

The second reason for the limitation of the scope of my paper is perhaps more important: There are significant differences between private law and public law, particularly constitutional law and European Union law. Thus, in many Civil Law countries there are specialized constitutional courts which can nullify laws if the court considers them unconstitutional. These decisions are binding on everybody, not just on the parties of the case. Significantly, in Germany, the law expressly provides that such decisions "have the force of a law" ("*Gesetzeskraft*").[3] The same holds true for court decisions overturning subordinate legislation (administrative regulations). This authority is often exercised by specialized administrative courts.[4]

2 See, e.g., Rüthers, *Die heimliche Revolution vom Rechtsstaat zum Richterstaat* (2014).

3 See § 31 para 2 German Constitutional Court Act (*Bundesverfassungsgerichts-Gesetz*).

4 I should point out that this authority of administrative courts is by no means a universal feature of all civil law countries. Thus, in Austria, only the Constitutional Court has the authority to nullify general norms, regardless of whether they were enacted by the legislature or issued by an administrative authority.

Similarly, many decisions of the CJEU are considered to have an *erga omnes* effect.[5]

Also, it has been suggested that "case law" has played an even larger role in the development of French administrative and constitutional law.[6]

On first glance, speaking of "case law" in a civil law system may sound inappropriate, perhaps even absurd.[7] Indeed, the Common Law is often characterized as being built on court decisions which are considered binding also for subsequent cases. On the other hand, it is often described as a "key feature" of Civil Law systems that in these countries, "[o]nly legislative enactments are considered binding for all. There is little scope for judge-made law in civil, criminal and commercial courts, although in practice judges tend to follow previous judicial decisions."[8]

Yet, when we take a closer look, also in civil law countries we find traces of "binding" precedent. It is the purpose of this paper to identify these traces in order to present a more accurate picture of the role of prior decisions in Civil Law countries. After a discussion of the position of the 19th century civil codes (section B) and academic authors of the time (section C) I'll move on to a discussion of factors that contribute to

5 B. Schima, *Das Vorabentscheidungsverfahren vor dem EuGH* (2015) 98.

6 Cohen-Tanugi, 'Case Law in a Legal System Without Binding Precedent: The French Example' (2006) 17 *Stanford Law School. Traditional Commentary*.

7 For a general discussion of "precedents" in Civil Law see Ancel, 'Case Law in France' (1934) 16 *Journal of Comparative Legislation and International Law*, 1; Ancel, 'Reflexions sur l'Etude Comparative des Cours Supremes et le Recours en Cassation' (1938) 3 *Annales de l'Institut de Droit Compare de l'Universite de Paris*, 285–302; C. Sumner Lobingier, 'Precedent in Past and Present Legal Systems' (1946) 44 *Michigan Law Review*, 955-996; Carbonnier, 'Authorities in civil law: France' in Brierley (trans) and Dainow (ed), *The role of judicial decisions and doctrine in civil law and in mixed jurisdictions* (1974); Troper and Grzegorczyk, 'Precedent in France' in MacCormick and Summers (eds), *Interpreting precedents: A comparative study* (1997) 103; Fon and Parisi, 'Judicial Precedents in Civil Law Systems: A Dynamic Analysis' (2006) 26 International Review of Law and Economics, 519 ff; Komarek, *Precedent and Judicial Lawmaking in Supreme Courts: The Court of Justice Compared to the US Supreme Court and the French Cour de Cassation* (2009); Igor Tokmadczic, 'The Case for Case Law: Recognising Precedent in Civil Law Systems' (2016), http://researcharchive.vuw.ac.nz/xmlui/bitstream/handle/10063/5228/paper.pdf?se (accessed 24 July 2021). For an epistemic justification of the use of precedents, see Bojan Spaić, 'The Authority of Precedents in Civil Law Systems' (2018) XXVII *Studia Iuridica Lubliensia*, 27- 44.

8 World Bank, *Key Features of Common Law or Civil Law Systems* <https://ppp.worldbank.org/public-private-partnership/legislation-regulation/framework-assessment/legal-systems/common-vs-civil-law> accessed 13 April 2021.

the "precedential effect" of court decisions. Here, the institutional framework (section D), the organization of the court system (section D II), the motivation of court decisions (section E) and the publication of decisions (section F) has to be taken into account. Also, in Civil Law systems there are mechanisms in place to ensure consistency of court decisions (section G). All these factors can contribute to court decisions having a stronger "effect" for the interpretation and development of the law. Finally, I'll try to show instances where in the Civil Law indeed a "binding" effect of "precedents" (or at least a close equivalent) can be discerned (section H). The final section of this short paper will attempt to elucidate the phenomenon of "authority" of court decisions in Civil Law legal systems in general (section I).

B. The Position of Early Civil Codes

The position of the early civil codes was clear: Judges were not allowed to create law; their decisions did not have any effect beyond the case in which they were rendered. Unity of law in Civil Law was to be achieved by way of codes, not by way of court decisions as is the case in the Common Law. Thus, the Prussian General Country Law (*Allgemeines Landrecht*) of 1792 flatly stated that "the opinions of academic lawyers or prior decisions of judges are not to be taken into account in future decisions."[9] A few years later, in 1804, the French Code Civil expressly prohibited judges from pronouncing general norms.[10] Also, the principle of res judicata was expressly limited to the object of the lawsuit.[11]

This was also the position of the Austrian Civil Code of 1811. There, it was expressly stipulated that decisions rendered in individual cases and judgments handed down by judges in particular lawsuits did not have the force of a law and could not be extended to other cases or other persons.[12]

---

9 Prussian ALR (1792) Einl § 6: „Auf Meinungen der Rechtslehrer oder ältere Aussprüche der Richter soll bei künftigen Entscheidungen keine Rücksicht genommen werden."

10 Art 5 Code Civil: Il est défendu aux juges de prononcer par voie de disposition générale et réglementaire sur les causes qui leur sont soumises.

11 Art 1351 Code Civil provided (until 2016): "L'autorité de la chose jugée n'a lieu qu'à l'égard de ce qui a fait l'objet du jugement. Il faut que la chose demandée soit la même; que la demande soit fondée sur la même cause; que la demande soit entre les mêmes parties, et formée par elles et contre elles en la même qualité."

12 § 12 Austrian Civil Code (*ABGB*): Die in einzelnen Fällen ergangenen Verfügungen und die von Richterstühlen in besonderen Rechtsstreitigkeiten gefällten Ur-

Indeed, until about the second half of the 19th century, not even judges of the Austrian Supreme Court were allowed access to prior decisions of this court,[13] the idea being that the Code is interpreted *de novo* in every single case. While this provision is still in force, it will be shown that actual practice as well as the entire legal framework have changed.

C. *Theoretical Approaches over Time*

When we look into theoretical approaches to the subject, developments in all countries show remarkable similarities. Initially, we always find very optimistic positions which overestimate to what degree a code could indeed determine the outcome of particular cases. This position was then universally abandoned in light of experience.

In France, according to Montesquieu, judges were to be "just the mouth of the law".[14] Indeed, the French view of the 18th and early 19th centuries was that the code, like a divine work, was to be regarded as a perfect and complete revelation of positive law, which ought a priori to be self-contained and cast in a system of mathematical exactitude.[15] On the other hand, Portalis, one of the drafters of the *Code civil*, correctly observed that

> "*[a] code, however complete it may seem, is no sooner finished than thousands of unexpected questions present themselves to the magistrate. For these laws, once drafted, remain as written. Men, on the other hand, never rest. They are always moving; and this movement, which never ceases and whose effects are variously modified by circumstances, continually produces some new fact, some new outcome. Many things are therefore necessarily left to the*

---

theile haben nie die Kraft eines Gesetzes, sie können auf andere Fälle oder auf andere Personen nicht ausgedehnet werden. The original draft of the Code had also provided that third parties were not allowed to assert such decisions. This was dropped in the final version, however. The revising committee felt that it would be conducive to consistency of decisions if the judges could be informed by the parties about prior decisions in similar cases (Ofner, *Der Ur-Entwurf und die Berathungs-Protokolle des Österreichischen Allgemeinen Bürgerlichen Gesetzbuches* [1889] I 33).

13 Wahle, 'Vorwort' in *Die Judikate und Sprüche des Obersten Gerichtshofes seit seinem Bestande* (1950) I, XXXIII; Kodek, 'Funktion und Arbeitsweise des OGH – die Binnensicht' in Kodek (ed), *Zugang zum OGH. Vorträge des Symposiums "Zugang zum OGH in Zivil- und Strafsachen"* (2012) 99 (104).

14 Montesquieu, *The Spirit of the Laws* (1748) bk XI ch 6, 73.

15 Gény, *Méthode d'interpretation et sources en droit privé positif* I (1919) para 96.

> *authority of custom, to the discussion of learned men, to the arbitration of judges*".[16]

In Austria, where the Code, like in France, restricted the effects of court decisions to the case in which they were rendered, the drafter of the Civil Code of 1811, Franz Zeiller, was opposed to awarding court decisions a binding effect beyond the case in which they were rendered. This, in his opinion, would lead to the evident danger to "perpetuate mistakes and injustices." Nonetheless he recognized the importance of consistency in judicial decisions, stating that it was desirable that courts, in order to avoid the impression of "justice being mutable", should remain steady and uniform ("*gleichförmig*") in their decisions.[17]

Almost 100 years later, when the German Civil Code of 1900 entered into force, codified law was widely perceived as perfect, being a complete and self-contained system, and thus being "gapless". At about the same time, the famous jurist Gierke stated that no court decision had binding authority. On the other hand, he recognized that court decisions may be important in that they constitute the "custom of the court" ("*usus fori*") and thus, a source of customary law.[18]

D. *Institutional Framework*

I. *The Role of Courts in a codified legal system*

When one wants to discuss the role of court decisions and of "case law" in Civil Law, one has to be aware of the institutional framework. First and foremost, Civil Law courts operate in a legal system which, in large measure, is based on written laws. Clearly, the idea of courts being limited to deciding individual cases whereas the passing of general norms is the prerogative of the legislature, relates to the separation of powers and, therefore, ultimately is of a constitutional dimension.[19] Thus, it can be argued that the members of parliament, rather than courts, because they

16 Preliminary Address on the First Draft of the Civil Code, presented by Messrs. Portalis, Tronchet, Bigot-Préameneu and Millville, members of the government-appointed commission, on 1 Pluviôse IX (21.01.1801), <https://www.justice.gc.ca/eng/rp-pr/csj-sjc/ilp-pji/code/index.html> accessed 13 April 2021.

17 Zeiller, *Commentar* I (1811) 85.

18 Gierke, *Deutsches Privatrecht* (1936) § 21, 177 ff.

19 See Payandeh, *Judikative Rechtserzeugung* (2017) 151 ff.

are elected by way of general elections, should be the only ones allowed to enact general norms in a democracy. Yet, it should be pointed out that this concern does not only apply to democracies. Rather, a power of the judges to shape general rules could be regarded also as incompatible, e.g., with the powers of an absolute monarch. This is graphically illustrated by the similar approaches taken by the French and the Austrian codes in the early 1900s: Both codes restricted the effect of court decisions to the case in which they were rendered.[20] Yet, in France this provision served to protect the prerogative of parliament, the National Assembly. There, the strict conception of separation of powers was due to the general distrust of courts that were manipulated by the king before the French revolution.[21] On the other hand in Austria, which was an absolute monarchy at this time, the provision wanted to prevent intrusions into the emperor's law-making authority.

In Civil Law countries, at least in principle, the most important decisions as to what the law should be, have been made by the legislature in enacting the civil code or other applicable law. This is also often spelt out in the constitution as being an essential part of the "rule of law" ("*Rechtsstaatsprinzip*"). Obviously, a law can never be "complete" in the sense that all possible situations are dealt with or no doubt can arise as to its meaning. Codified law may fail to provide a rule to meet a particular state of fact, or may deal with it in a manner which experience has proved to be inadequate.[22]

Yet, even if the statutory framework is sparse or out-dated (or both), at least some important questions will have been dealt with by the legislature. Therefore, courts and practitioners will refer to the code rather than to cases whenever there is a statutory provision on point. The importance of prior decisions is inversely proportional to the degree of specificity of the code or other statutory provisions.[23] The more detailed rules are set

---

20 See above section B.

21 Fon and Parisi, 'Judicial Precedents in civil law systems: A dynamic analysis' (2006) 26 *International Review of Law and Economics*, 519, 520, 522.

22 Gutteridge, *Comparative Law* (1946) 93.

23 Therefore, a meaningful comparison of the use of precedents in various legal systems also has to take into account the degree of specificity of statutory provisions. This cannot be done on a wholesale-basis, but has to be limited to certain areas of the law because the degree of specificity of statutory provisions can vary within a legal system. Clearly, when a statute only prohibits "unfair" trade practices, the role of court decisions is more important than in case of statute specifying the applicable rate of interest. Unfortunately, this aspect is sometimes overlooked in comparative research. For a suggestion of a more limited approach to research

forth in the code, the less need (and, indeed, leeway) is there for the courts to resolve questions of doubt. On the other hand, if the law remains silent or ambiguous, one has to resort to court decisions in order to learn what the law is.

A good example is the French law of delicts or tort. The *Code civil* devotes only a few articles (Articles 1382–1386) to this important area of the law. Thus, Article 1382 merely stated that any act whatever of a man, which causes damage to another, obliges the one by whose fault it occurred to compensate it.[24] Therefore, today, the substance of French tort law is to be found not in the provisions of the code, but in a very large number of judicial decisions.[25] The situation in Austria is similar. While the provisions on tort law in the Austrian Civil Code are more specific compared to France (sections 1293 to 1341), a lot of ambiguities remain. Similar to French law, the most important provision, section 1295, just provided that "anybody is entitled to ask for compensation from the tortfeasor for the damage inflicted to him by fault; no matter whether the loss was inflicted by way of violation of a contractual duty or without relation to a contract." Clearly, this leaves a lot of questions for the courts do decide. This includes the question of when a conduct is considered to be "fault", what duties of care are owed outside a contractual relationship or when a pure economic loss can be recovered. These defects of this part of the Austrian code led to several attempts of reform which, at least in part, was aimed at more clearly spelling out in the code the principles developed by the courts.[26]

Another example is insurance law. Until 1930 French law of non-marine insurance was entirely case law.[27] The same was true for Austria in the 19th century when insurance contracts were only briefly mentioned in the General Civil Code as "aleatory contracts".[28] Also, important types of contracts such as loan or lease were not regulated in the Civil Code. Heavily rooted in its Roman law origins and 18th century business practice,

---

only examining specific branches of the law, see Bell, 'Comparing Precedent' (1997) 82 *Cornell Law Review*, 1242, 1272.

24 "Tout fait quelconque de l'homme, qui cause à autrui un dommage, oblige celui par la faute duquel il est arrivé à le réparer".

25 Gutteridge, *Comparative Law* (1946) 93.

26 Griss et al., *Entwurf eines neuen österreichischen Schadenersatzrechts* (2005); an alternative proposal was published by Reischauer et al., *Reform des Schadenersatzrechts* (2006); for an alternative proposal by the Austrian Ministry of Justice see BMJ, *200 Jahre ABGB – RichterInnenwoche in Lochau* (2012) 151, 277.

27 Gutteridge, *Comparative Law* (1946) 93.

28 § 1269 Austrian Civil Code (*ABGB*).

the only form of loan dealt with in the original version of the Austrian Civil Code of 1811 was the Roman *mutuum*, a "real contract" ("*contractus in re*") for a loan for consumption. This was hardly satisfactory for modern business and, consequently, rules for other types of loans (based on simple consent of the parties, rather than on the money actually being paid out) were developed by courts and practice. Only in 2010 did the legislature step in and introduced rules on loans ("*Kreditvertrag*") into the Austrian Civil Code.[29] Similarly, the Austrian Code of 1811 did not (and even today, does not) mention leasing contracts. Consequently, rules for this form of contract had to be worked out by the courts, relying on analogy to other types of contract and on general principles.

II. Organization of the court system and case load

Another important aspect concerns the organization of the court system. Typically, Civil Law countries have not just one supreme court, but several highest courts with different functions. Thus, there often is a specialized constitutional court and often also a supreme administrative court in addition to a supreme court which is the court of last resort for civil and criminal cases. For example, in Germany, there are no less than six "supreme courts": the Constitutional Court (*Bundesverfassungsgericht*), the Supreme Court (*Bundesgerichtshof*), the Supreme Labour Court (*Bundesarbeitsgericht*), the Supreme Social Court (*Bundessozialgericht*), the Supreme Administrative Court (*Bundesverwaltungsgericht*) and the Supreme Fiscal Court (*Bundesfinanzhof*). While the German constitution envisages a "Supreme Federal Court" (*Oberstes Bundesgericht*) on top of these courts,[30] such a court has not been established so far. Rather, the function of this court is now exercised by a panel composed of judges of the six supreme courts, the "common panel of the supreme Federal courts".

In France, there is the Court of Cassation (*Cour de Cassation*) for civil and criminal matters, the State Council (*Conseil d'État*) for administrative matters and the Constitutional Council (*Conseil constitutionnel*) for constitutional matters. Similarly, in Austria there is the Supreme Court (*Oberster Gerichtshof*) for civil and criminal cases, the Court of Administrative Review (*Verwaltungsgerichtshof*) for administrative and tax cases and the Con-

29 In this year, the Austrian legislature enacted the Loan and Credit Amendment Act (Darlehens- und Kreditrechts-Änderungsgesetz – DaKrÄG).

30 See the original text of Art 95 of the German Constitution (*Grundgesetz*).

stitutional Court (*Verfassungsgerichtshof*) for review of laws and regulations as well as individual administrative decisions (but not court decisions) if a violation of a constitutional right is alleged. Similar systems are in place in most other Civil Law countries.

In addition, Civil Law supreme courts typically are very large and composed of several panels. These panels often have one or more areas of specialization. Thus, e.g., in the French Court of Cassation, there is a specialized commercial chamber, a social chamber and a penal chamber in addition to three civil chambers. In Germany, the Federal Supreme Court is composed of 13 highly specialized civil panels and 6 criminal panels. In Austria, the Supreme Court has 10 civil panels composed of five judges each (although some judges sit in more than one panel) and five criminal panels. The civil panels each have one or more special areas of expertise. In addition, cases categorized as "general civil cases" (such as, e.g., family law matters, sales contracts) not falling under one of the areas of special expertise are assigned to the various panels at a random basis.

Unlike in Common Law countries, supreme courts in civil law countries typically decide a large number of cases. Whereas the UK Supreme Court in 2019/20 only heard 82 appeals and decided 56 cases,[31] the Austrian Supreme Court in 2019 decided 2,786 civil cases (and some 800 criminal cases). The figures for the German Supreme Court are somewhat higher, with 3,782 civil cases heard in 2020, although to these one would have to add the cases decided by the Supreme Labour Court and the Supreme Social Court which exercise functions which in Austria are performed by the Supreme Court. As impressive as these figures are, they are easily topped by the French Court of Cassation which in 2017 heard a staggering 17,458 civil cases in 2017. In 2015 this figure was even higher at 22,890.

The large number of cases decided also requires a large number of judges even at the Supreme Court level. Thus, the French Cour de Cassation has 203 judges (121 *conseillers* and *82 conseillers référendaires)* for civil and criminal cases.[32] In other countries we find similarly impressive figures: The German Supreme Court has 152 judges for civil and criminal cases.[33] Yet these judges are not the sole arbiters of private law in Germany.

31 See, The Supreme Court Annual Report and Accounts 2019–202, 58 <https://www.supremecourt.uk/docs/annual-report-2019-20.pdf> accessed 13 April 2021.

32 https://www.courdecassation.fr/institution_1/presentation_2845/membres_cour_cassation_30991.html accessed 13 April 2021.

33 https://www.bundesgerichtshof.de/DE/DasGericht/Organisation/organisation_node.html accessed 13 April 2021.

In addition, there are the 38 judges of the Federal Labour Court[34] and the 42 judges of the Federal Social Court.[35] Similarly, in Austria the Supreme Court has 58 to 60 judges. This large number of judges, in and by itself, leads to courts being more "anonymous" than in Common Law countries. Thus, most lawyers in Civil Law countries would be hard-pressed to name more than perhaps two or three supreme court judges by name.

The large number of cases heard by Civil Law supreme courts has a number of important consequences for our enquiry: First, as a matter of simple arithmetic, the sheer number of decisions reduces the relative importance of every single decision. Second, because of the large number of decisions, it is more likely that a certain question of law has been addressed and developed not just by one decision, but by several decisions. This explains why comparative lawyers frequently find a chain of decisions on a single question of law in Civil Law systems.[36] Finally, because of the large number of decisions, reference to particular decisions may be impractical. Indeed, a principle may have been worked out not by a single decision but by a body of "case law". Particularly in France, the huge body of court decisions is often accessed indirectly by reference to treatises and commentaries which summarize and discuss the pertinent case law. Thus, the law is "distilled" from a large number of cases, not a single "leading" case. These observations, at least in part, explain why sometimes Civil Law courts refer to a "long standing line of decisions" rather than to single cases.

When we narrow our analysis from a general consideration of the entire legal system of a country to specific branches of the law,[37] we often find a different situation: Because of the high degree of specialization often found in the supreme courts of Civil Law countries, cases will be decided by a special panel of the supreme court. In their particular field of work, practitioners typically, from cases they litigated, but also from publications or seminars, know the judges. In a specialized area of the law it is also more likely that specialists (who are, of course, familiar with the general statutory framework) will focus their arguments and discussions (not on

---

34 https://www.bundesarbeitsgericht.de/dasgericht/richter.html accessed 13 April 2021.

35 https://www.bsg.bund.de/DE/Gericht/Rechtsprechung/recht-sprechung_node.html. While according to this website the number of judges is 44, it is currently only 42 (information from the court via email of 14 April 2021).

36 Gutteridge, *Comparative Law* (1946) 90.

37 This approach is recommended by Bell, 'Comparing Precedent' (1997) 82 *Cornell Law Review*, 1242, 1248.

lines of decisions or general "principles", but) on single decisions because that approach is necessary for the level of detail of their discussion. Examples for such areas of the law are, e.g., corporate law, unfair trade practices law or tax law.[38] In some of these areas, contrary to general practice in Civil Law systems, cases also are often referred to by catchy names rather than just by docket numbers, dates or publication.[39] In these areas, with a smaller number of judges and, consequently, a smaller number of decisions involved, the work of lawyers will often more closely resemble the situation in Common Law systems.

Finally, the style of judicial decisions[40] in Civil Law countries is different from the Common Law. Civil Law judges write in a purely impersonal style, rarely using the first person singular. Rather, even though, of course, the names of the judges are stated in judgments, the judgment would refer to "the Court" in the third person singular. This is by no means restricted to court decisions. Rather, in Germany and Austria as well as in France[41] students already learn in school and later in university that in essays and papers they are to avoid the first person singular and should adopt a more "objective" style of writing. This tendency is furthered by the fact that most Civil Law courts do not permit dissenting opinions, the most prominent exception being the German Constitutional Court. Observations like Lord Denning's "It was bluebell time in Kent"[42] or comments like Lord Roger's "I view the outcome with little enthusiasm"[43] are inconceivable in a Civil Law country. This seemingly "objective" style of reasoning, together with the attempt to demonstrate that the result achieved by the

38 For example, the discussion of the prohibition of "unfair" trade practices in the standard commentary on unfair trade practices in Austria (Wiebe and Kodek [eds], *UWG* [2nd edn, 2017]) comprises almost the entire first volume of two volumes.

39 For example, a seminal case in Austria on unfair trade practices and the selling of drugs via mail order is referred to as "Viagra", thereby making sure that every lawyer remembers the case. A full citation of the case would read "OGH 22.06.1999, 4 Ob 129/99w = ÖBl 2000, 64 – *Viagra*" (with the indication of the name of the court and the date often left out because the docket number and the name provide a sufficient, unequivocal identification of the decision). In order to avoid any possible confusion, I should point out that the presiding judge in this case, Dr. Kodek, was not this author, but rather my uncle.

40 On this, see Bell, 'Comparing Precedent' (1997) 82 *Cornell Law Review*, 1242, 1248.

41 I owe this information to my wife's sister who is a teacher in Paris.

42 *Hinz v. Berry* [1970] 2 QB 40 at 42.

43 Lord Roger in *R (Lewis) v Redcar and Cleveland Borough Council* (2010) UKSC 11 at para 97.

court is derived from the statute (or some statute-based general principle) sometimes conceals the fact that the court is indeed "creating" new law.

E. The Motivation of Court Decisions

I. Introduction

In order to determine whether, and if so, to what extent, there is a "case law" in Civil Law, one first has to look at what judges actually do. Obviously, in order to answer this question, one has to know whether, and again, if so, to what extent judges in practice actually follow prior decisions. But the answer to this question also depends on other factors which can contribute to the development of a "case law" . Here, the single most important factor is whether, and to what extent, judgments are motivated, i.e. whether, and to what extent, the reasons for the result reached by the court are spelt out in the judgment. Were decisions made by throwing a dice, this could not serve as a guideline for the outcome of future case. Perhaps more importantly, no rules could be derived from such a "judgment" which the "users" of the law could follow in the future. Also, a magisterial pronouncement without any reasons being given will provide little, if any guideline for future cases. On the other hand, clearly an extensive written motivation, in particular if it includes references to prior decisions, immensely contributes to the emergence of "case law". Indeed, publication and "motivation" have been described as the "two pillars of the integrity of case law".[44]

In this respect we find enormous differences among Civil Law countries.[45] The spectrum ranges from the highly compressed style of French decisions (which often consist of just one, albeit long, sentence) to the academic style of reasoning of German courts. Therefore, when it is said that in continental judgments precedents are very rarely referred to,[46] this is accurate only for France (and, perhaps, other countries influenced by the French legal system), but certainly not for other Civil Law countries such as Austria, Germany or Switzerland.

---

44 Cohen-Tanugi, 'Case Law in a Legal System Without Binding Precedent: The French Example' (2006) 17 *Stanford Law School. Traditional Commentary*.

45 S MacCormick and Summers, *Interpreting Precedents: A Comparative Study* (1997); Bell, 'Comparing Precedent' (1997) 82 *Cornell Law Review*, 1242.

46 Gutteridge, *Comparative Law* (1946) 89.

II. France

In France the original idea of judgments being based on the code alone is still very much alive. Even today, French judgments purport to be founded on the *lex scripta*. This notion contributes to the characteristic style of French judgments. They are typically very short and do not contain any references to authorities. Also, there is no publication of dissenting opinions, nor any trace of internal discussion or doubt.[47] Judgments are rightly described as being "highly compressed" and, consequently, "there is much to be read between the lines."[48] Indeed, in order to duly appreciate and understand a judgment of the Court of Cassation, one has to rely on commentaries or case notes. While there are no direct references to prior decisions, courts sometimes use a system of indirect citation by using verbatim quotes of prior decisions like formulas.[49] This also contributes to the formation of a *jurisprudence constante*. An example for this method is provided by Cohen-Tanugi:[50] The commercial chamber of the Cour de Cassation relied on a decision of the Plenary Assembly granting third parties the right to invoke the provisions of a contract as the basis of a tort claim. The commercial chamber did not mention the underlying case or the Plenary Assembly decision, but used the exact phrasing from the Plenary Assembly's decision at the beginning of its own decision, elevating the wording from the earlier decision to the level of a legal principle: "Whereas a third party can invoke a breach of contract as the basis of a tort claim when that breach of contract caused him a prejudice".[51]

---

47 See Cohen-Tanugi, *Le droit sans l'Etat (Law Without the State)* (1985) 79–82.

48 Allen, *Law in the Making*, 7th revised ed (1964) 180. The respective passage of the third edition of Sir Allen's book (Oxford 1939, pp. 168, 169) is cited approvingly by Gutteridge, *Comparative Law* (1946) 89.

49 Cohen-Tanugi, 'Case Law in a Legal System Without Binding Precedent: The French Example' (2006) 17 *Stanford Law School. Traditional Commentary*.

50 Cohen-Tanugi, 'Case Law in a Legal System Without Binding Precedent: The French Example' (2006) 17 *Stanford Law School. Traditional Commentary*.

51 Cour de cassation, commercial chamber, 6 March 2007, No. 04–13.689 ("*Attendu que le tiers à un contrat peut invoquer, sur le fondement de la responsabilité délictuelle, un manquement contractuel, dès lors que ce manquement lui a causé un dommage.*").

III. Germany and Austria

German and Austrian court decisions are characterized by their lengthy, erudite style. In both countries, court decisions rely heavily on, and extensively cite, authorities, both academic writings and prior decisions. The extensive motivation of judgments, particularly those of higher courts, makes it more likely that a decision is cited and used in other cases as well. Indeed, there is a "dialogue" between courts and academia with courts extensively discussing, and often following, academic writings and vice versa. Interestingly, this was not always the case. Until the 19th century, court judgments often were not motivated. In Austria, a mandatory motivation of court decisions was only introduced in 1853.[52]

F. Access to Court Decisions

If we examine whether, and to what extent, court decisions can have an effect beyond the case in which they were rendered and can actually constitute " law", an essential prerequisite is that these decisions are accessible in some form. Normally, this aspect is discussed under the heading of "publication" of court decisions.[53] This approach, however, is too narrow. The minimum requirement for prior court decisions to have an effect on decisions in later cases (and, thereby, warrant maybe to be regarded as "law") is that these decisions are accessible to the judges themselves. This aspect is normally not discussed because, apparently, it is taken for granted that a court's decisions are available to the judges themselves. Yet, legal history shows that at least in Civil Law countries this was by no means always the case. Thus, in Austria in the first half of the 19th century (and, therefore, for the first fifty years after the enactment of the Austrian Civil

---

52 Sprung, 'Die Entwicklung der zivilgerichtlichen Begründungspflicht' in Sprung and König (eds), *Entscheidungsbegründung* (1974) 43 (61); Kodek, 'Funktion und Arbeitsweise des OGH – die Binnensicht' in Kodek (ed), *Zugang zum OGH. Vorträge des Symposiums "Zugang zum OGH in Zivil- und Strafsachen"* (2012) 99 (113).

53 See, e.g., Bell, 'Comparing Precedent' (1997) 82 *Cornell Law Review*, 1243 (1270). For a history of the publication of court decisions, see Walker, 'Die Entwicklung der Publikationsmedien im modernen Staat' (1998) 97 *JurPC Web-Dok* <https://www.jurpc.de/jurpc/show?id=19980097> accessed 13 April 2021; see also Forgó-Feldner, 'Der OGH und der Zugang zu seinen Entscheidungen in historischer Perspektive' in Kodek (ed), *Zugang zum OGH. Vorträge des Symposiums „Zugang zum OGH in Zivil- und Strafsachen"* (2012) 1, 27 ff (citing further authority).

Code) the judges of the Supreme Court[54] did not know the decisions of other panels of that court.[55] During this time, the idea was still prevalent that judges decided every case afresh on the basis of the code itself. Therefore, access to prior decisions was regarded as unnecessary. Only in 1854 supreme court judges were allowed to inspect the "register of judgments" (*Judikatenbuch*) which contained important decisions.[56]

During the 19th century, the practice of selected publication of court decisions developed. At that time, this was a purely private initiative. Only from 1850, selected cases were published in an official publication once a year. The publication of court decisions was originally opposed by the government on the ground that this could lead to the case law becoming too rigid.[57] Interestingly, this argument suggests that a development of the jurisprudence was something desirable. This has to be pointed out because the president of the Supreme Court, Taaffe, had opposed the idea that the jurisprudence of courts should develop.[58]

Until the advent of wide-spread use of electronic databases, law journals were (and, to a certain extent, still are) the primary medium of publication of court decisions. This system was (and, in case of decisions of lower courts, still is) based on decisions being made available for publication ("sent in") by judges or lawyers. Only a relatively small number of all decisions was published in this form. All other decisions were indexed and referenced by way of a complex index with cardboard index cards.[59] Until 1990, a statutory provision restricted access to this index to judges and law professors. In 1990, the Austrian Constitutional Court overturned

54 In this time, the court of last resort was the "Supreme Justice Authority" (*Oberste Justizstelle*) which exercised both the functions of a supreme court and of a ministry of justice.

55 Wahle, 'Vorwort' in *Die Judikate und Sprüche des Obersten Gerichtshofes seit seinem Bestande* (1950) I, XXXIII; Kodek, 'Funktion und Arbeitsweise des OGH – die Binnensicht' in Kodek (ed), *Zugang zum OGH. Vorträge des Symposiums "Zugang zum OGH in Zivil- und Strafsachen"* (2012) 99 (104).

56 See also below section H.

57 Kodek, 'Funktion und Arbeitsweise des OGH – die Binnensicht' in Kodek (ed), *Zugang zum OGH. Vorträge des Symposiums "Zugang zum OGH in Zivil- und Strafsachen"* (2012) 99, 113.

58 Wahle, 'Vorwort' in *Die Judikate und Sprüche des Obersten Gerichtshofes seit seinem Bestande* (1950) XVII.

59 This system was introduced in 1907. See Forgó-Feldner, 'Der OGH und der Zugang zu seinen Entscheidungen in historischer Perspektive' in Kodek (ed), *Zugang zum OGH. Vorträge des Symposiums „Zugang zum OGH in Zivil- und Strafsachen"* (2012), 1 (21).

this provision as being unconstitutional.[60] According to the Court, the rule of law (*Rechtsstaatsprinzip*) required the efficiency of process[61] and the decisions of the Supreme Court as highest court in civil and criminal matters had a special function for assuring unity and legal certainty in the application of the law. The decisions of the Supreme Court served an essential function beyond the concrete case in which they had been rendered for the concretization of the law, for the interpretation of the law and for legal process. Therefore, according to the Court, it was evident that a reliable assessment of the admissibility of an appeal was only possible if it was possible to get access to the decisions of the Supreme Court.

On a similar line, the German Federal Administrative Tribunal (*Bundesverwaltungsgericht*) held that the duty of the state to grant access to justice (*Justizgewährungspflicht*), the principle of democracy and the principle of separation of powers required publication of court decisions.[62] Court decisions concretized legal provisions and developed the law. Therefore, according to the Court, publication of court decisions was as important as publication of laws. Another German decision held that publication of court decisions was important because of the principle of proceedings being public.[63]

In France there is no comprehensive official case reporting system. Rather, the presiding judge of the respective chamber decides whether or not to publish the decisions. There is a Reporter for civil cases and one for criminal cases (*Bulletin des Arrêts de la Cour de Cassation rendus en matiere civile* and *Bulletin des Arrêts de la Cour de Cassation rendus en matiere criminelle*, respectively). In addition, there are legal reviews (*revues juridiques generales*) which are published weekly and include various items including current news updates, legal writings, annotated full texts of court decisions, legislation, and summaries of new cases.[64]

Whereas traditionally there often only was a guarantee of court hearings being public,[65] nowadays Article 6 para 1 ECHR also requires that the judgment be pronounced publicly. While the text of Article 6 para 1 seems to require a public pronouncement of the decision, the Court,

---

60 VfGH 28.06.1990 - G 315/89, VfSlg 12.409.

61 The term used by the Court here is "*Rechtsschutz*" which literally means "legal protection".

62 BVerwG 26.02.1997 - 6 C 3/96, *NJW* 1997, 2694.

63 OLG Celle 12.06.1990 - 1 VAs 4/90, *NJW* 1990, 2570.

64 Cohen-Tanugi, 'Case Law in a Legal System Without Binding Precedent: The French Example' (2006) 17 *Stanford Law School. Traditional Commentary*.

65 See, e.g. Art 90 para 1 Austrian Constitution (*B-VG*).

quite pragmatically, has found, that "other means of rendering a judgment public" may also be compatible with Article 6 para1 ECHR.[66] In order to determine whether the forms of publicity provided for under domestic law are compatible with the requirement for judgments to be pronounced publicly within the meaning of this provision, "in each case the form of publicity to be given to the judgment under the domestic law [...] must be assessed in the light of the special features of the proceedings in question and by reference to the object and purpose of Article 6 para. 1".[67] The object pursued by Article 6 para 1 ECHR in this context – namely, to ensure scrutiny of the judiciary by the public with a view to safeguarding the right to a fair trial – must have been achieved during the course of the proceedings, which must be taken as a whole.[68] Where judgment is not pronounced publicly it must be ascertained whether sufficient publicity was achieved by other means.[69]

G. *Mechanisms to Ensure Consistency of Decisions*

I. *France*

All countries have adopted some mechanisms in order to ensure consistency of court decisions. In France, in case of contradictory decisions in similar cases by several chambers the Plenary Assembly of the Court of Cassation is convened to authoritatively resolve the conflicting interpretations. The Plenary Assembly is comprised of 19 judges, including the president of the court (*premier président*) and three representatives of each chamber.[70] The Plenary Assembly is also convened when an intermediate appellate court, after the Court of Cassation has overturned a decision

66 *Moser v. Austria*, ECHR 21.09.2006 – 12643/02, para 101.

67 ECHR, 7984/77, 08.12.1983, *Pretto and Others v. Italy*, para 26; ECHR, 8273/78, 08.12.1983, *Axen v. Germany*, para 31.

68 ECHR, 8273/78, 08.12.1983, *Axen v. Germany*, para 32.

69 For an overview of case law of the European Court of Human Rights on the publication of judgments, see European Court of Human Rights, Guide on Article 6 of the European Conventionon Human Rights – Right to a fair trial (civil limb) (2020) paras 408 ff <https://www.echr.coe.int/documents/guide_Art_6_eng.pdf> accessed 14 April 2021.

70 Cohen-Tanugi, 'Case Law in a Legal System Without Binding Precedent: The French Example' (2006) 17 *Stanford Law School. Traditional Commentary*.

and remanded the case, refuses to follow the decision of the Court of Cassation.

"Decisions of principle" ("*arrêts de principe*") of the Plenary Assembly are binding on all chambers of the Court of Cassation, and all lower judicial courts will generally apply the principles set forth in such decisions. Decisions by the Plenary Assembly are almost always considered to be decisions of principle. Decisions of principle do not differ in form from any other court decision. However, they will generally include a phrase explicitly stating a specific rule that applies to a particular situation.[71]

Another mechanism to ensure consistency of court decisions is a reference procedure which was introduced by the law of 15 May 1991. This procedure allows lower courts to request the opinion of the Supreme Court when they encounter new questions of serious difficulty.[72]

II. Germany

In the 19th century in some German states certain appellate decisions rendered by " plenary panels" were binding on lower courts.[73] However, this device seems to have been used only rarely. Contemporary observers noted that there seemed to exist a "*horror pleni*", i.e. a fear of convening the plenary panel.

Nowadays a complex mechanism is in place to avoid conflicting decisions between individual panels of the same court and with other courts. At the German Supreme Court, there are "enlarged panels" ("*Große Senate*") and "combined enlarged panels" ("*Vereinigte Große Senate*"). Also, if a panel wants to depart from a decision of another panel, the panels are to engage in a form of "dialogue". There is also a combined panel of all German highest courts ("*Gemeinsamer Senat der Obersten Gerichte des Bundes*"). In addition, there are reference proceedings available to other courts. Thus, an intermediate court of appeal can submit a request for a preliminary ruling to a special panel if it wants to depart from a decision of another court on the same level or of the Supreme Court ("*Divergenzvorlage*"). Also, a question can be referred to an enlarged panel if a large number of cases is

71 Cohen-Tanugi, 'Case Law in a Legal System Without Binding Precedent: The French Example' (2006) 17 *Stanford Law School. Traditional Commentary*.
72 Loi 91–491, Journal Officiel 18.05.1991. See Watt, 'Why French Law Rejects Judicial Precedent' (1997) *International Business Lawyer*, 18, 19.
73 See the examples listed by Gierke, *Deutsches Privatrecht* (1936) § 21, 177 fn. 3.

to be expected to be decided by different panels. This reference procedure is called "development of law reference" ("*Rechtsfortbildungsvorlage*").

III. Austria

Austria has a similar, although less elaborate, system to ensure consistency of judicial decisions. In spite of the restrictive position the Austrian Civil Code took against precedents,[74] the notion that court decisions may have an effect beyond the case in which they had been rendered seems to have come up quite early. Already Franz Zeiller, the drafter of the Austrian Civil Code, stated the importance of consistency of judicial decisions.[75]

In 1822 the Austrian emperor reprimanded the Supreme Court for departure from a prior decision. In an Imperial Decree ("*Allerhöchstes Handschreiben*") the emperor expressed his strongest disapproval because conflicting decisions were against the notion of justice and would undermine the authority of the Supreme Court. In order to avoid similar instances in the future, the presiding judge was ordered to stay a decision of a panel which was in conflict with an earlier decision and to refer the matter to a deliberation by a larger panel of 15 judges. If necessary, the matter was to be put before the emperor himself.[76] Similarly, in Austria under an imperial regulation of 1850 the Minister of Justice could authorize the Supreme Court to render plenary decisions which were binding on lower courts. This was abolished in 1872.[77]

In 1854 a register of important decisions (*Judikatenbuch*) was introduced. Departure of decisions registered there required a decision of a plenary panel of 15 judges.[78] Before the introduction of the *Judikatenbuch*, judges of the Supreme Court did not know (and could not get access to) the decisions of other panels.[79] According to a report by Haimberger, a

74 See above section B.

75 Zeiller, *Commentar I* (1811) 85. See also above section C.

76 This episode is related by Wahle, 'Vorwort' in *Die Judikate und Sprüche des Obersten Gerichtshofes seit seinem Bestande* (1950) V. Unfortunately, it is not clear anymore which decision triggered the emperor's disapproval and why this was the case.

77 See Unger, *Österreichisches Privatrecht I* (1856) § 45 Anm 13; Pfaff/Hofmann, *Commentar zum österreichischen allgemeinen bürgerlichen Gesetzbuche I* (1877) 213 ff.

78 Pfaff/Hofmann, *Commentar zum österreichischen allgemeinen bürgerlichen Gesetzbuche I* (1877) 213.

79 Wahle, 'Vorwort' in *Die Judikate und Sprüche des Obersten Gerichtshofes seit seinem Bestande* (1950) I, XXXIII; Kodek, 'Funktion und Arbeitsweise des OGH – die

well-known judge of that time, this led to "totally erroneous and unlawful" decisions being issued.[80] Specifically, the need for a register of decisions arose because the geographical area of jurisdiction of the Supreme Court was expanded to include Croatia and Hungary. As a result of this expansion, Croatian and Hungarian judges were appointed to the court who were said to be unfamiliar with Austrian law.[81]

Nowadays, a panel of five judges (the ordinary quorum for most cases) is enlarged by an additional six judges if the panel finds that prior Supreme Court decisions are in conflict with one another or if the panel wants to depart from an "established line of decisions".[82] In practice, however, such an enlargement of the panel rarely takes place, about once every two to three years.[83] While in theory a decision by an enlarged panel can be departed from later by another enlarged panel, this has never happened so far.

Binnensicht' in Kodek (ed), *Zugang zum OGH. Vorträge des Symposiums „Zugang zum OGH in Zivil- und Strafsachen"* (2012) 99 (104).

80 Wahle, 'Vorwort' in *Die Judikate und Sprüche des Obersten Gerichtshofes seit seinem Bestande* (1950) XIX.

81 Wahle, 'Vorwort' in *Die Judikate und Sprüche des Obersten Gerichtshofes seit seinem Bestande* (1950) VII; Kodek, 'Funktion und Arbeitsweise des OGH – die Binnensicht' in Kodek (ed), *Zugang zum OGH. Vorträge des Symposiums "Zugang zum OGH in Zivil- und Strafsachen"* (2012) 99 (104). It has to be pointed out that the Austrian Civil Code originally only was in force in Cisleithania, the part of Austria-Hungary situated west of the river Leitha. Only in 1851, the Civil Code was also introduced in Hungary, but there it remained in force only until 1861. See Olechowski, 'Das ABGB – Rechtseinheit für Zentraleuropa' in Kodek (ed), *200 Jahre Allgemeines Bürgerliches Gesetzbuch (ABGB) und Europäisches Vertragsrecht* (2012) 33, 40 ff. On Croatia, see Josipovic, 'Das ABGB in Kroatien – historische Geltung und Bedeutung für die kroatische Zivilrechtsgesetzgebung von heute' in Kodek (ed), *200 Jahre Allgemeines Bürgerliches Gesetzbuch (ABGB) und Europäisches Vertragsrecht* (2012) 55 ff.

82 § 8 Austrian Supreme Court Act (*Bundesgesetz über den Obersten Gerichtshof, OGHG*).

83 The decisions rendered by enlarged panels of the Austrian Supreme Court up to 2000 are discussed by Forgó-Feldner, *Verstärkte Senate beim Obersten Gerichtshof. Rechtsprechung im Spannungsfeld zwischen Unabhängigkeit, Richtigkeit und Einheitlichkeit* (2001).

H. *Binding Precedents? – A Search for Traces*

I. *Deviation from prior decisions*

When the civil codes were adopted, the prevailing (and, perhaps, universally accepted) view was that they constituted a sufficient guideline for courts and practice. Under this concept, it was thought that courts could decide cases on the sole basis of the code and would do so every time afresh without having to follow prior decisions. Yet, the original idea that judicial decisions do not have effects beyond the case in which they were rendered turned out to be too narrow. This change of views was brought about or at least furthered by radical developments of technology, of economy and of society as a whole with which the legislature could not always keep pace, thus leaving many decisions to the courts. Also, the traditional position that a statutory framework can be sufficiently "clear" and comprehensive so that courts simply have to "apply", rather than "create" or "shape" the law, has been recognized as being too optimistic. Rather, while still, at least in theory, being free to depart from and disregard prior decisions, courts in civil law countries nowadays often follow prior decisions. This point is clearly illustrated by a short look into any Civil Law commentary or treatise. There, very often (and, in case of publications aimed at practicing lawyers rather than academics, always) court decisions are prominently discussed. Also, such decisions are frequently relied on by lawyers and judges alike. Indeed, in practice, there is often little difference nowadays between Civil Law and Common Law in this respect. As Zweigert and Kötz, in their famous treatise on comparative law, observe, recently "the attitudes of Common Law and Continental Law have been drawing closer. On the Continent, [...] lawyers no longer see decision-making as a merely technical and automatic process, but accept that the comprehensive principles laid down by statutes call for broad interpretation, and have begun to treat the *jurisprudence constante* of the courts as an independent source of law."[84]

For prior decisions really constituting "precedents" in the full sense of the word, however, the empirical regularity of reference to previous decisions does not suffice.[85] Rather, the question is normative: Prior decisions are "precedents" only if judges not just regularly follow them in practice,

84 Zweigert and Kötz, *Introduction to Comparative Law* (2nd edn, 1987) 71.
85 Bell, 'Comparing Precedent' (1997) 82 *Cornell Law Review*, 1242, 1263.

but if they ought to do so.[86] Indeed, there are indications that also in Civil Law systems prior court decisions are more than just persuasive authority. This section will attempt to explore this aspect more fully.

With regard to the legal (as opposed to merely factual) effect of prior decisions it seems that the legal systems of the various Civil Law countries have developed differently. In France, the original concept that the code is the sole authority on which a court relies in its decision is still maintained.[87] A mere violation of *jurisprudence* does not constitute a ground for an appeal.[88] Rather, an appeal or cassation petition can only be based on a violation of the (statutory) law. Only occasionally does one find the notion that a prior decision (rather than codified law) is to be applied. Thus, an intermediate appellate court in one decision stated that „[t]he judges have made a just application of the terms of the judgment (sc. of the *cour de cassation* which was cited)".[89]

Indeed, the notion of judicial independence under which the judge is only bound by the written law is carried to its extremes in France. Technically, a lower court is not even bound by a decision of the *cour de cassation* if a decision is reversed and remanded. Only if the decision of the cassation court was rendered by the full court (*toutes chambres réunies*) would the lower court be bound to follow it. In practice, of course, appellate decisions (both rendered in the same proceeding and prior decisions) are usually followed. One reason (other than simple convenience) clearly is the hierarchical structure of French courts and the traditional concern of all judges worldwide to risk their decisions being overturned on appeal.[90] Thus, in practice a court will decide the case before it in conformity with earlier decisions to the extent to which they are similar.

---

86 Bell, 'Comparing Precedent' (1997) 82 *Cornell Law Review*, 1242, 1263.

87 See Watt, 'Why French Law Rejects Judicial Precedent' (1997) *International Business Lawyer*, 18; Lipstein, 'The Doctrine of Precedent in Continental Law with Special Reference to French and German Law' (1946) 28 *Journal of Comparative Legislation and International Law*, 34–44. See also Komarek, 'Precedent and Judicial Lawmaking in Supreme Courts: The Court of Justice Compared to the US Supreme Court and the French Cour de Cassation' in *Cambridge Yearbook of European Legal Studies* (2009) 399; McAuliffe, 'Precedent at the Court of Justice of the European Union: The Linguistic Aspect' (2013) 15 *Current Legal Issues*, 483.

88 Cour de cassation 21.12.1891 – Dalloz 1892 I 543.

89 Cour de Douai 05.03.1931 – Annales de Droit Commercial 1931, 348. The case is discussed by Ancel, *Case law in France* 11.

90 Watt, 'Why French Law Rejects Judicial Precedent' (1997) *International Business Lawyer*, 18, 19.

In its broadest sense *la jursprudence* is understood to mean the habit of the courts to decide similar cases in a similar manner.[91] While it is pointed out that *jurisprudence* cannot be considered an autonomous source of law, it exists in the form of the tendency to judge in a certain way in similar situations. As a result, *jurisprudence* is considered a source of law within the French legal system's "hierarchy of norms".[92] If there is a long line of concurring decisions, this is regarded as *jurisprudence constante.*[93] Along a similar line, Louisiana law provides that a precedent becomes a source of law when it has become "settled jurisprudence" (*jurisprudence constante*).[94]

In Austria the idea that consistency of court decisions was desirable was expressed quite early.[95] Presently in Germany and Austria it is postulated that there is a constitutional principle of "equality in the application of the law" (*Rechtsanwendungsgleichheit*).[96] This is a Civil Law equivalent of the Common Law principle that "like cases should be decided alike".[97]

In spite of consistency of court decisions being regarded as desirable, the position of courts varies as to the when departure from established jurisprudence is proper. A restrictive position was expressed by the German Supreme Court. According to a fundamental decision of the enlarged panel (*Großer Senat*) of the German Supreme Court of 1982, a departure or modification of a *jurisprudence constante* of many decades of jurisprudence requires "clearly prevailing or even compelling reasons".[98] If the interpretation of older statutory provisions was formed over time by a *jurisprudence*

---

91 Watt, 'Why French Law Rejects Judicial Precedent' (1997) *International Business Lawyer*, 18, 19.

92 Watt, 'Why French Law Rejects Judicial Precedent' (1997) *International Business Lawyer*, 18, 19. For an attempt to develop categories of judicial decisions, see Perreau, *Technique de la Jurisprudence en droit privé.*

93 Fon and Parisi, 'Judicial Precedents in civil law systems: A dynamic analysis' (2006) 26 *International Review of Law and Economics*, 519, 520.

94 For an analysis of precedential systems of *jurisprudence constante* see Dennis, 'The John Tucker Jr. Lecture in Civil Law: Interpretation and application of the civil code and the evaluation of judicial precedent' (1993) 54 *Louisiana Law Review*, 1; Moreno, 'Scott v. Cokern: Of precedent, jurisprudence constante, and the relationship between Louisiana commercial laws and Louisiana pledge jurisprudence' (1995) 10 *Tulane European and Civil Law Forum*, 31.

95 See section C above.

96 See Payandeh, *Judikative Rechtserzeugung* (2017) 173 ff, 353 f.

97 See, e.g., Marmor, *Law in the Age of Pluralism* (2007), chapter 7: "Should Like Cases Be Treated Alike?"

98 BGH 04.10.1982 – GSZ 1/82 = BGHZ 85, 64, 66. This view was affirmed by the Enlarged Panel for Civil Cases (Großer Senat für Zivilsachen), BGH 24.11.1994 – GSZ 1/94 = BGHZ 128, 85, 90 ff.

constante, legal certainty and the protection of legitimate expectations normally require that the existing jurisprudence be followed. A departure from this jurisprudence was only possible in exceptional circumstances.

Critics have remarked that the actual practice of the German Supreme Court does not live up to these restrictive criteria.[99] Yet, clearly protection of legitimate expectations of the public plays an important role in practice. This is achieved in various ways. Occasionally it is claimed that courts had to announce in advance that they intended to depart from a well-established jurisprudence.[100] In this debate, ideas similar to the Common Law concept of "prospective overruling" or the "future law approach" have been developed. Perhaps more importantly, departure from settled case law may lead to reversal on ground of "arbitrariness" (*Willkür*) by a Constitutional Court in some countries.[101]

In a relatively recent decision, the German Constitutional Court has adopted a more restrictive position as to the expectations of "constancy" of *jurisprudence constante*. The case concerned the question whether it was possible retroactively to deny to a trade union the capability to enter into collective agreements with employers or employers' associations. The Court declined to accept the trade unions application. It stated that the decisions of supreme courts were not statutory law and did not have a comparable binding force.[102] According to the Court, the effects of the interpretation of the law by these courts are based solely on the persuasive power of its reasons and the authority and competence of the court. Generally, the Court held, a significant change of circumstances or prevailing views is not a requirement for a court being permitted to depart from its prior decisions. The Court went on stating that "[f]rom a perspective of protection of legitimate expectations, an overruling of a *jurisprudence constante* is generally unobjectionable if there are sufficient reasons for this and the change takes place within expectable limits. Only in case of additional circumstances, in particular a firmly established line of decisions which has been followed for many years, a legitimate expectation as to a certain state of the law created by supreme court decisions can arise."[103]

99 Payandeh, *Judikative Rechtserzeugung* (2017) 313 ff.

100 This is heavily disputed. See Kodek, in Rummel and Lukas (eds), *ABGB* (2015), § 12, mn. 36 ff.

101 See Payandeh, *Judikative Rechtserzeugung* (2017) 264 ff, 297 ff. Furthermore, departure by a court or administrative authority from an established line of 'case law' may trigger a claim for damages against the state. See below section H.

102 BVerfG 25.04.2015 – 1 BvR 2314/12 para 13.

103 BVerfG 25.04.2015 – 1 BvR 2314/12 para 13.

Also in Austria the Supreme Court has repeatedly emphasized that "there always exists the theoretical possibility of a change of *jurisprudence constante*."[104] However, the Court went on to state that even in cases where a view repeatedly expressed in decisions was heavily criticized by academic writers, the likelihood of a change of jurisprudence in the near future cannot be predicted.[105] Therefore, a lawyer is only allowed "to engage in a risky attempt of challenging *jurisprudence constante*" if he advised the client on the risks associated with this attempt and the client consents to take these risks.[106]

Finally it has to be pointed out that the European Court for Human Rights has held that the existence of an established judicial practice should be taken into account in assessing the extent of the reasoning to be included in a decision.[107] In situations with well-established case law, courts must provide a detailed explanation as to why the case was determined contrary to existing case law. The court's failure to do so in that case meant that the court did not satisfy the requirements of a fair trial.

II. Precedents as a Means of Concretization of Statutes

In all legal systems court decisions are a means to concretize statutory provisions. In Germany, the existence of a body of "case law" explaining a law's meaning is also taken into account if a law is challenged on grounds of it being unconstitutional. Thus, a statute which otherwise would be unconstitutionally vague, will be upheld if there exist court decisions explaining the law's meaning.[108]

---

104 RIS-Justiz RS0026376.

105 RIS-Justiz RS0026376.

106 OGH 27.04.1989 – 7 Ob 568/89.

107 *Atanasovski v. The Former Yugoslav Republic of Macedonia,* ECHR 14.01.2010 – 36815/03. See also *Boumaraf v. France,* ECHR 30.08.2011 – 32820/08, where the principle established in *Atanasovski* was referred to. In this case, however, the Court, while noting that a more reasoned opinion would be desirable, held that the French court had satisfied the Article 6 requirements for a fair trial as the applicant had failed to prove that the case law at issue was sufficiently well-established. See also Cohen-Tanugi, 'Case Law in a Legal System Without Binding Precedent: The French Example' (2016) 17 *Stanford Law School. Traditional Commentary*, fn. 32.

108 Payandeh, *Judikative Rechtserzeugung* (2017) 336 ff.

III. Precedents and Leave to Appeal

While France has a cassation system which is based on the idea, that it should be possible, in principle, to have all decisions examined by the supreme court for any errors of law, in Germany and Austria access to the supreme court requires either a certification from the intermediate appellate court that the case involves an important question of law or leave to appeal from the supreme court. It is the criteria for admissibility of an appeal to the supreme court where the idea of "case law" is perhaps most clearly expressed in the text of the statute. In Austria, access to the Supreme Court requires a „question of substantive or procedural law which has significant importance for the uniform application of the law, legal certainty or development of the law, e.g. because the intermediate appellate court has departed from the *jurisprudence* of the Supreme Court, such *jurisprudence* are absent or inconsistent".[109]

It is within this statutory framework that the Austrian Supreme Court has expressly addressed the significance of single decisions or a small number or decisions which do not amount to *jurisprudence constante (ständige Rechtsprechung)*.[110] Specifically, the Court has held that in order for a question of law to be of significant importance it is necessary that there is no "reliable *jurisprudence*" (*gesicherte Rechtsprechung*). On the other hand, the Court emphasizes that the mere fact that there is no "*jurisprudence constante*" is not sufficient for leave to appeal to the Supreme Court.[111] For the existence of a "reliable jurisprudence" even a single decision which, although being the only one, was extensively motivated and published several times, in the absence of conflicting decisions and if this decision was also received in academic writings without criticism, is sufficient.[112]

---

109 § 502 para 1 Austrian Code of Civil Procedure (*ZPO*).

110 I deliberately use the French term *jurisprudence* and *jurisprudence constante* in order to avoid any misunderstandings that may be caused by the English terms 'case law' (which may be too strong) or just 'decisions' or 'line of decisions' which may be too weak to adequately define the concept of *jurisprudence*. Of course, the French term *jurisprudence* has a meaning entirely different from the English term "jurisprudence".

111 See Austrian Legal Information System (*Rechtsinformationssystem*) RIS-Justiz RS0042833.

112 RIS-Justiz RS0103384. According to the decisions listed there, this definition has been used by the Supreme Court some 90 times and therefore clearly has to be regarded as *jurisprudence constante*.

IV. Legal Malpractice and State Liability

Ignorance of (or failure to advise on) *jurisprudence constante* (*ständige Rechtsprechung*) can also give rise to a claim for damages in the law of delicts (tort law). Thus, if a lawyer fails to take into account, or advise his client on, *jurisprudence constante* he is liable for legal malpractice.[113] Of course this only shows that prior court decisions are important as a practical matter and have to be taken into account in practice. Thus, a lawyer's liability in tort law for ignorance of court decisions could, at least in theory, be explained by the mere factual importance of prior decisions but does not prove that the law *requires* that such decisions are actually followed.

A look into the concept of state liability (*Amtshaftung* or *Staatshaftung*), however, shows us that prior decisions are not merely important as a factual matter: In the Civil Law, the state is liable in damages for a harm inflicted by its officials. Sometimes this liability includes also courts. This rule is firmly established by statutes and has also been developed by the CJEU.[114] While there are differences between the various Civil Law countries, generally a party can claim damages from the state if a governmental officer deviated from *jurisprudence constante* without adequate reasons.[115] Under Austrian law, deviation from a clear statutory provision or *jurisprudence constante* which is unsupportable and does not show careful examination of the law can generally lead to a claim for damages against the state.[116] Interestingly, here ignorance of the law and of *jurisprudence constante* is treated in the same way. There is no difference in tort law between ignorance of laws and of "unanimous academic writings and court decisions" ("*einhellige Lehre und Rechtsprechung*").[117]

Yet, deviation from supreme court decisions does not constitute fault on part of the official per se. Rather, the official can depart from supreme

---

113 For Austria, see RIS-Justiz RS003863. Under this line of decisions, a lawyer is liable in case of ignorance of the law and of "unanimous academic writings and court decisions" (*einhellige Lehre und Rechtsprechung*).

114 For state liability under European Union law see, e.g. CJEU, Case C-6/90 and C-9/90, 19.11.1991, *Francovich*, ECLI:EU:C:1991:428; for state liability for the decisions of courts (even Supreme Courts) see CJEU, Case C-224/01, 30.09.2003, *Köbler*, ECLI:EU:C:2003:513 and CJEU, Case C-173/03, 13.06.2006, *Traghetti*, ECLI:EU:C:2006:391.

115 See, e.g. for Austria Koziol, *Haftpflichtrecht II* (2018) D/10/mn. 21; for Germany Payandeh, *Judikative Rechtserzeugung* (2017) 340 ff; Rebhahn, *Staatshaftung* (1997) 499 ff.

116 RIS-Justiz RS0049912.

117 RIS-Justiz RS0049912.

court decisions if he takes into account, and carefully considers, the jurisprudence and states his reasons for not following them.[118] In one case, the German Supreme Court even expressly stated that an official of the company register (*Rechtspfleger*), when deciding on an application for an entry into the commercial register, was under an obligation to follow the pertinent decisions of the Supreme Court. Only on the level of fault the Supreme Court examined whether there were sufficient reasons for not following the relevant *jurisprudence*.[119]

I. The "Authority" of Court Decisions

The mechanisms described above clearly show that court decisions go beyond just applying the law in individual cases.[120] Particularly decisions by supreme courts are enormously important for the application of the law.[121] Precedents should not be regarded as an independent legal phenomenon separate from statutory law, but as a contribution to the interpretation, concretization or development of statutory law.[122] Court decisions bridge the gap between abstract laws and concrete cases. In this way they contribute to the interpretation, concretization and development of the law. The degree of determinacy of abstract norms is necessarily limited. Here, court decisions fulfil an important compensatory function in that they contribute to the content and understanding of statutory provisions and reduce the uncertainty that comes with abstract-general legal provisions. Thereby, court decisions provide orientation for the application of the law and, from a perspective of the "user", make the law clearer and, thus, contribute to legal certainty.[123] Indeed, one can regard the functions of courts and legislature as a form of "division of labour". The relation to

---

118 For Germany, see BGH 17.10.1966 – II ZR 123/64, *VersR* 1967, 1150; Payandeh, *Judikative Rechtserzeugung* (2017) 345.

119 BGH 24.06.1982 – III ZR 19/81, *NJW* 1983, 222 (223).

120 For this section I rely in large measure on the insightful book by Payandeh, *Judikative Rechtserzeugung* (2017).

121 See, e.g., BGH 30.09.1993 – IX ZR 211/92, *NJW* 1993, 3323 (3324).

122 Payandeh, *Judikative Rechtserzeugung* (2017) 111 ff.

123 Payandeh, *Judikative Rechtserzeugung* (2017) 151 ff. It should be pointed out that the distinction between ratio decidendi and obiter dictum is not as important in Civil Law as it is in Common Law. However, the question of how important the legal considerations of a court were for its decision may well have a bearing on the authority of this part of the decision. See Payandeh, *Judikative Rechtserzeugung* (2017) 463 ff.

a particular case is the "added value" gained from the concretization of norms by way of court decisions compared to abstract statutory provisions. This aspect also has consequences for the interpretation of court decisions. Because court decisions are rendered in concrete cases, their interpretation always requires "contextualization" in that the factual and procedural context is taken into account.

Ultimately, the development of "case law" is a multi-faceted process. Factors required for (or at least facilitating) the development of "precedents" are rational decisions, "motivated" decisions (in the sense that the decisions set forth reasons) and publication and/or documentation of decisions. Institutional aspects contributing to the development of "precedents" are the hierarchical structure of the court system and the requirement that court decisions be "motivated".[124]

Even with all these factors present, the development of "precedents" is always a result of contribution of many "actors". Decisions are rendered by a high court, but subsequently these decisions are taken up by lower courts, but also by the legislature, by the administration and by practitioners and academic lawyers.[125] There is a "dialogue" with other courts and with the legislature. Court decisions show how laws enacted by the legislature work in practice and thus are a means of information for the legislature. The legislature then can react to court decisions in a variety of ways. It can enact laws simply reiterating results reached by the courts,[126] it can cite a decision approvingly in legislative materials, or it can remain silent and simply not act at all,[127] it may clarify the law or it can "overrule" *jurisprudence* by enacting a statutory provision to the contrary.

124 Payandeh, *Judikative Rechtserzeugung* (2017) 57 ff.

125 Payandeh, *Judikative Rechtserzeugung* (2017) 11 ff.

126 An example for this is the Austrian Non-Contentious Proceedings Act of 2003 which was described as a 'codification of judge-made law'. Similarly, the discussion about the reform of Austrian tort law in large measure is about codification of principles already developed by the courts. See also fn. 26.

127 There is a methodological discussion whether such 'silence' on part of the legislature should be regarded as legislative 'approval' of a certain *jurisprudence*. In the opinion of this author there is no simple answer to this question. Rather, the meaning (if any) of silence on part of the legislature depends on whether the decision was rendered in an area of the law in which the legislature considered reform proposals, on whether there was wide-spread public debate of a decision etc (see Kodek, in Rummel and Lukas (eds), *ABGB* (2015) § 6, mn. 109). One of the arguments against this position is that it is not the function of the legislature to 'police' the courts (Bollenberger, 'Drittpfandbestellung und Verbraucherschutz nach §§ 25c und 25d KSchG' (2008) *ÖBA*, 650, 652.

Also, decisions of higher courts are cited and followed by lower courts, or lower courts seek to limit the impact of certain decisions by way of distinguishing or carving out exceptions to the rule stated by the supreme court. In addition, in many countries there is a dialogue between courts and academic doctrine with courts picking up and reacting to academic writings and vice versa.

The effect of precedents depends on to what extent courts, the legislature, administrative authorities and other "users" of the law accept these decisions and base their own decisions on them. The effects of precedents are strengthened and stabilized by supreme courts referring to their own prior decisions, thereby affirming them, defending them against criticism and further developing them.[128] The acceptance of prior decisions may also depend on to what extent these decisions are perceived by the legal community to be convincing.[129] Therefore, the quality of reasoning and its "persuasive force" clearly plays an important role here. Thus, ultimately the "binding" nature of court decisions is a question of degree.

J. Conclusion

From the above it has become clear that even in civil law court decisions, while not formally "binding", often have effects that go far beyond the case in which they have been rendered. The rules on access to the supreme court, the various instruments to ensure consistency in the application of the law show that the function of supreme courts is not just the decision of individual cases, but also serves the interpretation, concretization and development of the law in general.

40 years ago, James Hardisty discussed stare decisis and non-stare decisis precedents from a perspective of American law. He stated that "[s]uperficially, the law draws a discrete line between stare decisis and non-stare decisis precedents; but underneath the surface, the law presents a continuum of degrees of influence along which precedents and parts of precedents are arrayed. Legal words, concepts and theories join in furnishing this surface appearance of stability while allowing subterranean change."[130] He concludes his observations by stating, long before the movie of that name, that "[w]hat the law presents as black and white resolves on analysis into

128 Payandeh, *Judikative Rechtserzeugung* (2017) 287 ff.
129 Payandeh, *Judikative Rechtserzeugung* 2017) 287 ff.
130 Hardisty, 'Reflections on Stare Decisis' (1979) 55 *Indiana Law Journal*, 40, 68.

shades of grey."[131] These observations are equally true for the Civil Law. Perhaps the best way of describing the functions of written laws on one hand and court decisions on the other hand, is still the explanation given by the commission that drafted the French Code Civil:

> *"The function of the statute is to set down, in broad terms, the general maxims of the law, to establish principles rich in consequences, and not to deal with the particulars of the questions that may arise on every subject. It is left to the magistrate and the jurisconsult, fully alive to the overall spirit of laws, to guide their application.*
> *Hence, in all civilized nations one always sees, alongside the sanctuary of laws and under the watchful eye of the lawmaker, the formation of a body of maxims, decisions and doctrine that is refined daily by practice and by the impact of judicial deliberations; that continually grows from all the knowledge acquired; and that has constantly been regarded as the true supplement of legislation.*"[132]

Bibliography

Sir Carleton Kemp Allen, *Law in the Making*, (7th revised edn, Oxford University Press 1964)

Marc Ancel, 'Case Law in France' (1934) 16 *Journal of Comparative Legislation and International Law*, 1

Marc Ancel, 'Reflexions sur l'Etude Comparative des Cours Supremes et le Recours en Cassation' (1938) 3 *Annales de l'Institut de Droit Compare de l'Universite de Paris*, 285

John Bell, 'Comparing Precedent' (1997) 82 *Cornell Law Review*, 1242

Raimund Bollenberger, 'Drittpfandbestellung und Verbraucherschutz nach §§ 25c und 25d KSchG' (2008) *ÖBA*, 650

Jean Carbonnier, 'Authorities in civil law: France' in J.E.C. Brierley (trans) and Joseph Dainow (ed), *The role of judicial decisions and doctrine in civil law and in mixed jurisdictions* (L.S.U. Press, Baton Rouge 1974)

Charles, Baron De Montesquieu, *The Spirit of the Laws* (Chez Barillot & Fils, Genf 1748)

---

131 Hardisty, 'Reflections on Stare Decisis' (1979) 55 *Indiana Law Journal*, 40, 68.

132 Preliminary Address on the First Draft of the Civil Code, presented by Messrs, Portalis, Tronchet, Bigot-Préameneu and Millville, members of the government-appointed commission, on 1 Pluviôse IX (21.01.1801), <https://www.justice.gc.ca/eng/rp-pr/csj-sjc/ilp-pji/code/index.html> accessed 13 April 2021.

Laurent Cohen-Tanugi, 'Case Law in a Legal System Without Binding Precedent: The French Example' (2006) 17 *Stanford Law School. Traditional Commentary* <https://cgc.law.stanford.edu/commentaries/17-laurent-cohen-tanugi> accessed 13 April 2021

Laurent Cohen-Tanugi, *Le droit sans l'Etat (Law Without the State)* (Presses Universitaires de France, Paris 1985), 79

James L. Dennis, 'Interpretation and application of the civil code and the evaluation of judicial precedent' (1993) 54 *Louisiana Law Review*, 1

Vincy Fon and Francesco Parisi, 'Judicial Precedents in Civil Law Systems: A Dynamic Analysis' (2006) 26 *International Review of Law and Economics*, 519

Birgit Forgó-Feldner, 'Der OGH und der Zugang zu seinen Entscheidungen in historischer Perspektive' in Georg Kodek (ed), *Zugang zum OGH. Vorträge des Symposiums „Zugang zum OGH in Zivil- und Strafsachen"* (Manz, Wien 2012) 1

Birgit Forgó-Feldner, *Verstärkte Senate beim Obersten Gerichtshof. Rechtsprechung im Spannungsfeld zwischen Unabhängigkeit, Richtigkeit und Einheitlichkeit* (Springer, Wien 2001)

François Gény, *Méthode d'interpretation et sources en droit privé positif I* (L.G.D.J, 1919)

Otto von Gierke, *Deutsches Privatrecht* (Duncker & Humblot, Berlin 1936)

Irmgard Griss, Georg Kathrein and Helmut Koziol, *Entwurf eines neuen österreichischen Schadenersatzrechts* (Verlag Österreich, Wien 2006)

Harold Cooke Gutteridge, *Comparative Law: An Introduction to the Comparative Method of Legal Study and Research* (Cambridge University Press, Cambridge 1946)

James Hardisty, 'Reflections on Stare Decisis' (1979) 55 *Indiana Law Journal*, 40

Tatjana Josipovic, 'Das ABGB in Kroatien – historische Geltung und Bedeutung für die kroatische Zivilrechtsgesetzgebung von heute' in Georg Kodek (ed), *200 Jahre Allgemeines Bürgerliches Gesetzbuch (ABGB) und Europäisches Vertragsrecht* (Manz, Wien 2012) 55

Georg Kodek, 'Funktion und Arbeitsweise des OGH – die Binnensicht' in Georg Kodek (ed), *Zugang zum OGH. Vorträge des Symposiums "Zugang zum OGH in Zivil- und Strafsachen"* (Manz, Wien 2012) 99

Jan Komarek, *Precedent and Judicial Lawmaking in Supreme Courts: The Court of Justice Compared to the US Supreme Court and the French Cour de Cassation* (Cambridge University Press, Cambridge 2009)

Helmut Koziol, *Haftpflichtrecht II* (3rd edn, Jan Sramek, Wien 2018)

Julius Ofner, *Der Ur-Entwurf und die Berathungs-Protokolle des Österreichischen Allgemeinen Bürgerlichen Gesetzbuches* (Hölder, Wien 1889)

D. K. Lipstein, 'The Doctrine of Precedent in Continental Law with Special Reference to French and German Law' (1946) 28 *Journal of Comparative Legislation and International Law*, 34

C. Sumner Lobingier, 'Precedent in Past and Present Legal Systems' (1946) 44 *Michigan Law Review*, 955

Karen McAuliffe, 'Precedent at the Court of Justice of the European Union: The Linguistic Aspect' (2013) 15 *Current Legal Issues*, 483

Andrei Marmor, *Law in the Age of Pluralism* (Oxford University Press, Oxford 2007)

Richard D. Moreno, 'Scott v. Cokern: Of precedent, jurisprudence constante, and the relationship between Louisiana commercial laws and Louisiana pledge jurisprudence' (1995) 10 *Tulane European and Civil Law Forum*, 31

Thomas Olechowski, 'Das ABGB – Rechtseinheit für Zentraleuropa' in Georg Kodek (ed), *200 Jahre Allgemeines Bürgerliches Gesetzbuch (ABGB) und Europäisches Vertragsrecht* (Manz, Wien 2012) 33

Mehrdad Payandeh, *Judikative Rechtserzeugung* (Mohr Siebeck, Tübingen 2017)

Leopold Pfaff and Franz Hofmann, *Commentar zum österreichischen allgemeinen bürgerlichen Gesetzbuche* (Manz, Wien 1877)

Robert Rebhahn, *Staatshaftung wegen mangelnder Gefahrenabwehr* (Manz, Wien 1997)

Rudolf Reischauer, Karl Spielbüchler and Rudolf Welser, *Reform des Schadenersatzrechts* (Manz, Wien 2006)

Peter Rummel and Meinhard Lukas (eds), *ABGB* (4th edn, Manz, Wien 2015)

Bernd Rüthers, *Die heimliche Revolution vom Rechtsstaat zum Richterstaat* (2nd edn, Mohr Siebeck, Tübingen 2016)

Bernhard Schima, *Das Vorabentscheidungsverfahren vor dem EuGH* (3rd edn, Ch. Beck in cooperation with Manz, München und Wien 2015)

Bojan Spaić, 'The Authority of Precedents in Civil Law Systems' (2018) XXVII *Studia Iuridica Lubliensia*, 27

Reinhard Sprung, 'Die Entwicklung der zivilgerichtlichen Begründungspflicht' in Reinhard Sprung and Bernhard König (eds), *Entscheidungsbegründung* (Springer-Verlag, Wien 1974) 43

Igor Tokmadczic, 'The Case for Case Law: Recognising Precedent in Civil Law Systems' (Wellington 2016), http://researcharchive.vuw.ac.nz/xmlui/bitstream/handle/10063/5228/paper.pdf?se

Michel Troper and Christophe Grzegorczyk, 'Precedent in France' in Neil MacCormick and Robert Summers (eds), *Interpreting precedents: A comparative study* (Ashgate/Dartmouth, Aldershot 1997) 103

Joseph Unger, *System des österreichischen allgemeinen Privatrechts I* (Breitkopf und Härtel, Leipzig 1856)

Karl Wahle, 'Vorwort' in *Die Judikate und Sprüche des Obersten Gerichtshofes seit seinem Bestande* (Manz, Wien 1950)

Reinhard Walker, 'Die Entwicklung der Publikationsmedien im modernen Staat' (1998) 97 *JurPC Web-Dok* <https://www.jurpc.de/jurpc/show?id=19980097> accessed 13 April 2021

Benjamin Watt, 'Why French Law Rejects Judicial Precedent' (1997) *International Business Lawyer*, 18

Andreas Wiebe and Georg Kodek (eds), *UWG* (2nd edn, Manz, Wien 2017)

Franz Zeiller, *Commentar über das Allgemeine bürgerliche Gesetzbuch* I (Geistinger Verlagsbuchhandlung, Wien und Triest 1811)

Konrad Zweigert and Heinz Kötz, *Introduction to Comparative Law* (2nd edn, Clarendon Press, Oxford 1987)

The Precedent in the ICC Jurisprudence

Raphaëlle Nollez-Goldbach

A classical definition of precedent circumscribes it as a previous decision that can be invoked as a reference to rule on a similar subsequent case. According to the different judicial systems, however, precedents are either binding or simply serve as examples, without mandatory effects, whose authority depends on the formation of the Court that rendered the decision. Besides, international law rejects the rule of the binding precedent. Yet it can be observed that International Courts do use some form of precedent, or at least construct a "*jurisprudence constante*" ("constant jurisprudence") by refering to their own judgments.

To study the role and practice of precedent by the International Criminal Court (ICC), this paper is relying on an empirical legal methodology, by the means of network analysis of the ICC jurisprudence, field studies and interviews held at the headquarters of the Court. It aims at enlightening the concept of precedent in ICC procedure and its specificity. Indeed precedent has a specific role in the ICC case-law: even if the rule of the binding precedent does not apply in international law, the ICC Statute authorizes the Court to «apply principles and rules of law as interpreted in its previous decisions».

A difficulty while working on precedent in ICC case-law is to identify what a precedent is, as almost every judgment brings a new interpretation of the statute (for being the first one applying a provision). These decisions can also be easily reversed, and even the Appeals Chamber departs from its previous judgments on the appeal. The first point of this paper is to present a definition of the value of precedent before the ICC. Is there a binding precedent rule or simply the right for the Court to refer to its previous decisions? Are the decisions of the Appeals Chamber binding upon lower chambers? In its second part, this paper will identify some practices of the ICC judges regarding precedent and how the Court pursues the objectives to ensure judicial security and to construct a «constant jurisprudence». Finally, in its third point, the paper will show how the ICC decisions are shifting from that objective of effectiveness and consistency by departing from precedent in a couple of very important recent acquittals.

1. *Definition of Precedent in the ICC Statute*

It is first necessary to address the question of the definition of precedent, by comparing precedent in the International Court of Justice (ICJ) and ICC Statutes.

The binding precedent – the *stare decisis* rule – has been ruled out in international law since the Statute of the Permanent Court of International Justice. This exclusion of the binding value of precedent was reproduced in the ICJ Statute: its famous article 38 provides in paragraph (d) that judicial decisions is only a « subsidiary means for the determination of rules of law ». Then the sources of international law explicitly exclude judicial decisions that can only play an auxiliary role. Besides, they are only binding between the parties and in respect of that particular case (according to article 59 of the ICJ Statute). The ICJ may refer to its precedents, but it has no binding character. Yet the Court refers to itself frequently to ensure "consistency of jurisprudence"[1].

However, the ICC definition of precedent, as it is included in its Statute, is different. Article 21 of the ICC Statute states that the Court in the determination of the rule of law applies in the first place its Statute; in the second place, international treaties and principles; and when appropriate, the national laws of States (that would normally exercise jurisdiction over the crime). But article 21 on applicable law contains another provision in its second paragraph. It allows the Court to apply « principles and rules of law as interpreted in its previous decisions ». Precedent seems to be here a source of law, which would be a first in international law – setting up a « precedent ».

Indeed the Statutes of the *ad hoc* International criminal tribunals did not include any provision on applicable law. In its famous *Tadic* proceedings, the ICTY judges pointed out this lack of guidance, qualified as « troubling » because of the « unique character of the Tribunal »[2]. As the first international criminal tribunal ever established by the United Nations, the ICTY had very little precedent to guide itself (its only predecessors being the International Military Tribunals at Nuremberg and Tokyo).

It seems then that the ICC Statute fills this gap and establishes the sources of international criminal law. However, we need to look deeper

---

1 Gilbert Guillaume, 'The Use of Precedent by International Judges and Arbitrators' (2011) 1 *Journal of International Dispute Settlement*, 2, 9–10.

2 ICTY, *Tadic case*, Decision on the Prosecutor's Motion Requesting Protective Measures for Victims and Witnesses, 10 August 1995, § 19.

into this definition and to focus on the choice of words. Paragraph 2 of article 21 of the ICC Statute reads as follow: the Court *may* apply its previous decisions; not the Court *shall* apply. A classic use of grammar (of verb tenses and modalities) in international law. It indicates that precedents are not binding, as they are in national common law systems. Then the ICC Statute rejects the binding precedent doctrine. Article 21.2 is « not a mandatory provision. Nor does the provision explicitly establish any hierarchy in terms of the decisions of the various Chambers of the Court »[3].

What the ICC can do, however, is to decide whether or not to apply precedents, a compromise settled during the Rome negotiations that balances the common law and roman-german law approaches[4]. Indeed neither the International Law Commission (ILC) nor the UN Committee for the creation of the International Criminal Court included in their draft Statutes in 1953 and 1994 the reference to previous decisions[5]. The ILC's special referee proposed though to mention jurisprudence, but only as a subsidiary means[6]. The mention of the ICC previous decisions as sources of law was included as the second paragraph of article 21 by the Preparatory Comity eventually just before the Rome Conference[7]. It was adopted to authorize the Court to « apply principles and rules of law as interpreted in its previous decisions ».

Thus precedent in the ICC system is not a « subsidiary means » for the determination of law as it is for the ICJ. But it is not mandatory either and the *stare decisis* rule is not established. It is something in between. And the choice whether or not to apply precedent is left to the Court for each case. The use of precedent is to the discretion of the judges.

---

3 Schabas, *The International Criminal Court: A Commentary on the Rome Statute* (2016) 526.

4 Callejon, 'Article 21. Droit applicable', in Fernandez and Pacreau (eds), *Commentaire du Statut de Rome* (2012) 766.

5 Article 2 of the Draft Statute, *Report of the UN Committee* (1953), 24 and Article 33 of the ICL Draft Statute, *Yearbook of the ILC*, vol. II (1994), 54.

6 A proposal that was not adopted anyway. *Yearbook of the ILC*, vol. II (1992), 14, § 78.

7 *Report of the Preparatory Committee on the Establishment of an International Criminal Court*, 14 April 1998, 46–47.

2. Identification of Precedent in ICC Case-Law

It follows from this definition of precedent that the judges have to decide in each case whether or not to retain the solutions they previously adopted, as there is no binding precedent rule, but a discretionary right for the judges to apply previous decisions. The Pre-Trial Chambers, the Trial Chambers and even the Appeals Chamber are not bound by their previous decisions. We can note, however, that they, most of the time, do follow precedents in practice. Doing so, their objective is to build an efficient and stable jurisprudence, without constructing any binding precedent doctrine.

Analyses of the ICC case-law on article 21.2 of the Statute[8] shows that judges are allowed to choose to apply or not previous decisions of the Court. Chambers interpreted this right as an obligation to verify, first, the principles established to date by the Court and, second, whether and to which extend they apply to the case.

Concerning whether and how to apply « the principles established so far by the Court », the Chambers often lean on the jurisprudence of Pre-Trial Chamber I in the situation in the Democratic Republic of the Congo. Due to its position as the first Chamber to have rendered decisions in the first situation under proceedings before the Court, the Pre-Trial Chamber I has produced one of the most cited jurisprudence. In the *Kony* case, for example, when the first decision was to be rendered on applications for victims participation – one area in which the ICC is innovative for being the first Court to allow such victims participation –, the Court took « into account the principles established and the practice followed so far by the Court in the area of victims participation »[9]. In that regard, it is noteworthy that the Court had a particular focus on the determination of those jurisprudence principles that « appear to be relevant to the Situation and/or to the case and may assist the Court [...] to establish whether

---

8 The author has been able to analyse the ICC decisions citing article 21.1 by the means of network analysis of this jurisprudence. See for methodology: Tarissan and Nollez-Goldbach, 'Analysing the first case of the International Criminal Court from a network-science perspective' (2016) 4 *Journal of Complex Networks*, 616–634.

9 Situation in Uganda, Pre-Trial Chamber II, Decision on victims' applications for participation a/0010/06, a/0064/06 to a/0070/06, a/0081/06 to a/0104/06 and a/0111/06 to a/0127/06, ICC-02/04–01/05–252, 10 August 2007, § 5.

such principles maybe supplemented with a view to further enhancing the efficiency and predictability of proceedings »[10].

ICC Chambers have thus held that – even though they are not required to apply previous decisions – they can do so on their own discretion. They ruled on the necessity to take into account principles and rules of laws established so far by the Court[11]. They also ensured that their interpretation of articles of the Statute is consistent with the jurisprudence of the Court[12] and that they applied the rights of the parties as recognized by the jurisprudence of the Court[13].

What needs also to be emphasized is that ICC decisions are subject to an internal review mechanism, contrary to the ICJ. Parties can appeal the decisions and they can be reversed. This raises the question of whether the judgments after appeal to a higher authority are not only mandatory in the case in question obviously, but whether, more generally, lower chambers obey Appeal Chambers previous decisions.

This issue was resolved in the affirmative by the Appeals Chamber of the Tribunal for the former Yugoslavia in the *Aleksovski* case[14]. Yet the ICTY Statute did not contain any provision about applicable law. Contrary to the ICC Statute, binding precedent was not excluded, allowing judges to create this solution. The Appeals chamber considered that the *ratio decidendi* of its decisions is binding on trial chambers to ensure certainty and predictability (but the trial chambers decisions have no binding force on each others). The Appeals Chamber also held that it should follow its previous decisions but is free to depart from them for cogent reasons in the interest of justice.

Regarding the ICC some of its case-law provides insights on this question of the value of higher chamber judgments. The Appeals Chamber underlined that it is not required to follow its previous interpretations

---

10 *Ibid.*

11 *Katanga* Case, Trial Chamber II, Judgment pursuant to article 74 of the Statute, ICC-01/04–01/07–3436-tENG, 7 March 2014, §. 42; *Kenyatta* Case, Pre-Trial Chamber II, Decision on the Confinnation of Charges Pursuant to Article 61(7) (a) and (b) of the Rome Statute, ICC-01/09–02/11–382-Red, 23 January 2012, §. 66.

12 See for example, Situation in Birma, Pre-Trial Chamber I, Decision on the "Prosecution's Request for a Ruling on Jurisdiction Under Article 19(3) of the Statute", ICC-RoC46(3)-01/18–37, 6 September 2018, § 59.

13 Situation in Uganda, Pre-Trial Chamber II, Decision on victims' applications for participation, op. cit., § 100.

14 *Aleksovski* Case, Appeals Chamber, Judgment, n° IT-95–14/1-A, 24 mars 2000, §§ 113–114.

of principles and rules of law through binding *stare decisis*. It has held that it is rather vested with discretion as to whether to do so or not[15]. If the Appeals Chamber has discretion to depart from its previous case-law, it will not do so, however, given « the need to ensure predictability of the law and the fairness of adjudication to foster public reliance on its decisions »[16]. In order to ensure consistency and predictability – here again –, it ruled that « without "convincing reasons" it will not depart from its previous decisions »[17].

The Appeals chamber has mainly applied its previous decisions in numerous matters: victims participation, powers of the chambers, right of the accused, numerous questions of proceedings... And the decisions of the Appeals Chamber have been regularly applied by lower chambers. However, the Chambers did not feel bound to follow mandatorily previous decisions, even from higher Chambers. ICC judges, acting as single Judge on behalf of a Pre-Trial Chamber, departed from previous Trial Chamber or even Appeals Chamber decisions[18], underlying that « Trial Chamber Decision is not *per se* binding upon the Pre-Trial Chamber »[19]. Besides, in a couple of major decisions, leading to the significant acquittals of two main accused, the Appeals Chamber has departed from previous decisions, revealing a very inconstant jurisprudence when it comes to the standard of proof.

15 *Gbagbo* Case, Appeals Chamber, Victims Participation Decision, ICC-02/11-01/15-172, 31 July 2015, § 14; *Bemba* case, Appeals Chamber, Victims Participation Decision, ICC-01/05-01/08-566, 20 October 2009, § 16.

16 *Ibid.*

17 *Bemba* case, Appeals Chamber, Victims Participation Decision, *op. cit.*, § 16; *Bemba* case, Appeals Chamber, Prosecution's Response to Mr Bemba's Request to the Appeals Chamber to hold an Oral Hearing in the Re-sentencing appeal proceedings, 15 July 2009, § 14; *Gbagbo* Case, Victims Participation Decision, *op. cit.*, § 14.

18 *Ongwen* Case, Pre-Trial Chamber II, Decision on the "Defence Request for the Interim Release of Dominic Ongwen", ICC-02/04-01/15-349-Red, 27 November 2015, § 7; *Katanga and Ngudjolo* Case, Pre-Trial Chamber I, Decision on Article 54(3)(e) Documents Identified as Potentially Exculpatory or Otherwise Material to the Defence's Preparation for the Confirmation Hearing, ICC-01/04-01/07-621, 20 June 2008, § 59.

19 *Ibid.*.

3. *From Constant Jurisprudence to a Constant Change of Jurisprudence on the Standard of Proof*

Some recent decisions rendered in the most important ICC cases led to acquittals of famous accused by the reversal of the ICC jurisprudence. Judges depart from former jurisprudence, each time on the appreciation of the standard of proof.

The very first acquittal rendered by the Appeals Chamber, in the *Bemba* case on 8 June 2018[20], sparked surprise and controversy[21] and was based on the reversal of the jurisprudence of the Court. Jean-Pierre Bemba, the former vice-President of the Democratic Republic of Congo, had been found guilty of war crimes and crimes against humanity and convicted to 18 years's imprisonment. But he got acquitted of all charges on appeal. The appeals judges considered that the verdict exceeded the Confirmation Decision's charges and that the elements of proofs did not reach the new (and controversial) interpretation of the military commander responsibility they established[22].

---

20 *Bemba* Case, Appeals Chamber, Judgment, ICC-01/05–01/08–3636-Red, 8 June 2018.

21 See in French: Nollez-Goldbach, 'Acquittement en appel de Jean-Pierre Bemba devant la CPI: une décision contestée sur la responsabilité du chef militaire' (2018) 28 *La Semaine juridique (JCP G)*, 369 and a case commentary in 'Chronique de jurisprudence internationale' (2013) 3 *Revue générale de droit internaional public*, 755–757. In English: Sadat, 'Fiddling While Rome Burns? The Appeals Chamber's Curious Decision in Prosecutor v. Jean-Pierre Bemba Gombo', *EJIL:Talk*, 12 June 2018 <https://www.ejiltalk.org/fiddling-while-rome-burns-the-appeals-chambers-curious-decision-in-prosecutor-v-jean-pierre-bemba-gombo> accessed 31 May 2021; Amann, "In Bemba and Beyond, Crimes Adjudged to Commit Themselves", *EJIL:Talk*, 13 June 2018 <https://www.ejiltalk.org/in-bemba-and-beyond-crimes-adjudged-to-commit-themselves> accessed 31 May 2021; Jackson, "Commander's Motivations in Bemba", *EJIL:Talk*, 15 June 2018 <https://www.ejiltalk.org/commanders-motivations-in-bemba> accessed 31 May 2021; Heller, 'A Fascinating But Meritless OTP Gambit in Bemba' (2018) *OpinioJuris* <http://opiniojuris.org/2018/07/04/a-fascinating-if-meritless-otp-gambit-in-bemba> accessed 31 May 2021; Trahan, 'Bemba Acquittal Rests on Erroneous Application of Appellate Review Standard' (2018) *OpinioJuris* <http://opiniojuris.org/2018/06/25/bemba-acquittal-rests-on-erroneous-application-of-appellate-review-standard/> accessed 31 May 2021; Miles Jackson, "Geographical Remoteness in Bemba", *EJIL:Talk*, 30 July 2018 <https://www.ejiltalk.org/geographical-remoteness-in-bemba> accessed 31 May 2021; Leila Sadat, "Prosecutor v. Jean-Pierre Bemba Gombo" (2019) 113 *AJIL*, 353–361.

22 Nollez-Goldbach, 'Un précédent dans la jurisprudence de la CPI ?' (2018) *AJ Pénal*, 451–453.

The Bemba acquittal departs from the previous precedent set up by the Appeals Chamber on the standard of proof. Appeals judges lowered the standard of proof in order to be authorized to carry out a new examination of the proofs if the one of the trial chamber raised any « doubt »[23]. However the Appeals Chamber previous decisions stated that « without "convincing reasons" it will not depart from its previous decisions » and that it was allowed to interfere « only in the case where it cannot discern how the Chamber's conclusion could have reasonably been reached from the evidence before it »[24]. To concur with these previous decisions, the appeal judges in the Bemba acquittal relied on a major convincing reason compelling them to interfere: to avoid what judges called « miscarriage of justice »[25]. Based on this reasoning, appeals judges carried out a new examination of the proofs, as they were trier of the facts, and concluded to the weakness of the proofs leading to part of the acquittal.

But this very decision that set up a new precedent on facts evaluation and standard of proof by departing from the previous ones is not certain to last. Indeed the composition of the Appeals Chamber just changed after the judgment and two new judges replaced two former ones (especially the President of the Appeals Chamber whose mandate ended the day after the judgment and who influenced strongly this acquittal[26]). No one can know at this point what majority will emerge about the standard of proof if the chamber has to rule on it again. A situation in serious contradiction with the objective of the predictability of jurisprudence.

Another resounding acquittal was the Gbagbo's one on 15 January 2019[27], granted at mid-trial by the Trial Chamber I. It was granted after a « no case to answer » Defense request, based on the lack of evidence presented by the accusation. Here again the majority departed from previous decisions on the standard of proof for this particular stage of proceedings. The Defense request for a « no case to answer » at mid-trial is to the discretion of the Chamber, as it is not provided by the Statute and a

---

23 *Bemba* Case, Appeals Chamber, Judgment, *op. cit.*, §§ 2, 3 45, 46.

24 *Lubanga* Case, Appeals Chamber, Judgment, ICC-01/04–01/06–3121-Red, 1st December 2014, § 21. The ICC first decision on factual findings and evaluation of the fact of the first-instance Chamber. A solution confirmed in the *Ngudjolo* Case, Appeals Chamber, Judgment, ICC-01/04–02/12–271-Corr, 7 April 2015, § 22.

25 *Bemba* Case, Appeals Chamber, Judgment, *op. cit.*, *ibid.*, § 40.

26 This work is based on interviews and observations made by the author on that case and judgment at the seat of the ICC.

27 *Gbagbo* Case, Trial Chamber I, Oral Decision, Transcript of the hearing, ICC-02/11–01/15-T-234-ENG, 15 December 2019.

common law procedure imported by common law lawyers. The central question in this case was to decide which standard of proof should apply to examine the elements of proof at mid-trial (because the lack of proofs was at the center of the acquittal). Should the judges be convinced behind any reasonable doubt, as for the final judgment? Or is there sufficient « evidence on which a reasonable Trial Chamber *could* convict »[28], as stated in a previous decision in the Ruto case (the first and only at that time « no case to answer » that led to an acquittal at mid-trial)?

That question was at the core of the dispute between the judges' majority and the third judge who relied, in her dissenting opinion, on the previous Ruto decision. She underlied the duty for the Chamber to consider « the relevance, probative value and potential prejudice of each item of evidence » and that led her to conclude that a « reasonable Trial Chamber might enter a conviction »[29] and therefore she ruled out an acquittal at this stage. In the oral decision, the President judge even replied to the dissenting opinion, stating that the dissenting judge « is mistaken in stating that the majority has applied the beyond a reasonable doubt standard of proof » and debating with her about the standard of proof for motions for acquittal at this stage of the proceedings[30].

The President also contemplated in the oral decision the possibility that the Appeals Chamber would reverse the decision. For the majority, if it is « possible that the Appeals Chamber will agree with the dissenting judge in respect of the applicable standard for motions for acquittal at this stage of the proceedings [...] this is entirely speculative and unexceptional and, therefore, cannot serve as a reason to maintain the accused in detention »[31]. It clearly points out here the role of the Appeals Chamber in setting precedent, or at least constant jurisprudence, in a matter that has never been applied before nor interpreted. But it also shows that lower chambers do not feel intighten to agree or follow Appeals Chamber decisions. Indeed « recent jurisprudence tends to further demonstrate that Chambers do not feel bound by the jurisprudence of other Chambers. Even more interesting to note, Chambers have deviated from previous jurisprudence either explicitly or implicitly, simply ignoring the jurispru-

28 *Ruto* Case, Trial Chamber V, Decision on the Conduct of Trial Proceedings (Principles and Procedure on 'No Case to Answer' Motions), ICC-01/09–01/11–1334, 3 June 2014, § 32.

29 *Gbagbo* Case, Trial Chamber I, Oral Decision, *op. cit.*, p. 4.

30 *Ibid.*, pp. 4–5.

31 *Ibid.*, p. 5.

dence of other Chambers »[32]. In the Gbagbo case, as an appeal has been filed by the Prosecutor, the position of the Appeals Chamber on the « no case to answer » standard of proof will be of great interest regarding that question of precedent, but also on the binding effect of Appeals Chamber decisions on lower chambers.

In the written full reasons for the acquittal that were published six months after the oral decision, on 16 July 2019[33], and were strangely composed of the three judges separated reasons[34], the Chamber decided on the applicable standard of proof. The majority found that « the legal basis for the decision that the accused has no case to answer is article 66.2 of the Statute, which places the onus of proving the guilt of the accused squarely on the Prosecutor »[35]. A burden that never shifts.

Has then the Prosecutor submitted sufficient evidence to support a conviction on each charge? The majority found that she failed to satisfy the burden of proof to the requisite standard, departing from the Ruto decision. For the Chamber, « the Prosecutor has not satisfied the burden of proof in relation to several core constitutive elements of the crimes as charged »[36]. In particular the Prosecutor has failed to demonstrate that there was a common plan or the existence of the alleged policy to attack a civilian population.

---

32 Bitti, 'Article 21 and the Hierarchy of Sources of Law before the ICC', in Carsten Stahn (ed), *The Law and Practice of the International Criminal Law* (2015) 411, 422–424.

33 *Gbagbo* Case, Trial Chamber I, Reasons for oral decision of 15 January 2019 on the Requête de la Défense de Laurent Gbagbo afin qu'un jugement d'acquittement portant sur toutes les charges soit prononcé en faveur de Laurent Gbagbo et que sa mise en liberté immédiate soit ordonnée, and on the Blé Goudé Defence no case to answer motion, ICC-02/11-01/15-1263, 16 July 2019.

34 The majority's analysis of the evidence is contained in Judge Henderson's reasons (Annex B). Judge Tarfusser's opinion can be found in Annex A. Judge Herrera Carbuccia's dissenting opinion can be found in Annex C.

35 *Gbagbo* Case, Trial Chamber I, Reasons for oral decision of 15 January 2019, *op. cit.*, § 15.

36 *Gbagbo* Case, Trial Chamber I, Reasons for oral decision of 15 January 2019, *op. cit.*, § 28.

Conclusion

Significant changes have occurred recently in ICC case-law, in particular regarding the standard of proof or the definition of charges. The Chambers have reconsidered previous decisions, departing from earlier jurisprudence to establish a new one. It shows clearly that the ICC judges used the margin of appreciation granted by Article 21.2 about the use of precedents.

One could have expected the opposite: a young court willing to establish a constant and settled jurisprudence in order to strengthen its legitimacy and efficiency. A path partly followed by the Chambers but mainly restricted to preliminary phase decisions and on topics such as the powers of the Chambers, the rights of the parties or the participation of the victims. However, at the other end of the procedural scale, on appeal or during the course of trial, some of the judges choices led to striking reversal of previous decisions. This can be explained by the internal context of the ICC: the disagreement and disputes between judges on fundamental legal questions, such as the standard of proof or the determination of charges. Those topics were not randomly chosen by judges: they symbolized the division between ICC judges on the question of the grounding of a conviction in international criminal law.

This internal debate led to acquittals by departing from previous decisions. The reversal of the jurisprudence on the determination of charges in the Bemba acquittal set a strict control of charges modification during proceedings and an obligation to detail them geographically and temporally. A former confrontation on that point already divided the Trial Chamber II in 2014 about the Katenga verdict that was grounded on a modification of charges in the course of the trial. Christine Van den Wyngaert, one of the three judges, opposed to the conviction in a very strong dissenting opinion. She even refused to sign the verdict (an unprecedented act). This judge became later the President of the Appeals Chamber and brought all her weight to bear in order to set a new precedent on that question of charges modification. The reversal of precedent seems then to depend on some geopolitics of the ICC judges and leads to a very unstable jurisprudence on specific matters. The Appeals Judgment in the Gbagbo case will provide a glimpse on the new orientation of the jurisprudence about the standard of proof and, if the Trial Chamber decision is reversed, on the binding effect of Appeals Chamber decisions.

Bibliography

Diane Marie Amann, 'In Bemba and Beyond, Crimes Adjudged to Commit Themselves', *EJIL:Talk*, 13 June 2018 <https://www.ejiltalk.org/in-bemba-and-beyond-crimes-adjudged-to-commit-themselves> accessed 31 May 2021.

Gilbert Bitti, 'Article 21 and the Hierarchy of Sources of Law before the ICC', in Carsten Stahn (ed.), *The Law and Practice of the International Criminal Law* (Oxford University Press, Oxford 2015) 411

Claire Callejon, 'Article 21. Droit applicable', in Julian Fernandez and Xavier Pacreau (eds.), *Commentaire du Statut de Rome* (Éditions Pedone, Paris 2012) 763

Nathalie Clarenc Bicudo, 'Article 21. Droit applicable', in Julian Fernandez, Xavier Pacreau and Muriel Ubéda-Saillard (eds.), *Commentaire du Statut de Rome*, (Éditions Pedone, Paris 2019) 957

Gilbert Guillaume, 'The Use of Precedent by International Judges and Arbitrators', (2011) 2 *Journal of International Dispute Settlement*, 5 ['Le précédent dans la justice et l'arbitrage international' (2010) 3 *Journal du droit international*, 687]

Kevin Jon Heller, 'A Fascinating But Meritless OTP Gambit in Bemba' (2018) *OpinioJuris* <http://opiniojuris.org/2018/07/04/a-fascinating-if-meritless-otp-gambit-in-bemba> accessed 31 May 2021

Miles Jackson, 'Commander's Motivations in Bemba', *EJIL:Talk*, 15 June 2018 <https://www.ejiltalk.org/commanders-motivations-in-bemba> accessed 31 May 2021

Miles Jackson, "Geographical Remoteness in Bemba", *EJIL:Talk*, 30 July 2018 <https://www.ejiltalk.org/geographical-remoteness-in-bemba> accessed 31 May 2021

Leila Sadat, 'Fiddling While Rome Burns? The Appeals Chamber's Curious Decision in Prosecutor v. Jean-Pierre Bemba Gombo', *EJIL:Talk*, 12 June 2018 < https://www.ejiltalk.org/fiddling-while-rome-burns-the-appeals-chambers-curious-decision-in-prosecutor-v-jean-pierre-bemba-gombo> accessed 31 May 2021.

Leila Sadat, 'Prosecutor v. Jean-Pierre Bemba Gombo' (2019) 113 *AJIL*, 353

William Schabas, 'Article 21. Applicable law / Droit applicable', in Schabas (ed), *The International Criminal Court: A Commentary on the Rome Statute* (Oxford University Press, Oxford 2016) 511

Société française de droit international, *Le précédent en droit international* (Éditions Pedone, Paris 2016)

Jennifer Trahan, 'Bemba Acquittal Rests on Erroneous Application of Appellate Review Standard' (2018) *OpinioJuris* <http://opiniojuris.org/2018/06/25/bemba-acquittal-rests-on-erroneous-application-of-appellate-review-standard/> accessed 17 May 2021